THE GRACE THAT MAKES US HOLY

Gloria Copeland

D1173203

THE GRACE THAT MAKES US HOLY

Gloria Copeland

Harrison House

Tulsa, Oklahoma

10 09 08 07 06 05 04 03 02 01   10 9 8 7 6 5 4 3 2 1

The Grace That Makes Us Holy
ISBN 1-57794-330-9   KC-30-0552

©2002 Gloria Copeland
Kenneth Copeland Ministries
Fort Worth, Texas 76192-0001

Published by Harrison House, Inc.
P.O. Box 35035
Tulsa, Oklahoma 74153

THE GRACE THAT
MAKES US HOLY

Jesus is coming soon!

I know some people scoff at that idea. (That's no surprise; the Bible said they would.) But it doesn't matter what people say. The signs are clear. We are at the end of the end!

The final outpouring of the Holy Spirit has already begun. Reports of miracles, signs and wonders, dreams and visions like those prophesied in Acts 2 are coming in from around the world. And even greater manifestations of God are on the way.

This is the greatest time in all of history. This is the time the prophets of old longed to see. I'm telling you, Elijah would love it down here now. I'm sure he wishes he could get right in the middle of it all. He enjoyed great manifestations of God's power in his lifetime. He saw God do signs and wonders. But nothing like this last-of-the-last days. We will see more of the power of God, more signs, more wonders and more glory than anyone has ever seen before.

God is manifesting Himself to us and among us in marvelous ways! And there's more to come.

Actually, our situation today is much like the one the Israelites found themselves in after Moses led them out of Egypt. When they reached the foot of Mount Sinai, God spoke and told them, *I'm coming down. Be ready.* He said:

> Lo, I come unto thee in a thick cloud, that the people may hear when I speak with thee, and believe thee for ever.... Go unto the people, and sanctify them today and tomorrow, and let them wash their clothes, And be ready against the third day: for the third day the Lord will come down in the sight of all the people upon mount Sinai (Exodus 19:9-11).

Right now, God is saying much the same thing to us. He's saying, *Get ready! I'm about to manifest Myself in your midst!* He's telling us to sanctify ourselves unto Him, to separate from the unclean things of this world.

Our robes of righteousness must be bright and spotless because the Lord is coming down to us in these last days. When His power comes in fullness, it brings life to what's good and death to what's bad. We haven't seen much of that kind of power in our day, so we don't usually think in those terms. But it's time we start to. It's time we realized that when God manifests Himself in great measure among us, His glory will destroy sin in a moment's time. So those who are clinging to sin will be in trouble.

Someone might say, "Now wait a minute, that sounds like Old Testament theology to me."

No, it isn't. Do you remember what happened to Ananias and Sapphira in Acts 5? As far as I know, they were members in good standing of the New Testament Church. (It was a big church and Peter knew Ananias by name.) But they conspired together to lie to the Holy Ghost and, as a result, they both died in church on the same day! That would not have happened in a cold, dead church.

We haven't seen anything like that in recent times because, up to this point, the power of God hasn't been in manifestation as powerfully among us as it was in the early Church. If there's just a little power being manifested, then people get away with more, longer. But when great power of God is being manifested, you better be going with God and not against Him.

Sin in the Church was dealt with quickly in that day. Of course, it didn't have to be that way. Ananias and Sapphira could have repented on the spot. Each could have said, "I was wrong. Forgive me!" But they didn't. They clung to their sin. So when the power of God extinguished that sin in the Church, their physical lives were extinguished, too.

Disconnect From Worldliness

I realize that's a sobering thought. But the Bible instructs us to be sober in these last days. It teaches that we should be serious about sanctifying ourselves; that we should *"follow...holiness, without which no man shall see the Lord"* (Hebrews 12:14).

Do you want to be ready when Jesus comes to catch His Church away? Do you want to see and move in manifestations of His power and glory in the days that lead up to His coming? Then live holy and without blame before Him in love (Ephesians 1:4).

In other words, if you and I want to get in on this great move of God, we must follow after holiness. Those who are obedient to Him will be able to stand in the midst of this great work.

Exactly what does the word *holiness* mean? It simply means "separation to God" or "conduct befitting those so separated."

To *separate* means "to set apart, to dis-unite, to divide, to sever, to disconnect, to part company, to go in a different direction, to cease to be associated, to become distinct or disengage as cream separates from milk and rises to the top."

If we want to be holy, we must be discon-nected from the world and its ways, and con-nected to God and His ways.

"But we're just human beings," you may say. "Is it really possible for us to be holy?"

Yes, it is, because we've been born again. When that happened we were separated to God on the *inside.* Now God expects us to walk out that separation so that it will take effect on the *outside.* Holiness isn't a scary thing that only a few people achieve. Everyone in the Body of Christ should walk in holiness. We have been given the robe of righteousness, but we have to maintain it. We have the HOLY Spirit living inside us for that purpose—He directs us in holiness. We can do our part if we choose to obey Him.

We ought not look like the world and talk and act like the world. We ought to look and talk and act like God, Who fathered us! The Bible says, *"As the One Who called you is holy, you yourselves also be holy in all your conduct and manner of living"* (1 Peter 1:15, AMP). Honestly, I'm surprised at how some Christians live. When I see believers who go to church and act nice on Sunday, then live like the world the rest of the week, it disturbs me. I don't believe that's normal behavior for a believer and I'm not used to it.

Ken and I haven't been raised spiritually around people who live one way at church and another way at home. Those we have followed and the people we run with act the same all the time. When we take off on our motorcycle trips, we might look like the world with our helmets and our leathers on, but we praise God, talk faith and act in love just like we do when we're preaching at a convention. And we have a wonderful time and lots of fun!

If your friends don't do that, you need to get some new friends. If your friends are worldly, you need to separate yourself from them and find some others, because your associates will pull you down to their level. You need to get away and break off from people who live in sin—whether they call themselves Christians or not.

I can prove it to you from the Word. In his two letters to the Corinthians, the Apostle Paul wrote:

> Now I have written unto you not to keep company, if any man that is called a brother be a fornicator, or covetous, or an idolater, or a railer, or a drunkard, or an extortioner... (1 Corinthians 5:11).

> Be ye not unequally yoked together with unbelievers: for what fellowship hath righteousness with unrighteousness? and what communion hath light with darkness? And what concord hath Christ with Belial? or what part hath he that believeth with an infidel? And what

agreement hath the temple of God with idols? for ye are the temple of the living God; as God hath said, I will dwell in them, and walk in them; and I will be their God, and they shall be my people. Wherefore come out from among them, and be ye separate, saith the Lord, and touch not the unclean thing; and I will receive you, And will be a Father unto you, and ye shall be my sons and daughters, saith the Lord Almighty. Having therefore these promises, dearly beloved, let us cleanse ourselves from all filthiness of the flesh and spirit, perfecting holiness in the fear of God (2 Corinthians 6:14-7:1).

We should minister to the unrighteous. It's good to go to sinners and bring them the good news. But these scriptures tell us not to have ongoing fellowship with them. Don't hang out or let your hair down with that group. They'll end up having a negative effect on you.

They'll start influencing you toward their unholy way of thinking. Pretty soon, you'll be watching the television shows and the movies they watch. You'll be feeding your mind on things that are full of sin. You'll begin to talk like them and act like them.

Walk in love and be an example. Then you can bring them up to a higher level. Listen, you and I don't have any business feeding on the world's sin. We've been set apart for God and for His sacred use! We don't need to be watching television sitcoms that make light of immorality. Those things are intended to desensitize people to sin. They applaud evil. But Proverbs 3:7 says to *"depart from evil."* If we want to perfect holiness in the fear of God, we'll have to shut off that kind of thing!

I realize some people will argue about that. They'll say, "It's just a little harmless fun. It's nothing serious. They're just playing around."

The Bible warns us about that attitude. It says we're not to be like the children of Israel were when they indulged in the sinful ways of the world and *"sat down to eat and drink, and rose up to play"* (1 Corinthians 10:7).

Instead, we are to follow Psalm 101:2-3, *"I will behave myself wisely in a perfect way. O when wilt thou come unto me? I will walk within my house with a perfect heart. I will set no wicked thing before mine eyes: I hate the work of them that turn aside; it shall not cleave to me."*

Don't play around like the people in the world do. It will get you in trouble. You might start out on a small scale. For example, you might indulge in just a little glass of wine after dinner now and then, and say, "Well, Gloria, I don't think there's anything wrong with that."

That may be, but you have to admit that many others do consider it wrong. And we're under obligation to live right before other people. You may think no one will find out, but they will. Those things won't remain a secret, because Jesus said what is done in the dark will be made known in the light.

Maybe *you* could have just one glass of wine and never overindulge, but what about the people to whom you are an example? Wine is alcohol. It is addictive. It is easy for people to become alcoholics. If you really want, or have a strong desire, to drink, you could very well fit in this category. You don't want to be responsible for that. The Bible says to avoid the very appearance of evil (1 Thessalonians 5:22). Besides, Jesus said He would drink no more wine *"until that day when I drink it new with you in my Father's kingdom"* (Matthew 26:29). It would be good to follow Him!

What's more, compromising ourselves for something as silly as a drink of alcohol is foolishness. Why would we want something like that in our way when we can walk in the glory of God? Why would we go after some stupid, fleshly indulgence when we can go after the power and glory of God? The Bible says for us *not* to be drunk with wine, but to be filled with the Holy Spirit! That is so much better and more exciting! (See Ephesians 5:18.)

Nothing Legalistic About It

If you think I'm being legalistic, think again. There is nothing legalistic about holiness. In fact, under the Law, holiness was totally unattainable.

That's because holiness doesn't come by simply observing outward rules or laws. Holiness comes as the result of the work of grace God does in our hearts! It manifests in our lives as we live out, by grace, what God has put within us. Titus 2:11-14 says it this way:

> **For the grace of God that bringeth salvation hath appeared to all men, Teaching us that,**

denying ungodliness and worldly lusts, we should live soberly, righteously, and godly, in this present world; Looking for that blessed hope, and the glorious appearing of the great God and our Saviour Jesus Christ; Who gave himself for us, that he might redeem us from all iniquity, and purify unto himself a peculiar people, zealous of good works.

The grace of God means the favor of God. God is showing us favor when He corrects us by His Spirit.

If we want to enjoy the favor of God in one area, we need to have it in the other areas. If we want to enjoy the blessing and favor of God in our midst, then we will have to receive the grace of God that teaches us to deny ungodliness.

You can learn more about how grace works if you'll read the book of Romans. There, the Apostle Paul says that *"if ye live after the flesh, ye shall die: but if ye through the Spirit do mortify the deeds of the body, ye shall live. For as many as are led by the Spirit of God, they are the sons of God"* (Romans 8:13-14).

Paul is telling us that, while grace has freed us from the Law, it obligates us to walk in obedience to the Holy Spirit. And the Holy Spirit will never condone sin in our lives. On the contrary, He will lead us to put to death ungodly desires and activities of the body.

If you will fellowship with God and stay in living contact with Him, the Holy Spirit will lead you into holiness. He will say to you, for example, *Stop using that profane language. Use words that glorify the Lord. Or, Stop reading those worldly novels and read more of the Word.*

Now that may sound like a legalistic requirement, but it's not. Here's why: God's suggestions always bring life. And you don't have to do it in your own strength. Whatever the Holy Ghost asks us to do, He also empowers us to do. The Bible says in 1 Corinthians 10:13 that God gives us the strength to overcome every temptation.

That's why the New Testament speaks to us in such strong terms about holiness. Nowhere does it say, "Well, I know you Christians have been sinning a lot lately, but, hey, I understand. Life is tough and at least you're trying."

No! It just says, "Be ye holy; for I am holy" (1 Peter 1:15-16). We have no excuse for living unholy lives. By grace and by His Spirit, God not only prompts us to be holy—He enables us to live the holy lifestyle He's called us to!

And, I'm telling you, it is high time we take advantage of the power of God's Holy Spirit that indwells us. We've reached the end of this age. Jesus is coming sooner than we think. It is time to get the slack out of our lives and become absolutely focused on God. It's time to drop everything that pulls us away from Him. It's time to get our flesh under control and yield only to the Holy Spirit.

Don't Be an Unholy Tare

Peter said, *"For the time is come that judgment must begin at the house of God: and if it first begin at us, what shall the end be of them that obey not the gospel of God?"* (1 Peter 4:17).

We haven't heard a lot about that judgment in recent years. But that's not because the New Testament doesn't teach about it. It does! In fact, Jesus Himself talked about that judgment in Matthew 13. In years past, I didn't understand that chapter because I kept thinking He was referring to the catching away of the Church in the last days. But I knew that couldn't be right because He refers to the *wicked* being removed first—not the righteous.

Recently, I've come to believe that He is talking about the separation of the holy from the unholy that will take place in the final days of this age. Read His words for yourself.

The kingdom of heaven is likened unto a man which sowed good seed in his field: But while men slept, his enemy came and sowed tares among the wheat, and went his way. But when the blade was sprung up, and brought forth fruit, then appeared the tares also. So the servants of the householder came and said unto him, Sir, didst not thou sow good seed in thy field? from whence then hath it tares? He said unto them, An enemy hath done this. The servants said unto him, Wilt thou then that we go and gather them up? But he said, Nay; lest while ye gather up the tares, ye root up also the wheat with them. Let both grow together until the harvest: and in the time of harvest I will say to the reapers, Gather ye together first the tares, and bind them in bundles to burn them: but gather the wheat into my barn (verses 24-30).

Now, the disciples who were listening to this parable didn't understand it. So later they asked Jesus to explain it to them and He said:

He that soweth the good seed is the Son of man; The field is the world; the good seed are the children of the kingdom; but the tares are the children of the wicked one; The enemy that sowed them is the devil; the harvest is the end of the world; and the reapers are the angels. As therefore the tares are gathered and burned in the fire; so shall it be in the end of this world. The Son of man shall send forth his angels, and they shall gather out of his kingdom all things that offend, and them which do iniquity; And shall cast them into a furnace of fire: there shall be wailing and gnashing of teeth. Then shall the righteous shine forth as the sun in the kingdom of their Father (verses 37-43).

According to Jesus, there is coming a time at the end of the world, at the harvest time, when the tares will be bundled together and burned. In other words, it will be a time of separation. Impostors in the Church will not be able to stand the presence of God. It's the time when the righteous will shine with the glory of God. It's the time when Jesus will sanctify His Church and cleanse it so that He *"might present it to himself a glorious church, not having spot, or wrinkle, or any such thing; but that it should be holy and without blemish"* (see Ephesians 5:26-27).

If you're an unholy tare, that's a frightening thought. But if you've set your heart on being holy, it's exciting. You will be part of that glorious Church.

Now, you might say, "But I don't know if I can be holy, without spot or blemish!" We could never be that Church, except the blood of Jesus is always available to cleanse us from sin. When you sin and miss the mark, be quick to repent. Turn away from sin and turn to the Father.

This then is the message which we have heard of him, and declare unto you, that God is light, and in him is no darkness at all. If we say that we have fellowship with him, and walk in darkness, we lie, and do not the truth: But if we walk in the light, as he is in the light, we have fellowship one with another, and the blood of Jesus Christ his Son cleanseth us from all sin. If we say that we have no sin, we deceive ourselves, and the truth is not in us. If we confess our sins, he is faithful and just to forgive us our sins, and to cleanse us from all unrighteousness. If we say that we have not sinned, we make him a liar, and his word is not in us. My little children, these things write I unto you, that ye sin not. And if any man sin, we have an advocate with the Father, Jesus Christ the righteous: And he is the propitiation for our sins: and not for ours only, but also for the sins of the whole world (1 John 1:5-2:2).

By the grace of God, Jesus is coming for a glorious Church. We have to be glorious. If this is the end, then there's no one else to do it. We're it! We're all God has, and because He is God, He can bring it forth in us!

God *is* able! So, let's believe that. Let's act on it. Let's pray for ourselves and each other the inspired words of the Apostle Paul:

May the God of peace Himself sanctify you through and through [separate you from profane things, make you pure and wholly consecrated to God]; and may your spirit and soul and body be preserved sound and complete [and found] blameless at the coming of our Lord Jesus Christ (the Messiah). Faithful is He Who is calling you [to Himself] and utterly trustworthy, and He will also do it (1 Thessalonians 5:23-24, AMP).

Hallelujah! Amen!!

Scriptures for Living Holy

"Be ye holy; for I am holy" (1 Peter 1:16).

God has not only called you to be holy or separated unto Him, but He has also made it possible. If you're born again, the blood of Jesus has cleansed you from all unrighteousness and, as Hebrews 10 says, through this new and living way, you can now draw near to God (verses 19-22). You can actually fellowship with God in His presence.

This vital fellowship and contact with God is your key to living a holy life. When you live vitally united to God, you yield to and obey His Word and what He speaks to you directly. No matter how hard you try, you can't walk holy in your own strength. But when you are connected to God and His way of thinking, then you are strong spiritually.

When you are in vital fellowship with God, you spend time in prayer and in His Word. John 17:14-17 says, *"I have given them thy word; and the world hath hated them, because they are not of the world, even as I am not of the world. I pray not that thou shouldest take them out of the world, but that thou shouldest keep them from the evil. They are not of the world, even as I am not of the world. Sanctify them through thy truth: thy word is truth."*

God's Word sanctifies or separates you from the world's way of thinking and living. When you abide in it, study it, meditate on it and obey what it says, it sanctifies you and makes you holy. To the degree that you hear and obey God's Word, that is the degree you will be separated unto God. Although there are different degrees of separation, full separation is available to everyone.

You actually became separated unto God when you were born again. According to 1 Corinthians 1:30, Jesus has been made unto us wisdom, righteousness, sanctification and redemption. Now, you have to walk that separation out.

Allow the Word to separate you. Study the following scriptures and use your faith to activate them in your life. Put them in your heart and speak them out of your mouth. Begin to walk in holiness one step at a time. Learn to recognize any disobedience, or weight or sin in your life that is standing between you and

God—and let it go! With the leading and help of the Holy Spirit and the Word of God as your firm foundation, you will not fail!

Exodus 19:5-6

If ye will obey my voice indeed, and keep my covenant, then ye shall be a peculiar treasure unto me above all people: for all the earth is mine: And ye shall be unto me a kingdom of priests, and an holy nation.

Exodus 20:2-5

I am the Lord thy God, which have brought thee out of the land of Egypt, out of the house of bondage. Thou shalt have no other gods before me. Thou shalt not make unto thee any graven image, or any likeness of any thing that is in heaven above, or that is in the earth beneath, or that is in the water under the earth: Thou shalt not bow down thyself to them, nor serve them: for I the Lord thy God am a jealous God.

Deuteronomy 6:18

Thou shalt do that which is right and good in the sight of the Lord: that it may be well with thee.

Deuteronomy 28:9, 14

The Lord shall establish thee an holy people unto himself, as he hath sworn unto thee, if thou shalt keep the commandments of the Lord thy God, and walk in his ways.... And thou shalt not go aside from any of the words which I command thee this day, to the right hand, or to the left, to go after other gods to serve them.

Joshua 24:15

Choose you this day whom ye will serve...but as for me and my house, we will serve the Lord.

1 Chronicles 28:9

Know thou the God of thy father, and serve him with a perfect heart and with a willing mind: for the Lord searcheth all hearts, and understandeth all the imaginations of the thoughts: if thou seek him, he will be found of thee.

Psalm 4:3, NIV

Know that the Lord has set apart the godly for himself.

Psalm 19:12-14

Who can understand his errors? cleanse thou me from secret faults. Keep back thy servant also from presumptuous sins; let them not have dominion over me: then shall I be upright, and I shall be innocent from the great transgression. Let the words of my mouth, and the meditation of my heart, be acceptable in thy sight, O Lord, my strength, and my redeemer.

Psalm 24:3-5

Who shall ascend into the hill of the Lord? or who shall stand in his holy place? He that hath clean hands, and a pure heart; who hath not lifted up his soul unto vanity, nor sworn deceitfully. He shall receive the blessing from the Lord, and righteousness from the God of his salvation.

Psalm 32:8-9, NKJV

I will instruct you and teach you in the way you should go; I will guide you with My eye. Do not be like the horse or like the mule, Which have no understanding, Which must be harnessed with bit and bridle, Else they will not come near you.

Psalm 37:27-28

Depart from evil, and do good; and dwell for evermore. For the Lord loveth judgment, and forsaketh not his saints; they are preserved for ever: but the seed of the wicked shall be cut off.

Psalm 40:6-8

Sacrifice and offering thou didst not desire; mine ears hast thou opened: burnt offering and sin offering hast thou not required. Then said I, Lo, I come: in the volume of the book it is written of me, I delight to do thy will, O my God: yea, thy law is within my heart.

Psalm 51:10-11

Create in me a clean heart, O God; and renew a right spirit within me. Cast me not away from thy presence; and take not thy holy spirit from me.

Psalm 119:9, AMP

How shall a young man cleanse his way? By taking heed and keeping watch [on himself] according to Your word [conforming his life to it].

Psalm 132:9, 13-16

Let thy priests be clothed with righteousness; and let thy saints shout for joy.... For the Lord hath chosen Zion; he hath desired it for his habitation. This is my rest for ever: here will I dwell; for I have desired it. I will abundantly bless her provision: I will satisfy her poor with bread. I will also clothe her priests with salvation: and her saints shall shout aloud for joy.

Proverbs 3:7-8, NKJV

Do not be wise in your own eyes; Fear the Lord and depart from evil. It will be health to your flesh, And strength to your bones.

Proverbs 4:24-27, AMP

Put away from you false and dishonest speech, and willful and contrary talk put far from you. Let your eyes look right on [with fixed purpose], and let your gaze be straight before you. Consider well the path of your feet, and let all your ways be established and ordered aright. Turn not aside to the right hand or to the left; remove your foot from evil.

Proverbs 6:16-19

These six things doth the Lord hate: yea, seven are an abomination unto him: A proud look, a lying tongue, and hands that shed innocent blood, An heart that deviseth wicked imaginations, feet that be swift in running to mischief,

A false witness that speaketh lies, and he that soweth discord among brethren.

Proverbs 16:6, AMP

By mercy and love, truth and fidelity [to God and man—not by sacrificial offerings], iniquity is purged out of the heart, and by the reverent, worshipful fear of the Lord men depart from and avoid evil.

Proverbs 20:11, NIV

Even a child is known by his actions, by whether his conduct is pure and right.

Proverbs 21:8, AMP

The way of the guilty is exceedingly crooked, but as for the pure, his work is right and his conduct is straight.

Proverbs 30:12

There is a generation that are pure in their own eyes, and yet is not washed from their filthiness.

Isaiah 1:16-19

Wash you, make you clean; put away the evil of your doings from before mine eyes; cease to do evil; Learn to do well.... Come now, and let us reason together, saith the Lord: though your sins be as scarlet, they shall be as white as snow; though they be red like crimson, they shall be as wool. If ye be willing and obedient, ye shall eat the good of the land.

Isaiah 3:10-11

Say ye to the righteous, that it shall be well with him: for they shall eat the fruit of their doings. Woe unto the wicked! it shall be ill with him: for the reward of his hands shall be given him.

Isaiah 43:21

This people have I formed for myself; they shall show forth my praise.

Isaiah 55:6-9

Seek ye the Lord while he may be found, call ye upon him while he is near: Let the wicked forsake his way, and the unrighteous man his thoughts: and let him return unto the Lord, and he will have mercy upon him; and to our God, for he will abundantly pardon. For my thoughts are not your thoughts, neither are your ways my ways, saith the Lord. For as the heavens are higher than the earth, so are my ways higher than your ways, and my thoughts than your thoughts.

Jeremiah 15:19

Thus saith the Lord, If thou return, then will I bring thee again, and thou shalt stand before me: and if thou take forth the precious from the vile, thou shalt be as my mouth.

Jeremiah 18:11

Return ye now every one from his evil way, and make your ways and your doings good.

Daniel 1:8

But Daniel purposed in his heart that he would not defile himself with the portion of the king's meat, nor with the wine which he drank: therefore he requested of the prince of the eunuchs that he might not defile himself.

Matthew 5:8

Blessed are the pure in heart: for they shall see God.

Matthew 5:48, AMP

You, therefore, must be perfect [growing into complete maturity of godliness in mind and character, having reached the proper height of virtue and integrity], as your heavenly Father is perfect.

Matthew 6:33

Seek ye first the kingdom of God, and his righteousness; and all these things shall be added unto you.

Matthew 10:24-25

The disciple is not above his master, nor the servant above his lord. It is enough for the disciple that he be as his master, and the servant as his lord.

Matthew 15:8

This people draweth nigh unto me with their mouth, and honoureth me with their lips; but their heart is far from me.

Mark 8:34-38

Whosoever will come after me, let him deny himself, and take up his cross, and follow me. For whosoever will save his life shall lose it; but whosoever shall lose his life for my sake and the gospel's, the same shall save it. For what shall it profit a man, if he shall gain the whole world, and lose his own soul? Or what shall a man give in exchange for his soul? Whosoever therefore shall be ashamed of me and of my words in this adulterous and sinful generation; of him also shall the Son of man be ashamed, when he cometh in the glory of his Father with the holy angels.

Luke 1:15

For he shall be great in the sight of the Lord, and shall drink neither wine nor strong drink.

Luke 3:8, AMP

Bear fruits that are deserving and consistent with [your] repentance [that is, conduct worthy of a heart changed, a heart abhorring sin].

Luke 6:40

The disciple is not above his master: but every one that is perfect shall be as his master.

Luke 11:2

He said unto them, When ye pray, say, Our Father which art in heaven, Hallowed be thy name.

John 14:21, 23-24

He that hath my commandments, and keepeth them, he it is that loveth me: and he that loveth me shall be loved of my Father, and I will love him, and will manifest myself to him.... Jesus answered and said unto him, If a man love me, he will keep my words: and my Father will love him, and we will come unto him, and make our abode with him. He that loveth me not keepeth not my sayings: and the word which ye hear is not mine, but the Father's which sent me.

John 15:2-4

Every branch in me that beareth not fruit he taketh away: and every branch that beareth fruit, he purgeth it, that it may bring forth more fruit. Now ye are clean through the word which I have spoken unto you. Abide in me, and I in you. As the branch cannot bear fruit of itself, except it abide in the vine; no more can ye, except ye abide in me.

John 15:5-8

I am the vine, ye are the branches: He that abideth in me, and I in him, the same bringeth forth much fruit: for without me ye can do nothing. If a man abide not in me, he is cast forth as a branch, and is withered; and men gather them, and cast them into the fire, and they are burned. If ye abide in me, and my words abide in you, ye shall ask what ye will, and it shall be done unto you. Herein is my Father glorified, that ye bear much fruit; so shall ye be my disciples.

John 17:15-20

I pray not that thou shouldest take them out of the world, but that thou shouldest keep them from the evil. They are not of the world, even as I am not of the world. Sanctify them through thy truth: thy word is truth. As thou hast sent me into the world, even so have I also sent them into the world. And for their sakes I sanctify myself, that they also might be sanctified through the truth. Neither pray I for these alone, but for them also which shall believe on me through their word.

Acts 20:32

Now, brethren, I commend you to God, and to the word of his grace, which is able to build you up, and to give you an inheritance among all them which are sanctified.

Acts 26:18

To open their eyes, and to turn them from darkness to light, and from the power of Satan unto God, that they may receive forgiveness of sins, and inheritance among them which are sanctified by faith that is in me [Jesus].

Romans 6:1-6

Shall we continue in sin, that grace may abound? God forbid. How shall we, that are dead to sin, live any longer therein? Know ye not, that so many of us as were baptized into Jesus Christ were baptized into his death? Therefore we are buried with him by baptism into death: that like as Christ was raised up from the dead by the glory of the Father, even so we also should walk in newness of life. For if we have been planted together in the likeness of his death, we shall be also in the likeness of his resurrection: Knowing this, that our old man is crucified with him, that the

body of sin might be destroyed, that henceforth we should not serve sin.

Romans 6:11-14, NKJV

Likewise you also, reckon yourselves to be
dead indeed to sin, but alive to God in Christ
Jesus our Lord. Therefore do not let sin reign
in your mortal body, that you should obey it
in its lusts. And do not present your members
as instruments of unrighteousness to sin, but
present yourselves to God as being alive from
the dead, and your members as instruments
of righteousness to God. For sin shall not have
dominion over you.

Romans 6:15-16, Moffatt

Are we "to sin, because we live under grace,
not under law"? Never! Do you not know

you are servants of the master you obey, of the master to whom you yield yourselves obedient, whether it is Sin, whose service ends in death, or Obedience, whose service ends in righteousness?

Romans 6:15-18, NKJV

What then? Shall we sin because we are not under law but under grace? Certainly not! Do you not know that to whom you present yourselves slaves to obey, you are that one's slaves whom you obey, whether of sin leading to death, or of obedience leading to right-eousness? But God be thanked that though you were slaves of sin, yet you obeyed from the heart that form of doctrine to which you were delivered. And having been set free from sin, you became slaves of righteousness.

Romans 6:19, 22

I speak after the manner of men because of the infirmity of your flesh: for as ye have yielded your members servants to uncleanness and to iniquity unto iniquity; even so now yield your members servants to righteousness unto holiness.... But now being made free from sin, and become servants to God, ye have your fruit unto holiness, and the end everlasting life.

Romans 8:6, 13-14

To be carnally minded [to think as the world thinks] is death; but to be spiritually minded

[to think as God thinks] is life and peace....
For if ye live after the flesh, ye shall die: but if
ye through the Spirit do mortify the deeds of
the body, ye shall live. For as many as are led
by the Spirit of God, they are the sons of God.

Romans 8:29

Whom he did foreknow, he also did predes-
tinate to be conformed to the image of his
Son, that he might be the firstborn among
many brethren.

Romans 12:1-2

I beseech you therefore, brethren, by the
mercies of God, that ye present your bodies a
living sacrifice, holy, acceptable unto God,
which is your reasonable service. And be not

conformed to this world: but be ye transformed by the renewing of your mind, that ye may prove what is that good, and acceptable, and perfect, will of God.

Romans 15:16

That I should be the minister of Jesus Christ to the Gentiles, ministering the gospel of God, that the offering up of the Gentiles might be acceptable, being sanctified by the Holy Ghost.

1 Corinthians 1:2

To them that are sanctified in Christ Jesus, called to be saints, with all that in every place call upon the name of Jesus Christ our Lord, both theirs and ours.

1 Corinthians 1:10

Now I beseech you, brethren, by the name of our Lord Jesus Christ, that ye all speak the same thing, and that there be no divisions among you; but that ye be perfectly joined together in the same mind and in the same judgment.

1 Corinthians 1:30

But of him [God] are ye in Christ Jesus, who of God is made unto us wisdom, and righteousness, and sanctification, and redemption.

1 Corinthians 3:1-3

I, brethren, could not speak unto you as unto spiritual, but as unto carnal, even as unto babes in Christ. I have fed you with milk, and not with meat: for hitherto ye were not able to bear it, neither yet now are ye able. For ye are yet carnal: for whereas there is among you envying, and strife, and divisions, are ye not carnal, and walk as men?

1 Corinthians 3:16-17

Know ye not that ye are the temple of God, and that the Spirit of God dwelleth in you? If any man defile the temple of God, him shall God destroy; for the temple of God is holy, which temple ye are.

1 Corinthians 6:9-11, NKJV

Do you not know that the unrighteous will not inherit the kingdom of God? Do not be deceived. Neither fornicators, nor idolaters, nor adulterers, nor homosexuals, nor sodomites, nor thieves, nor covetous, nor drunkards, nor revilers, nor extortioners will inherit the kingdom of God. And such were some of you. But you were washed, but you were sanctified, but you were justified in the name of the Lord Jesus and by the Spirit of our God.

1 Corinthians 6:13-20, NIV

The body is not meant for sexual immorality, but for the Lord, and the Lord for the body. By his power God raised the Lord from the dead, and he will raise us also. Do you not know that your bodies are members of Christ himself? Shall I then take the members of Christ and unite them with a prostitute? Never! Do you not know that he who unites himself with a prostitute is one with her in body? For it is said, "The two will become one flesh." But he who unites himself with the Lord is one with him in spirit. Flee from sexual immorality. All other sins a man commits are outside his body, but he who sins sexually sins against his own body. Do you not know that your body is a temple of the Holy Spirit, who is in you, whom you have received from God? You are not your own; you were bought at a price. Therefore honor God with your body.

1 Corinthians 7:14

For the unbelieving husband is sanctified by the wife, and the unbelieving wife is sanctified by the husband: else were your children unclean; but now are they holy.

1 Corinthians 9:24-27, NKJV

Do you not know that those who run in a race all run, but one receives the prize? Run in such a way that you may obtain it. And everyone who competes for the prize is temperate in all things. Now they do it to obtain a perishable crown, but we for an imperishable crown. Therefore I run thus: not with uncertainty. Thus I fight: not as one who beats the air. But I discipline my body and bring it into subjection, lest, when I have preached to others, I myself should become disqualified.

1 Corinthians 10:1, 4-11, NKJV

All our fathers were under the cloud, all passed through the sea, all were baptized into Moses in the cloud and in the sea.... They drank of that spiritual Rock that foll...

that Rock was Christ. But with ...

God was not well pleased, for the...

were scattered in the wilderness. Now these things became our examples, to the intent that we should not lust after evil things as they also lusted. And do not become idolaters as were some of them.... Nor let us commit sexual immorality, as some of them did, and in one day twenty-three thousand fell; nor let us tempt Christ, as some of them also tempted, and were destroyed by serpents; nor complain, as some of them also complained, and were destroyed by the destroyer. Now all these things happened to them as examples, and they were written for our admonition.

1 Corinthians 10:13, NKJV

No temptation has overtaken you except such
as is common to man; but God is faithful,
who will not allow you to be tempted beyond
what you are able, but with the temptation
will also make the way of escape, that you may
be able to bear it.

1 Corinthians 10:21

Ye cannot drink the cup of the Lord, and the
cup of devils: ye cannot be partakers of the
Lord's table, and of the table of devils.

1 Corinthians 15:33-34, AMP

Do not be so deceived and misled! Evil com-
panionships (communion, associations)
corrupt and deprave good manners and

morals and character. Awake...to sober sense and your right minds, and sin no more.

2 Corinthians 4:10

Always bearing about in the body the dying of the Lord Jesus, that the life also of Jesus might be made manifest in our body.

2 Corinthians 10:3-5

Though we walk in the flesh, we do not war after the flesh: (For the weapons of our warfare are not carnal, but mighty through God to the pulling down of strong holds;) Casting down imaginations, and every high thing that exalteth itself against the knowledge of God, and bringing into captivity every thought to the obedience of Christ.

Galatians 2:20

I am crucified with Christ: nevertheless I live; yet not I, but Christ liveth in me: and the life which I now live in the flesh I live by the faith of the Son of God, who loved me, and gave himself for me.

Galatians 4:3-7

Even so we, when we were children, were in bondage under the elements of the world: But when the fulness of the time was come, God sent forth his Son, made of a woman, made under the law, To redeem them that were under the law, that we might receive the adoption of sons. And because ye are sons, God hath sent forth the Spirit of his Son into your hearts, crying, Abba, Father. Wherefore thou art no more a servant, but a son; and if a son, then an heir of God through Christ.

Galatians 4:19

My little children, of whom I travail in birth again until Christ be formed in you.

Galatians 5:13, 16-18, NIV

You, my brothers, were called to be free. But do not use your freedom to indulge the sinful nature; rather, serve one another in love.... Live by the Spirit, and you will not gratify the desires of the sinful nature. For the sinful nature desires what is contrary to the Spirit, and the Spirit what is contrary to the sinful nature. They are in conflict with each other, so that you do not do what you want. But if you are led by the Spirit, you are not under law.

Galatians 5:19-25

Now the works of the flesh are manifest, which are these; Adultery, fornication, uncleanness, lasciviousness, Idolatry, witchcraft, hatred, variance, emulations, wrath, strife, seditions, heresies, Envyings, murders, drunkenness, revellings, and such like: of the which I tell you before, as I have also told you in time past, that they which do such things shall not inherit the kingdom of God. But the fruit of the Spirit is love, joy, peace, longsuffering, gentleness, goodness, faith, Meekness, temperance: against such there is no law. And they that are Christ's have crucified the flesh with the affections and lusts. If we live in the Spirit, let us also walk in the Spirit.

Galatians 6:1

Brethren, if a man be overtaken in a fault, ye which are spiritual, restore such an one in the spirit of meekness; considering thyself, lest thou also be tempted.

Galatians 6:7-8

Be not deceived; God is not mocked: for whatsoever a man soweth, that shall he also reap. For he that soweth to his flesh shall of the flesh reap corruption; but he that soweth to the Spirit shall of the Spirit reap life everlasting.

Ephesians 1:4, AMP

[In His love] He [God] chose us—actually picked us out for Himself as His own—in Christ before the foundation of the world, that we should be holy (consecrated and set apart for Him) and blameless in His sight, even above reproach, before Him in love.

Ephesians 1:7, AMP

In Him we have redemption (deliverance and salvation) through His blood, the remission (forgiveness) of our offenses (shortcomings and trespasses), in accordance with the riches and the generosity of His gracious favor.

Ephesians 2:19-21

Now therefore ye are no more strangers and foreigners, but fellowcitizens with the saints, and of the household of God; And are built upon the foundation of the apostles and prophets, Jesus Christ himself being the chief corner stone; In whom all the building fitly framed together groweth unto an holy temple in the Lord.

Ephesians 4:11-15

He gave some, apostles; and some, prophets; and some, evangelists; and some, pastors and teachers; For the perfecting of the saints...for the edifying of the body of Christ: Till we all come in the unity of the faith, and of the knowledge of the Son of God, unto a perfect man, unto the measure of the stature of the fulness of Christ: That we henceforth be no more children, tossed to and fro...But speaking the truth in love, may grow up into him in all things, which is the head, even Christ.

Ephesians 4:17-24, NIV

So I tell you this, and insist on it in the Lord, that you must no longer live as the Gentiles do, in the futility of their thinking. They are darkened in their understanding and separated from the life of God because of the ignorance that is in them due to the hardening of their hearts. Having lost all sensitivity, they have given themselves over to sensuality so as to indulge in every kind of impurity, with a continual lust for more. You, however, did not come to know Christ that way. Surely you heard of him and were taught in him in accordance with the truth that is in Jesus. You were taught, with regard to your former way of life, to put off your old self, which is being corrupted by its deceitful desires; to be made new in the attitude of your minds; and to put on the new self, created to be like God in true righteousness and holiness.

Ephesians 4:25-28

Putting away lying, speak every man truth with his neighbour: for we are members one of another. Be ye angry, and sin not: let not the sun go down upon your wrath: Neither give place to the devil. Let him that stole steal no more: but rather let him labour, working with his hands the thing which is good.

Ephesians 4:29-32

Let no corrupt communication proceed out of your mouth, but that which is good to the use of edifying…. And grieve not the holy Spirit of God, whereby ye are sealed unto the day of redemption. Let all bitterness, and wrath, and anger, and clamour, and evil speaking, be put away from you, with all malice: And be ye kind one to another, tenderhearted, forgiving one another, even as God for Christ's sake hath forgiven you.

Ephesians 5:1-7

Be ye therefore followers of God, as dear children; And walk in love.... But fornication, and all uncleanness, or covetousness, let it not be once named among you, as becometh saints; Neither filthiness, nor foolish talking, nor jesting, which are not convenient: but rather giving of thanks. For this ye know, that no whoremonger, nor unclean person, nor covetous man, who is an idolater, hath any inheritance in the kingdom of Christ and of God. Let no man deceive you with vain words: for because of these things cometh the wrath of God upon the children of disobedience. Be not ye therefore partakers with them.

Ephesians 5:8-15, Moffatt

While once upon a time you were darkness, now in the Lord you are light; lead the life of those who are children of the light (for the fruit of light consists in all that is good and right and true), verifying what pleases the Lord. Have nothing to do with the fruitless enterprises of darkness; rather expose them. One is indeed ashamed even to speak of what such men do in secret; still, whatever the light exposes becomes illuminated.... Thus it is said, "Wake up, O sleeper, and rise from the dead; so Christ will shine upon you." Be strictly careful then about the life you lead; act like sensible men, not like thoughtless.

Ephesians 5:18, NIV

Do not get drunk on wine, which leads to debauchery. Instead, be filled with the Spirit.

Ephesians 5:21-24

Submitting yourselves one to another in the fear of God. Wives, submit yourselves unto your own husbands, as unto the Lord. For the husband is the head of the wife, even as Christ is the head of the church: and he is the saviour of the body. Therefore as the church is subject unto Christ, so let the wives be to their own husbands in every thing.

Ephesians 5:25-27

Christ also loved the church, and gave himself for it; That he might sanctify and cleanse it with the washing of water by the word, That he might present it to himself a glorious church, not having spot, or wrinkle, or any such thing; but that it should be holy and without blemish.

Philippians 4:8

Finally, brethren, whatsoever things are true, whatsoever things are honest, whatsoever things are just, whatsoever things are pure, whatsoever things are lovely, whatsoever things are of good report; if there be any virtue, and if there be any praise, think on these things.

Colossians 1:10, 12-14, 21-23

Walk worthy of the Lord unto all pleasing, being fruitful in every good work...Giving thanks unto the Father, which hath made us meet to be partakers of the inheritance of the saints in light: Who hath delivered us from the power of darkness, and hath translated us into the kingdom of his dear Son: In whom we have redemption through his blood, even the forgiveness of sins.... And you, that were sometime alienated and enemies in your mind by wicked works, yet now hath he reconciled In the body of his flesh through death, to present you holy and unblameable and unreproveable in his sight: If ye continue in the faith grounded and settled, and be not moved away from the hope of the gospel, which ye have heard.

Colossians 2:6

As ye have therefore received Christ Jesus the
Lord, so walk ye in him.

Colossians 3:1-2, AMP

If then you have been raised with Christ [to a
new life, thus sharing His resurrection from
the dead], aim at and seek the [rich, eternal
treasures] that are above, where Christ is,
seated at the right hand of God. And set your
minds and keep them set on what is above
(the higher things), not on the things that are
on the earth.

Colossians 3:5-10

Mortify therefore your members which are
upon the earth; fornication, uncleanness,

inordinate affection, evil concupiscence, and covetousness, which is idolatry: For which things' sake the wrath of God cometh on the children of disobedience: In the which ye also walked some time, when ye lived in them. But now ye also put off all these; anger, wrath, malice, blasphemy, filthy communication out of your mouth. Lie not one to another, seeing that ye have put off the old man with his deeds; And have put on the new man, which is renewed in knowledge after the image of him that created him.

Colossians 3:12

Put on therefore, as the elect of God, holy and beloved, bowels of mercies, kindness, humbleness of mind, meekness, longsuffering.

1 Thessalonians 3:12-13

The Lord make you to increase and abound in love one toward another, and toward all men, even as we do toward you: To the end he may stablish your hearts unblameable in holiness before God, even our Father, at the coming of our Lord Jesus Christ with all his saints.

1 Thessalonians 4:1-7

We beseech you, brethren, and exhort you...that as ye have received of us how ye ought to walk and to please God, so ye would abound more and more. For ye know what commandments we gave you by the Lord Jesus. For this is the will of God, even your sanctification, that ye should abstain from fornication: That every one of you should know how to possess his vessel in sanctification and honour; Not in the lust of concupiscence, even as the Gentiles which know not God: That no man go beyond and defraud his brother in any matter: because that the Lord is the avenger of all such.... For God hath not called us unto uncleanness, but unto holiness.

1 Thessalonians 5:15

See that none render evil for evil unto any man; but ever follow that which is good, both among yourselves, and to all men.

1 Thessalonians 5:21-22

Prove all things; hold fast that which is good. Abstain from all appearance of evil.

2 Thessalonians 2:13, NIV

Brothers loved by the Lord...from the beginning God chose you to be saved through the sanctifying work of the Spirit and through belief in the truth.

1 Timothy 2:8

I will therefore that men pray every where, lifting up holy hands, without wrath and doubting.

1 Timothy 4:1-5, NKJV

Now the Spirit expressly says that in latter times some will depart from the faith, giving heed to deceiving spirits and doctrines of demons, speaking lies in hypocrisy, having their own conscience seared with a hot iron...commanding to abstain from foods which God created to be received with thanksgiving by those who believe and know the truth. For every creature of God is good, and nothing is to be refused if it is received with thanksgiving; for it is sanctified by the word of God and prayer.

1 Timothy 4:14-16, Wuest

Do not keep on neglecting the spiritual enduement which is in you, which was given to you through prophecy in connection with the imposition of the hands of the body of elders. Be diligently attending to these things; be constantly engrossed in them, in order that your progress may be evident to all. Keep on paying careful attention to yourself and to the teaching. Constantly stay by them, for in doing this you will both save yourself and those who hear you [from the false doctrines of demons].

1 Timothy 6:11

Follow after righteousness, godliness, faith, love, patience, meekness.

2 Timothy 1:9, AMP

[For it is He] Who delivered and saved us and called us with a calling in itself holy and leading to holiness [to a life of consecration, a vocation of holiness]; [He did it] not because of anything of merit that we have done, but because of and to further His own purpose and grace (unmerited favor) which was given us in Christ Jesus before the world began.

2 Timothy 2:19-22

The Lord knoweth them that are his.... Let every one that nameth the name of Christ depart from iniquity. But in a great house there are not only vessels of gold and of silver, but also of wood and of earth; and some to honour, and some to dishonour. If a man therefore purge himself from these, he shall be a vessel unto honour, sanctified, and meet for the master's use, and prepared unto every good work. Flee also youthful lusts: but follow righteousness, faith, charity, peace, with them that call on the Lord out of a pure heart.

2 Timothy 3:16-17

All scripture is given by inspiration of God, and is profitable for doctrine, for reproof, for correction, for instruction in righteousness: That the man of God may be perfect, thoroughly furnished unto all good works.

Hebrews 2:1-3

Therefore we ought to give the more earnest heed to the things which we have heard, lest at any time we should let them slip. For if the word spoken by angels was stedfast, and every transgression and disobedience received a just recompence of reward; How shall we escape, if we neglect so great salvation; which at the first began to be spoken by the Lord, and was confirmed unto us by them that heard him?

Hebrews 2:9, 11, AMP

We are able to see Jesus...crowned with glory and honor because of His having suffered death, in order that by the grace (unmerited favor) of God [to us sinners] He might experience death for every individual person.... For both He Who sanctifies [making men holy] and those who are sanctified all have one [Father]. For this reason He is not ashamed to call them brethren.

Hebrews 2:18-3:1, NIV

Because he [Jesus] himself suffered when he was tempted, he is able to help those who are being tempted. Therefore, holy brothers, who share in the heavenly calling, fix your thoughts on Jesus, the apostle and high priest whom we confess.

Hebrews 3:14, 18

We are made partakers of Christ, if we hold the beginning of our confidence stedfast unto the end.... And to whom sware he that they should not enter into his rest, but to them that believed not?

Hebrews 4:14-16

Seeing then that we have a great high priest, that is passed into the heavens, Jesus the Son of God, let us hold fast our profession. For we have not an high priest which cannot be touched with the feeling of our infirmities; but was in all points tempted like as we are, yet without sin. Let us therefore come boldly unto the throne of grace, that we may obtain mercy, and find grace to help in time of need.

Hebrews 5:7-9, NIV

During the days of Jesus' life on earth, he offered up prayers and petitions with loud cries and tears to the one who could save him from death, and he was heard because of his reverent submission. Although he was a son, he learned obedience from what he suffered and, once made perfect, he became the source of eternal salvation for all who obey him.

Hebrews 5:12-6:1, AMP

For even though by this time you ought to be teaching others, you actually need someone to teach you over again the very first principles of God's Word. You have come to need milk, not solid food. For everyone who continues to feed on milk is obviously inexperienced and unskilled in the doctrine of righteousness (of conformity to the divine will in purpose, thought, and action), for he is a mere infant [not able to talk yet]! But solid food is for full-grown men, for those whose senses and mental faculties are trained by practice to discriminate and distinguish between what is morally good and noble and what is evil and contrary either to divine or human law. Therefore let us go on and get past the elementary stage in the teachings and doctrine of Christ (the Messiah), advancing steadily toward the completeness and perfection that belong to spiritual maturity. Let us not again be laying the foundation of repentance and abandonment of dead works (dead formalism), and of the faith [by which you turned] to God.

Hebrews 7:19

For the law made nothing perfect, but the bringing in of a better hope did; by the which we draw nigh unto God.

Hebrews 9:13-14

If the blood of bulls and of goats, and the ashes of an heifer sprinkling the unclean, sanctifieth to the purifying of the flesh: How much more shall the blood of Christ, who through the eternal Spirit offered himself without spot to God, purge your conscience from dead works to serve the living God?

Hebrews 9:24-26

For Christ is not entered into the holy places made with hands, which are the figures of the true; but into heaven itself, now to appear in the presence of God for us: Nor yet that he should offer himself often, as the high priest entereth into the holy place every year with blood of others; For then must he often have suffered since the foundation of the world: but now once in the end of the world hath he appeared to put away sin by the sacrifice of himself.

Hebrews 10:10, 14, AMP

In accordance with this will [of God], we have been made holy (consecrated and sanctified) through the offering made once for all of the body of Jesus Christ (the Anointed One)....

For by a single offering He has forever completely cleansed and perfected those who are consecrated and made holy.

Hebrews 10:19-22, NIV

Therefore, brothers, since we have confidence to enter the Most Holy Place by the blood of Jesus, by a new and living way opened for us through the curtain, that is, his body, and since we have a great priest over the house of God, let us draw near to God with a sincere heart in full assurance of faith, having our hearts sprinkled to cleanse us from a guilty conscience and having our bodies washed with pure water.

Hebrews 10:23-26

Let us hold fast the profession of our faith without wavering; (for he is faithful that promised;) And let us consider one another to provoke unto love and to good works: Not forsaking the assembling of ourselves together, as the manner of some is; but exhorting one another: and so much the more, as ye see the day approaching. For if we sin wilfully after that we have received the knowledge of the truth, there remaineth no more sacrifice for sins.

Hebrews 12:1-2

Seeing we also are compassed about with so great a cloud of witnesses, let us lay aside every weight, and the sin which doth so easily beset us, and let us run with patience the race that is set before us. Looking unto Jesus the author and finisher of our faith.

Hebrews 12:3-4

For consider him that endured such contradiction of sinners against himself, lest ye be wearied and faint in your minds. Ye have not yet resisted unto blood, striving against sin.

Hebrews 12:9-11, NKJV

We have had human fathers who corrected us, and we paid them respect. Shall we not much more readily be in subjection to the Father of spirits and live? For they indeed for a few days chastened [instructed, disciplined, educated, corrected, taught] us as seemed best to them, but He for our profit, that we may be partakers of His holiness. Now no chastening seems to be joyful for the present, but painful; nevertheless, afterward it yields the peaceable fruit of righteousness to those who have been trained by it.

Hebrews 12:14-15

Follow peace with all men, and holiness, without which no man shall see the Lord: Looking diligently lest any man fail of the grace of God; lest any root of bitterness springing up trouble you, and thereby many be defiled.

Hebrews 12:28

Wherefore we receiving a kingdom which cannot be moved, let us have grace, whereby we may serve God acceptably with reverence and godly fear.

Hebrews 13:12, AMP

Jesus also suffered and died outside the [city's] gate in order that He might purify and consecrate the people through [the shedding of] His own blood and set them apart as holy [for God].

Hebrews 13:20-21

Now the God of peace, that brought again from the dead our Lord Jesus, that great shepherd of the sheep, through the blood of the everlasting covenant, Make you perfect in every good work to do his will, working in you that which is wellpleasing in his sight, through Jesus Christ.

James 1:19-27

Wherefore, my beloved brethren, let every man be swift to hear, slow to speak, slow to wrath: For the wrath of man worketh not the righteousness of God. Wherefore lay apart all filthiness and superfluity of naughtiness, and receive with meekness the engrafted word, which is able to save your souls. But be ye doers of the word, and not hearers only, deceiving your own selves. For if any be a hearer of the word, and not a doer, he is like unto a man beholding his natural face in a glass: For he beholdeth himself, and goeth his way, and straightway forgetteth what manner of man he was. But whoso looketh into the perfect law of liberty, and continueth therein, he being not a forgetful hearer, but a doer of the work, this man shall be blessed in his deed. If any man among you seem to be religious, and bridleth not his tongue, but deceiveth his own heart, this man's religion is vain. Pure religion and undefiled before God and the Father is this, To visit the fatherless and widows in their affliction, and to keep himself unspotted from the world.

James 3:2, AMP

For we all often stumble and fall and offend in many things. And if anyone does not offend in speech [never says the wrong things] he is a fully developed character and a perfect man, able to control his whole body and to curb his entire nature.

James 3:13-16, NIV

Who is wise and understanding among you?
Let him show it by his good life, by deeds
done in the humility that comes from
wisdom. But if you harbor bitter envy and
selfish ambition in your hearts, do not boast
about it or deny the truth. Such "wisdom"
does not come down from heaven but is
earthly, unspiritual, of the devil. For where
you have envy and selfish ambition, there you
find disorder and every evil practice.

James 4:1-3

From whence come wars and fightings among
you? come they not hence, even of your lusts
that war in your members? Ye lust, and have
not: ye kill, and desire to have, and cannot

obtain: ye fight and war, yet ye have not, because ye ask not. Ye ask, and receive not, because ye ask amiss, that ye may consume it upon your lusts.

James 4:4-8, 10

Know ye not that the friendship of the world is enmity with God? whosoever therefore will be a friend of the world is the enemy of God. Do ye think that the scripture saith in vain, The spirit that dwelleth in us lusteth to envy? But he giveth more grace. Wherefore he saith, God resisteth the proud, but giveth grace unto the humble. Submit yourselves therefore to God. Resist the devil, and he will flee from you. Draw nigh to God, and he will draw nigh to you. Cleanse your hands, ye sinners; and

purify your hearts, ye double minded....
Humble yourselves in the sight of the Lord,
and he shall lift you up.

1 Peter 1:1-2, AMP

Peter, an apostle (a special messenger) of Jesus
Christ, [writing] to the elect exiles of the dis-
persion scattered (sowed) abroad...Who were
chosen and foreknown by God the Father and
consecrated (sanctified, made holy) by the
Spirit to be obedient to Jesus Christ (the
Messiah) and to be sprinkled with [His]
blood: May grace (spiritual blessing) and
peace be given you in increasing abundance
[that spiritual peace to be realized in and
through Christ, freedom from fears, agitating
passions, and moral conflicts].

1 Peter 1:13-17, AMP

Brace up your minds; be sober (circumspect, morally alert,... [Live] as children of obedience [to God]; do not conform yourselves to the evil desires [that governed you] in your former ignorance [when you did not know the requirements of the Gospel]. But as the One Who called you is holy, you yourselves also be holy in all your conduct and manner of living. For it is written, You shall be holy, for I am holy. And if you call upon Him as [your] Father Who judges each one impartially according to what he does, [then] you should conduct yourselves with true reverence.

1 Peter 1:18-19, AMP

You must know (recognize) that you were redeemed (ransomed) from the useless (fruitless) way of living inherited by tradition from [your] forefathers, not with corruptible things [such as] silver and gold, But [you were purchased] with the precious blood of Christ (the Messiah), like that of a [sacrificial] lamb without blemish or spot.

1 Peter 2:1-2

Laying aside all malice, and all guile, and hypocrisies, and envies, and all evil speakings, As newborn babes, desire the sincere milk of the word, that ye may grow thereby.

1 Peter 2:5, 9, NKJV

You also, as living stones, are being built up a spiritual house, a holy priesthood, to offer up spiritual sacrifices acceptable to God through Jesus Christ.... You are a chosen generation, a royal priesthood, a holy nation, His own special people, that you may proclaim the praises of Him who called you out of darkness into His marvelous light.

1 Peter 2:11-12, NIV

Dear friends, I urge you, as aliens and strangers in the world, to abstain from sinful desires, which war against your soul. Live such good lives among the pagans that, though they accuse you of doing wrong, they may see your good deeds and glorify God.

1 Peter 3:10-12, NKJV

He who would love life And see good days, Let him refrain his tongue from evil, And his lips from speaking deceit. Let him turn away from evil and do good; Let him seek peace and pursue it. For the eyes of the Lord are on the righteous, And His ears are open to their prayers; But the face of the Lord is against those who do evil.

1 Peter 3:15-18, NKJV

But sanctify the Lord God in your hearts, and always be ready to give a defense to everyone who asks you a reason for the hope that is in you, with meekness and fear; having a good conscience, that when they defame you as evildoers, those who revile your good conduct in Christ may be ashamed. For it is better, if it is the will of God, to suffer for doing good than for doing evil. For Christ also suffered once for sins, the just for the unjust, that He might bring us to God, being put to death in the flesh but made alive by the Spirit.

1 Peter 4:1, AMP

So, since Christ suffered in the flesh for us, for you, arm yourselves with the same thought and purpose [patiently to suffer rather than fail to please God]. For whoever has suffered in the flesh [having the mind of Christ] is done with [intentional] sin [has stopped pleasing himself and the world, and pleases God].

1 Peter 4:7-8

But the end of all things is at hand: be ye therefore sober, and watch unto prayer. And above all things have fervent charity among yourselves: for charity shall cover the multitude of sins.

1 Peter 4:15-16

Let none of you suffer as a murderer, or as a thief, or as an evildoer, or as a busybody in other men's matters. Yet if any man suffer as a Christian, let him not be ashamed; but let him glorify God on this behalf.

2 Peter: 1:3-4

His divine power hath given unto us all things that pertain unto life and godliness, through the knowledge of him that hath called us to glory and virtue: Whereby are given unto us exceeding great and precious promises: that by these ye might be partakers of the divine nature, having escaped the corruption that is in the world through lust.

2 Peter 2:9

The Lord knoweth how to deliver the godly out of temptations.

2 Peter 3:9-14

The Lord is not slack concerning his promise, as some men count slackness; but is longsuffering to us-ward, not willing that any should perish, but that all should come to repentance. But the day of the Lord will come as a thief in the night; in the which the heavens shall pass away with a great noise, and the elements shall melt with fervent heat, the earth also and the works that are therein shall be burned up. Seeing then that all these things shall be dissolved, what manner of persons ought ye to be in all holy conversation and godliness, Looking for and hasting unto the coming of the day of God, wherein the heavens being on fire shall be dissolved, and the elements shall melt with fervent heat? Nevertheless we, according to his promise, look for new heavens and a new earth, wherein dwelleth righteousness. Wherefore, beloved, seeing that ye look for such things, be diligent that ye may be found of him in peace, without spot, and blameless.

1 John 2:1, 3, 6, AMP

If anyone should sin, we have an Advocate (One Who will intercede for us) with the Father—[it is] Jesus Christ [the all] righteous [upright, just, Who conforms to the Father's will in every purpose, thought, and action].... And this is how we may discern [daily, by experience] that we are coming to know Him...if we keep (bear in mind, observe, practice) His teachings (precepts, commandments).... Whoever says he abides in Him ought [as a personal debt] to walk and conduct himself in the same way in which He walked and conducted Himself.

1 John 2:9-11

He that saith he is in the light, and hateth his brother, is in darkness even until now. He that loveth his brother abideth in the light, and there is none occasion of stumbling in him. But he that hateth his brother is in darkness, and walketh in darkness, and knoweth not whither he goeth, because that darkness hath blinded his eyes.

1 John 2:15-17

Love not the world, neither the things that are in the world. If any man love the world, the love of the Father is not in him. For all that is in the world, the lust of the flesh, and the lust of the eyes, and the pride of life, is not of the Father, but is of the world. And the world passeth away, and the lust thereof: but he that doeth the will of God abideth for ever.

1 John 2:20, 24, 28-29, NKJV

But you have an anointing from the Holy One, and you know all things.... Therefore let that abide in you which you heard from the beginning. If what you heard from the beginning abides in you, you also will abide in the Son and in the Father.... Now, little children, abide in Him, that when He appears, we may have confidence and not be ashamed before Him at His coming. If you know that He is righteous, you know that everyone who practices righteousness is born of Him.

1 John 3:1-3

Behold, what manner of love the Father hath bestowed upon us, that we should be called the sons of God: therefore the world knoweth us not, because it knew him not. Beloved, now are we the sons of God, and it doth not yet appear what we shall be: but we know that, when he shall appear, we shall be like him; for we shall see him as he is. And every man that hath this hope in him purifieth himself, even as he is pure.

1 John 3:18-22

My little children, let us not love in word, neither in tongue; but in deed and in truth. And hereby we know that we are of the truth, and shall assure our hearts before him. For if our heart condemn us, God is greater than our heart, and knoweth all things. Beloved, if our heart condemn us not, then have we confidence toward God. And whatsoever we ask, we receive of him, because we keep his commandments, and do those things that are pleasing in his sight.

1 John 5:17-18, 21, AMP

All wrongdoing is sin.... We know [absolutely] that anyone born of God does not [deliberately and knowingly] practice committing sin, but the One Who was begotten of God carefully watches over and protects him [Christ's divine presence within him preserves him against the evil], and the wicked one does not lay hold (get a grip) on him or touch [him].... Little children, keep yourselves from idols (false gods)—[from anything and everything that would occupy the place in your heart due to God, from any sort of substitute for Him that would take first place in your life].

Revelation 22:10-11

He saith unto me, Seal not the sayings of the prophecy of this book: for the time is at hand. He that is unjust, let him be unjust still: and he which is filthy, let him be filthy still: and he that is righteous, let him be righteous still: and he that is holy, let him be holy still.

Prayer for Salvation and
Baptism in the Holy Spirit

Heavenly Father, I come to You in the Name of Jesus. Your Word says, *"Whosoever shall call on the name of the Lord shall be saved"* (Acts 2:21). I am calling on You. I pray and ask Jesus to come into my heart and be Lord over my life according to Romans 10:9-10. *"If thou shalt confess with thy mouth the Lord Jesus, and shalt believe in thine heart that God hath raised him from the dead, thou shalt be saved."* I do that now. I confess that Jesus is Lord, and I believe in my heart that God raised Him from the dead.

I am now reborn! I am a Christian—a child of Almighty God! I am saved! You also said in Your Word, *"If ye then, being evil, know how to give good gifts unto your children: HOW MUCH MORE shall your heavenly Father give the Holy Spirit to them that ask him?"* (Luke 11:13). I'm also asking You to fill me with the Holy Spirit. Holy Spirit, rise up within me as I praise God. I fully expect to speak with other tongues as You give me the utterance (Acts 2:4).

Begin to praise God for filling you with the Holy Spirit. Speak those words and syllables you receive—not in your own language, but the language given to you by the Holy Spirit. You have to use your own voice. God will not force you to speak. Worship and praise Him in your heavenly language—in other tongues.

Continue with the blessing God has given you and pray in tongues each day.

You are a born-again, Spirit-filled believer. You'll never be the same!

Find a good Word of God preaching church, and become a part of a church family who will love and care for you as you love and care for them.

We need to be connected to each other. It increases our strength in God. It's God's plan for us.

About the Author

Gloria Copeland is an author and minister of the gospel whose teaching ministry is known throughout the world. Believers worldwide know her through Believers' Conventions, Victory Campaigns, magazine articles, teaching tapes and videos, and the daily and Sunday *Believer's Voice of Victory* television broadcast, which she hosts with her husband, Kenneth Copeland. She is known for "Healing School," which she began teaching and hosting in 1979 at KCM meetings. Gloria delivers the Word of God and the keys to victorious Christian living to millions of people every year.

Gloria has written many books, including *God's Will for You, Walk With God, God's Will Is Prosperity, Hidden Treasures* and *Are You*

Listening. She has also co-authored several books with her husband, including *Family Promises, Healing Promises* and the best-selling daily devotionals, *From Faith to Faith* and *Pursuit of His Presence.*

She holds an honorary doctorate from Oral Roberts University. In 1994, Gloria was voted Christian Woman of the Year, an honor conferred on women whose example demonstrates outstanding Christian leadership. Gloria is also the co-founder and vice president of Kenneth Copeland Ministries in Fort Worth, Texas.

Learn more about
Kenneth Copeland Ministries
by visiting our Web site at **www.kcm.org**.

Materials to Help You
Receive Your Healing
by Gloria Copeland

Books

* And Jesus Healed Them All

  God's Prescription for Divine Health

  God's Will for Your Healing

* Harvest of Health

Audiotapes

  God Is a Good God

  God Wants You Well

  Healing School

Videotapes

  Healing School: God Wants You Well

  Know Him As Healer

Other Books Available
From Kenneth Copeland Ministries

by Gloria Copeland

* And Jesus Healed Them All
  Are You Listening?
  Are You Ready?
  Build Your Financial Foundation
  Build Yourself an Ark
  Fight On!
  Go With the Flow
  God's Prescription for Divine Health
  God's Success Formula
  God's Will for You
  God's Will for Your Healing
  God's Will Is Prosperity
* God's Will Is the Holy Spirit
* Harvest of Health
  Hearing From Heaven
  Hidden Treasures
  Living Contact
  Living in Heaven's Blessings Now
* Love—The Secret to Your Success
  No Deposit—No Return
  Pleasing the Father
  Pressing In—It's Worth It All
  Shine On!

The Power to Live a New Life
The Unbeatable Spirit of Faith
* Walk in the Spirit (Available in Spanish Only)
Walk With God
Well Worth the Wait

by Kenneth Copeland

* A Ceremony of Marriage
  A Matter of Choice
  Covenant of Blood
  Faith and Patience—The Power Twins
* Freedom From Fear
  Giving and Receiving
  Honor—Walking in Honesty, Truth and Integrity
  How to Conquer Strife
  How to Discipline Your Flesh
  How to Receive Communion
  Living at the End of Time—A Time of Supernatural
    Increase
  Love Never Fails
  Managing God's Mutual Funds
* Now Are We in Christ Jesus
* Our Covenant With God
  Partnership, Sharing the Vision—Sharing the Grace
* Prayer—Your Foundation for Success
* Prosperity: The Choice Is Yours
  Rumors of War
* Sensitivity of Heart
* Six Steps to Excellence in Ministry
* Sorrow Not! Winning Over Grief and Sorrow
* The Decision Is Yours
* The Force of Faith
* The Force of Righteousness

The Image of God in You

The Laws of Prosperity

* The Mercy of God

The Miraculous Realm of God's Love

The Outpouring of the Spirit—The Result of Prayer

* The Power of the Tongue

The Power to Be Forever Free

The Troublemaker

* The Winning Attitude

Turn Your Hurts Into Harvests

* Welcome to the Family

* You Are Healed!

Your Right-Standing With God

Books Co-Authored by Kenneth and Gloria Copeland

Family Promises

Healing Promises

Prosperity Promises

Protection Promises

* From Faith to Faith—A Daily Guide to Victory

From Faith to Faith—A Perpetual Calendar

One Word From God Series

- One Word From God Can Change Your Destiny
- One Word From God Can Change Your Family
- One Word From God Can Change Your Finances
- One Word From God Can Change Your Formula for Success
- One Word From God Can Change Your Health
- One Word From God Can Change Your Nation
- One Word From God Can Change Your Prayer Life
- One Word From God Can Change Your Relationships

Over The Edge—A Youth Devotional

Pursuit of His Presence—A Daily Devotional

Pursuit of His Presence—A Perpetual Calendar

Other Books Published by KCP

Products Designed for Today's Children and Youth

Baby Praise Board Book

Baby Praise Christmas Board Book

Noah's Ark Coloring Book

The Best of *Shout!* Adventure Comics

The *Shout!* Joke Book

The *Shout!* Super-Activity Book

*Commander Kellie and the Superkids*_{SM} **Books:**

*Commander Kellie and the Superkids*_{SM} Series

Middle Grade Novels by Christopher P.N. Maselli

#1 The Mysterious Presence

#2 The Quest for the Second Half

#3 Escape From Jungle Island

#4 In Pursuit of the Enemy

#5 Caged Rivalry

#6 Mystery of the Missing Junk

The SWORD Adventure Book

*Available in Spanish

World Offices
of Kenneth Copeland Ministries

For more information about KCM and a free
catalog, please write the office nearest you:

Kenneth Copeland Ministries
Fort Worth, Texas 76192-0001

Kenneth Copeland
Locked Bag 2600
Mansfield Delivery Centre
QUEENSLAND 4122
AUSTRALIA

Kenneth Copeland
Post Office Box 15
BATH
BA1 3XN
ENGLAND U.K.

Kenneth Copeland
Private Bag X 909
FONTAINEBLEAU
2032
REPUBLIC OF
   SOUTH AFRICA

Kenneth Copeland
Post Office Box 378
Surrey, B.C.
V3T 5B6
CANADA

UKRAINE
L'VIV 290000
Post Office Box 84
Kenneth Copeland Ministries
L'VIV 290000
UKRAINE

We're Here for You!

Believer's Voice of Victory Television Broadcast

Join Kenneth and Gloria Copeland and the *Believer's Voice of Victory* broadcasts Monday through Friday and on Sunday each week, and learn how faith in God's Word can take your life from ordinary to extraordinary. This teaching from God's Word is designed to get you where you want to be—*on top!*

You can catch the *Believer's Voice of Victory* broadcast on your local, cable or satellite channels.

*Check your local listings for times and stations in your area.

Believer's Voice of Victory Magazine

Enjoy inspired teaching and encouragement from Kenneth and Gloria Copeland and guest ministers each month in the *Believer's Voice of Victory* magazine. Also included are real-life testimonies of God's miraculous power and divine intervention into the lives of people just like you!

It's more than just a magazine—it's a ministry.

Shout! ...The dynamic magazine just for kids!

Shout! The Voice of Victory for Kids is a Bible-charged, action-packed, bimonthly magazine available FREE to kids everywhere! Featuring *Wichita Slim* and *Commander Kellie and the Superkids, Shout!* is filled with colorful adventure comics, challenging games and puzzles, exciting short stories, solve-it-yourself mysteries and much more!!

Stand up, sign up and get ready to *Shout!*

To receive a FREE subscription to *Believer's Voice of Victory,* or to give a child you know a FREE subscription to *Shout!,* write:

Kenneth Copeland Ministries
Fort Worth, Texas 76192-0001

Or call:
1-800-600-7395
(9 a.m.-5 p.m. CT)

Or visit our Web site at:
www.kcm.org

If you are writing from outside the U.S., please contact the KCM office nearest you. Addresses for all Kenneth Copeland Ministries offices are listed on the previous page.

The Harrison House Vision

Proclaiming the truth and the power

Of the Gospel of Jesus Christ

With excellence;

Challenging Christians to

Live victoriously,

Grow spiritually,

Know God intimately.

W9-BGL-287

THE BOOK

Translated from the Dutch into nearly a score of languages including German, *ANNE FRANK: THE DIARY OF A YOUNG GIRL* has sold over 5 million copies in its American edition alone.

THE AUTHOR

Anne Frank's life was cut tragically short three months before her sixteenth birthday, two months before the liberation of Holland, in the concentration camp at Bergen-Belsen.

The Reader's Supplement to this ENRICHED CLASSICS edition appears in the center insert. It has been prepared under the supervision of an editorial committee directed by Harry Shefter, Professor of English, M.S.Ed.

THE ACCLAIM

In addition to its many translations, there have been two dramatic versions of Anne Frank's diary. The 1959 movie version won an Academy Award (best supporting actress) and the Broadway play was awarded the Pulitzer Prize, the New York Drama Critics' Circle Award and the Antoinette Perry Award.

Anne Frank:

The Diary
of a Young Girl

**TRANSLATED FROM THE DUTCH
BY B. M. MOOYAART**

WASHINGTON SQUARE PRESS
PUBLISHED BY POCKET BOOKS NEW YORK

Produced as a Broadway Play October 5, 1955,
under the title *The Diary of Anne Frank*

Anne Frank: The Diary of a Young Girl has been
published in the following countries: Argentina,
Brazil, Czechoslovakia, Denmark, Finland, France,
Germany, Great Britain, Greece, Iceland, Israel,
Italy, Japan, The Netherlands, Norway, Poland,
Portugal, Spain, Sweden, Turkey.

WSP

A Washington Square Press Publication of
POCKET BOOKS, a Simon & Schuster division of
GULF & WESTERN CORPORATION
1230 Avenue of the Americas, New York, N.Y. 10020

ISBN: 0-671-43029-7

First Pocket Books printing (Enriched Classics edition) June, 1972

15   14   13   12   11

WASHINGTON SQUARE PRESS, WSP and colophon are
trademarks of Simon & Schuster.

Printed in the U.S.A.

FIRST PUBLISHED IN 1947 IN HOLLAND
BY CONTACT, AMSTERDAM, UNDER THE TITLE *Het Achterhuis*

Het Achterhuis, the Dutch title of this book, refers to
that part of the building which served as a hiding place
for the two families who took shelter there between 1942
and 1944. *Achter* means "behind" or "in back of" and *huis*
is Dutch for "house." In Amsterdam's old buildings the
apartments overlooking a garden or court may be divided
from those overlooking the street, thus providing two
separate suites within the same apartment. Het Achterhuis or, literally, "the house behind" is situated on the
Prinsengracht, one of the city's canals.

To simplify the English text, we have called that part
of the house the Secret Annexe, although it is not an annex in the proper sense of the word.

This is a remarkable book. Written by a young girl—and the young are not afraid of telling the truth—it is one of the wisest and most moving commentaries on war and its impact on human beings that I have ever read. Anne Frank's account of the changes wrought upon eight people hiding out from the Nazis for two years during the occupation of Holland, living in constant fear and isolation, imprisoned not only by the terrible outward circumstances of war but inwardly by themselves, made me intimately and shockingly aware of war's greatest evil—the degradation of the human spirit.

At the same time, Anne's diary makes poignantly clear the ultimate shining nobility of that spirit. Despite the horror and the humiliation of their daily lives, these people never gave up. Anne herself—and, most of all, it is her portrait which emerges so vividly and so appealingly from this book—matured very rapidly in these two years, the crucial years from thirteen to fifteen in which change is so swift and so difficult for every young girl. Sustained by her warmth and her wit, her intelligence and the rich resources of her inner life, Anne wrote and thought much of the time about things which very sensitive and talented adolescents without the threat of death will write—her relations with her parents, her developing self-awareness, the problems of growing up.

These are the thoughts and expression of a young girl living under extraordinary conditions, and for this reason her diary tells us much about ourselves and about our own children. And for this reason, too, I felt how close we all are to Anne's experience, how very much involved we are in her short life and in the entire world.

Anne's diary is an appropriate monument to her fine

spirit and to the spirits of those who have worked and are working still for peace. Reading it is a rich and rewarding experience.

ELEANOR ROOSEVELT

Ik zal hoop ik aan jou allerkinneen hoeverbrouwen, daals ik het nog aan niemand gekund heb, en ik hoop dat je elar grote stuen voor me zult zijn.

Anne Frank. 12 Juni 1942.

I hope I shall be able to confide in you completely, as I have never been able to do in anyone before, and I hope that you will be a great support and comfort to me.

Anne Frank:
The Diary
of a Young Girl

Sunday, 14 June, 1942

On Friday, June 12th, I woke up at six o'clock and no wonder; it was my birthday. But of course I was not allowed to get up at that hour, so I had to control my curiosity until a quarter to seven. Then I could bear it no longer, and went to the dining room, where I received a warm welcome from Moortje (the cat).

Soon after seven I went to Mummy and Daddy and then to the sitting room to undo my presents. The first to greet me was *you*, possibly the nicest of all. Then on the table there were a bunch of roses, a plant, and some peonies, and more arrived during the day.

I got masses of things from Mummy and Daddy, and was thoroughly spoiled by various friends. Among other things I was given *Camera Obscura,* a party game, lots of sweets, chocolates, a puzzle, a brooch, *Tales and Legends of the Netherlands* by Joseph Cohen, *Daisy's Mountain Holiday* (a terrific book), and some money. Now I can buy *The Myths of Greece and Rome*—grand!

Then Lies called for me and we went to school. During recess I treated everyone to sweet biscuits, and then we had to go back to our lessons.

Now I must stop. Bye-bye, we're going to be great pals!

Monday, 15 June, 1942

I had my birthday party on Sunday afternoon. We showed a film *The Lighthouse Keeper* with Rin-Tin-Tin, which my school friends thoroughly enjoyed. We had a lovely time. There were lots of girls and boys. Mummy always wants to know whom I'm going to marry. Little

1

does she guess that it's Peter Wessel; one day I managed, without blushing or flickering an eyelid, to get that idea right out of her mind. For years Lies Goosens and Sanne Houtman have been my best friends. Since then, I've got to know Jopie de Waal at the Jewish Secondary School. We are together a lot and she is now my best girl friend. Lies is more friendly with another girl, and Sanne goes to a different school, where she has made new friends.

Saturday, 20 June, 1942

I haven't written for a few days, because I wanted first of all to think about my diary. It's an odd idea for someone like me to keep a diary; not only because I have never done so before, but because it seems to me that neither I—nor for that matter anyone else—will be interested in the unbosomings of a thirteen-year-old schoolgirl. Still, what does that matter? I want to write, but more than that, I want to bring out all kinds of things that lie buried deep in my heart.

There is a saying that "paper is more patient than man"; it came back to me on one of my slightly melancholy days, while I sat chin in hand, feeling too bored and limp even to make up my mind whether to go out or stay at home. Yes, there is no doubt that paper is patient and as I don't intend to show this cardboard-covered notebook, bearing the proud name of "diary," to anyone, unless I find a real friend, boy or girl, probably nobody cares. And now I come to the root of the matter, the reason for my starting a diary: it is that I have no such real friend.

Let me put it more clearly, since no one will believe that a girl of thirteen feels herself quite alone in the world, nor is it so. I have darling parents and a sister of sixteen. I know about thirty people whom one might call friends—I have strings of boy friends, anxious to catch a glimpse of me and who, failing that, peep at me through mirrors in class. I have relations, aunts and uncles, who

2

are darlings too, a good home, no—I don't seem to lack anything. But it's the same with all my friends, just fun and joking, nothing more. I can never bring myself to talk of anything outside the common round. We don't seem to be able to get any closer, that is the root of the trouble. Perhaps I lack confidence, but anyway, there it is, a stubborn fact and I don't seem to be able to do anything about it.

Hence, this diary. In order to enhance in my mind's eye the picture of the friend for whom I have waited so long, I don't want to set down a series of bald facts in a diary like most people do, but I want this diary itself to be my friend, and I shall call my friend Kitty. No one will grasp what I'm talking about if I begin my letters to Kitty just out of the blue, so albeit unwillingly, I will start by sketching in brief the story of my life.

My father was thirty-six when he married my mother, who was then twenty-five. My sister Margot was born in 1926 in Frankfort-on-Main, I followed on June 12, 1929, and, as we are Jewish, we emigrated to Holland in 1933, where my father was appointed Managing Director of Travies N.V. This firm is in close relationship with the firm of Kolen & Co. in the same building, of which my father is a partner.

The rest of our family, however, felt the full impact of Hitler's anti-Jewish laws, so life was filled with anxiety. In 1938 after the pogroms, my two uncles (my mother's brothers) escaped to the U.S.A. My old grandmother came to us, she was then seventy-three. After May 1940 good times rapidly fled: first the war, then the capitulation, followed by the arrival of the Germans, which is when the sufferings of us Jews really began. Anti-Jewish decrees followed each other in quick succession. Jews must wear a yellow star,[1] Jews must hand in their bicycles, Jews are banned from trains and are forbidden to drive. Jews are only allowed to do their shopping between three and five o'clock and then only in shops which bear the placard "Jewish shop." Jews must be indoors by eight o'clock and

[1] To distinguish them from others, all Jews were forced by the Germans to wear, prominently displayed, a yellow six-pointed star.

3

cannot even sit in their own gardens after that hour. Jews are forbidden to visit theaters, cinemas, and other places of entertainment. Jews may not take part in public sports. Swimming baths, tennis courts, hockey fields, and other sports grounds are all prohibited to them. Jews may not visit Christians. Jews must go to Jewish schools, and many more restrictions of a similar kind.

So we could not do this and were forbidden to do that. But life went on in spite of it all. Jopie used to say to me, "You're scared to do anything, because it may be forbidden." Our freedom was strictly limited. Yet things were still bearable.

Granny died in January 1942; no one will ever know how much she is present in my thoughts and how much I love her still.

In 1934 I went to school at the Montessori Kindergarten and continued there. It was at the end of the school year, I was in form 6B, when I had to say good-by to Mrs. K. We both wept, it was very sad. In 1941 I went, with my sister Margot, to the Jewish Secondary School, she into the fourth form and I into the first.

So far everything is all right with the four of us and here I come to the present day.

Saturday, 20 June, 1942

Dear Kitty,

I'll start straight away. It is so peaceful at the moment, Mummy and Daddy are out and Margot has gone to play ping-pong with some friends.

I've been playing ping-pong a lot myself lately. We ping-pongers are very partial to an ice cream, especially in summer, when one gets warm at the game, so we usually finish up with a visit to the nearest ice-cream shop, Delphi or Oasis, where Jews are allowed. We've given up scrounging for extra pocket money. Oasis is usually full and among our large circle of friends we always

4

manage to find some kindhearted gentleman or boy friend, who presents us with more ice cream than we could devour in a week.

I expect you will be rather surprised at the fact that I should talk of boy friends at my age. Alas, one simply can't seem to avoid it at our school. As soon as a boy asks if he may bicycle home with me and we get into conversation, nine out of ten times I can be sure that he will fall head over heels in love immediately and simply won't allow me out of his sight. After a while it cools down of course, especially as I take little notice of ardent looks and pedal blithely on.

If it gets so far that they begin about "asking Father" I swerve slightly on my bicycle, my satchel falls, the young man is bound to get off and hand it to me, by which time I have introduced a new topic of conversation.

These are the most innocent types; you get some who blow kisses or try to get hold of your arm, but then they are definitely knocking at the wrong door. I get off my bicycle and refuse to go further in their company, or I pretend to be insulted and tell them in no uncertain terms to clear off.

There, the foundation of our friendship is laid, till tomorrow!

Yours, Anne

Sunday, 21 June, 1942

Dear Kitty,

Our whole class B1 is trembling, the reason is that the teachers' meeting is to be held soon. There is much speculation as to who will move up and who will stay put. Miep de Jong and I are highly amused at Wim and Jacques, the two boys behind us. They won't have a florin left for the holidays, it will all be gone on betting. "You'll move up," "Shan't," "Shall," from morning till night. Even Miep pleads for silence and my angry outbursts don't calm them.

According to me, a quarter of the class should stay

where they are; there are some absolute cuckoos, but teachers are the greatest freaks on earth, so perhaps they will be freakish in the *right* way for once.

I'm not afraid about my girl friends and myself, we'll squeeze through somehow, though I'm not too certain about my math. Still we can but wait patiently. Till then, we cheer each other along.

I get along quite well with all my teachers, nine in all, seven masters and two mistresses. Mr. Keptor, the old math master, was very annoyed with me for a long time because I chatter so much. So I had to write a composition with "A Chatterbox" as the subject. A chatterbox! Whatever could one write? However, deciding I would puzzle that out later, I wrote it in my notebook, and tried to keep quiet.

That evening, when I'd finished my other homework, my eyes fell on the title in my notebook. I pondered, while chewing the end of my fountain pen that anyone can scribble some nonsense in large letters with the words well spaced but the difficulty was to prove beyond doubt the necessity of talking. I thought and thought and then, suddenly having an idea, filled my three allotted sides and felt completely satisfied. My arguments were that talking is a feminine characteristic and that I would do my best to keep it under control, but I should never be cured, for my mother talked as much as I, probably more, and what can one do about inherited qualities? Mr. Keptor had to laugh at my arguments, but when I continued to hold forth in the next lesson, another composition followed. This time it was "Incurable Chatterbox," I handed this in and Keptor made no complaints for two whole lessons. But in the third lesson it was too much for him again. "Anne, as punishment for talking, will do a composition entitled 'Quack, quack, quack, says Mrs. Natterbeak.'" Shouts of laughter from the class, I had to laugh too, although I felt that my inventiveness on this subject was exhausted. I had to think of something else, something entirely original. I was in luck, as my friend Sanne writes good poetry and offered to help by doing the whole composition in verse. I jumped for joy. Keptor wanted to make a fool of me with this absurd theme, I would get my own back and make him the laughing-stock of the whole class. The poem was finished and was perfect. It was about a mother duck and a father swan who had three baby ducklings. The baby ducklings were bitten to death by Father because they chattered too much. Luckily Keptor saw the joke, he read the poem out loud to the class, with comments, and also to various other classes.

Since then I am allowed to talk, never get extra work, in fact Keptor always jokes about it.

Yours, Anne

Wednesday, 24 June, 1942

Dear Kitty,

It is boiling hot, we are all positively melting, and in this heat I have to walk everywhere. Now I can fully appreciate how nice a tram is; but that is a forbidden luxury for Jews—shank's mare is good enough for us. I had to visit the dentist in the Jan Luykenstraat in the lunch hour yesterday. It is a long way from our school in the Stadstimmertuinen; I nearly fell asleep in school that afternoon. Luckily, the dentist's assistant was very kind and gave me a drink—she's a good sort.

We are allowed on the ferry and that is about all. There is a little boat from the Josef Israelskade, the man there took us at once when we asked him. It is not the Dutch people's fault that we are having such a miserable time.

I do wish I didn't have to go to school, as my bicycle was stolen in the Easter holidays and Daddy has given Mummy's to a Christian family for safekeeping. But thank goodness, the holidays are nearly here, one more week and the agony is over. Something amusing happened yesterday, I was passing the bicycle sheds when someone called out to me. I looked around and there was the nice-looking boy I met on the previous evening, at my girl friend Eva's home. He came shyly towards me and introduced himself as Harry Goldberg. I was rather surprised and wondered what he wanted, but I didn't have to wait

7

long. He asked if I would allow him to accompany me to school. "As you're going my way in any case, I will," I replied and so we went together. Harry is sixteen and can tell all kinds of amusing stories. He was waiting for me again this morning and I expect he will from now on.

Yours, Anne

Tuesday, 30 June, 1942

Dear Kitty,

I've not had a moment to write to you until today. I was with friends all day on Thursday. On Friday we had visitors, and so it went on until today. Harry and I have got to know each other well in a week, and he has told me a lot about his life; he came to Holland alone, and is living with his grandparents. His parents are in Belgium.

Harry had a girl friend called Fanny. I know her too, a very soft, dull creature. Now that he has met me, he realizes that he was just daydreaming in Fanny's presence. I seem to act as a stimulant to keep him awake. You see we all have our uses, and queer ones too at times!

Jopie slept here on Saturday night, but she went to Lies on Sunday and I was bored stiff. Harry was to have come in the evening, but he rang up at 6 P.M. I went to the telephone, he said, "Harry Goldberg here, please may I speak to Anne?" "Yes, Harry, Anne speaking."

"Hullo, Anne, how are you?"

"Very well, thank you."

"I'm terribly sorry I can't come this evening, but I would like to just speak to you; is it all right if I come in ten minutes?"

"Yes, that's fine, good-by!"

"Good-by, I'll be with you soon."

Receiver down.

I quickly changed into another frock and smartened up my hair a bit. Then I stood nervously at the window watching for him. At last I saw *him* coming. It was a wonder I didn't dash down at once; instead I waited patiently until he rang. Then I went down and he positively burst in when I opened the door. "Anne, my grandmother thinks you are too young to go out regularly with me, and that I should go to the Leurs, but perhaps you know that I am not going out with Fanny any more!"

"No, why is that, have you quarreled?"

"No, not at all. I told Fanny that we didn't get on well together, so it was better for us not to go out together any more, but she was always welcome in our home, and I hope I should be in hers. You see, I thought Fanny had been going out with another boy and treated her accordingly. But that was quite untrue. And now my uncle says I should apologize to Fanny, but of course I didn't want to do that so I finished the whole affair. That was just one of the many reasons. My grandmother would rather I went with Fanny than you, but I shan't; old people have such terribly old-fashioned ideas at times, but I just can't fall into line. I need my grandparents, but in a sense they need me too. From now on I shall be free on Wednesday evenings. Officially I go to wood-carving lessons to please my grandparents, in actual fact I go to a meeting of the Zionist Movement. I'm not supposed to, because my grandparents are very much against the Zionists. I'm by no means a fanatic, but I have a leaning that way and find it interesting. But lately it has become such a mess there that I'm going to quit, so next Wednesday will be my last time. Then I shall be able to see you on Wednesday evenings, Saturday afternoon, Sunday afternoon, and perhaps more."

"But your grandparents are against it, you can't do it behind their backs!"

"Love finds a way."

Then we passed the bookshop on the corner, and there stood Peter Wessel with two other boys; he said "Hello" —it's the first time he has spoken to me for ages, I was really pleased.

Harry and I walked on and on and the end of it all was that I should meet him at five minutes to seven in the front of his house next evening.

Yours, Anne

9

Friday, 3 July, 1942

Dear Kitty,

Harry visited us yesterday to meet my parents. I had bought a cream cake, sweets, tea, and fancy biscuits, quite a spread, but neither Harry nor I felt like sitting stiffly side by side indefinitely, so we went for a walk, and it was already ten past eight when he brought me home. Daddy was very cross, and thought it was very wrong of me because it is dangerous for Jews to be out after eight o'clock, and I had to promise to be in by ten to eight in future.

Tomorrow I've been invited to his house. My girl friend Jopie teases me the whole time about Harry. I'm honestly not in love, oh, no, I can surely have boy friends—no one thinks anything of that—but one boy friend, or beau, as Mother calls him, seems to be quite different.

Harry went to see Eva one evening and she told me that she asked him, "Who do you like best, Fanny or Anne?" He said, "It's nothing to do with you!" But when he left (they hadn't chatted together any more the whole evening), "Now listen, it's Anne, so long, and don't tell a soul." And like a flash, he was gone.

It's easy to see that Harry is in love with me, rather fun for a change. Margot would say, "Harry is a decent lad." I agree, but he is more than that. Mummy is full of praise: a good-looking boy, a well-behaved, nice boy. I'm glad that the whole family approves of him. He likes them too, but he thinks my girl friends are very childish, and he's quite right.

Yours, Anne

Sunday morning, 5 July, 1942

Dear Kitty,

Our examination results were announced in the Jewish Theater last Friday. I couldn't have hoped for better. My

10

report is not at all bad, I had one *vix satis*, a five for algebra, two sixes, and the rest were all sevens or eights. They were certainly pleased at home, although over the question of marks my parents are quite different from most. They don't care a bit whether my reports are good or bad as long as I'm well and happy, and not too cheeky: then the rest will come by itself. I am just the opposite. I don't want to be a bad pupil; I should really have stayed in the seventh form in the Montessori School, but was accepted for the Jewish Secondary. When all the Jewish children had to go to Jewish schools, the headmaster took Lies and me conditionally after a bit of persuasion. He relied on us to do our best and I don't want to let him down. My sister Margot has her report too, brilliant as usual. She would move up with *cum laude* if that existed at school, she is so brainy. Daddy has been at home a lot lately, as there is nothing for him to do at business; it must be rotten to feel so superfluous. Mr. Koophuis has taken over Travies and Mr. Kraler the firm Kolen & Co. When we walked across our little square together a few days ago, Daddy began to talk of us going into hiding. I asked him why on earth he was beginning to talk of that already. "Yes, Anne," he said, "you know that we have been taking food, clothes, furniture to other people for more than a year now. We don't want our belongings to be seized by the Germans, but we certainly don't want to fall into their clutches ourselves. So we shall disappear of our own accord and not wait until they come and fetch us."

"But, Daddy, when would it be?" He spoke so seriously that I grew very anxious.

"Don't you worry about it, we shall arrange everything. Make the most of your carefree young life while you can." That was all. Oh, may the fulfillment of these somber words remain far distant yet!

Yours, Anne

Dear Kitty,

Years seem to have passed between Sunday and now. So much has happened, it is just as if the whole world had turned upside down. But I am still alive, Kitty, and that is the main thing, Daddy says.

Yes, I'm still alive, indeed, but don't ask where or how. You wouldn't understand a word, so I will begin by telling you what happened on Sunday afternoon.

At three o'clock (Harry had just gone, but was coming back later) someone rang the front doorbell. I was lying lazily reading a book on the veranda in the sunshine, so I didn't hear it. A bit later, Margot appeared at the kitchen door looking very excited. "The S.S. have sent a call-up notice for Daddy," she whispered. "Mummy has gone to see Mr. Van Daan already." (Van Daan is a friend who works with Daddy in the business.) It was a great shock to me, a call-up; everyone knows what that means. I picture concentration camps and lonely cells—should we allow him to be doomed to this? "Of course he won't go," declared Margot, while we waited together. "Mummy has gone to the Van Daans to discuss whether we should move into our hiding place tomorrow. The Van Daans are going with us, so we shall be seven in all." Silence. We couldn't talk any more, thinking about Daddy, who, little knowing what was going on, was visiting some old people in the Joodse Invalide; waiting for Mummy, the heat and suspense, all made us very overawed and silent.

Suddenly the bell rang again. "That is Harry," I said. "Don't open the door." Margot held me back, but it was not necessary as we heard Mummy and Mr. Van Daan downstairs, talking to Harry, then they came in and closed the door behind them. Each time the bell went, Margot or I had to creep softly down to see if it was Daddy, not opening the door to anyone else.

Margot and I were sent out of the room. Van Daan

wanted to talk to Mummy alone. When we were alone together in our bedroom, Margot told me that the call-up
was not for Daddy, but for her. I was more frightened
than ever and began to cry. Margot is sixteen; would they
really take girls of that age away alone? But thank goodness she won't go, Mummy said so herself; that must be
what Daddy meant when he talked about us going into
hiding.

Into hiding—where would we go, in a town or the
country, in a house or a cottage, when, how, where . . . ?

These were questions I was not allowed to ask, but I
couldn't get them out of my mind. Margot and I began to
pack some of our most vital belongings into a school
satchel. The first thing I put in was this diary, then hair
curlers, handkerchiefs, schoolbooks, a comb, old letters; I
put in the craziest things with the idea that we were going
into hiding. But I'm not sorry, memories mean more to
me than dresses.

At five o'clock Daddy finally arrived, and we phoned
Mr. Koophuis to ask if he could come around in the evening. Van Daan went and fetched Miep. Miep has been
in the business with Daddy since 1933 and has become a
close friend, likewise her brand-new husband, Henk.
Miep came and took some shoes, dresses, coats, underwear, and stockings away in her bag, promising to return
in the evening. Then silence fell on the house; not one
of us felt like eating anything, it was still hot and everything was very strange. We let our large upstairs room
to a certain Mr. Goudsmit, a divorced man in his thirties,
who appeared to have nothing to do on this particular evening; we simply could not get rid of him without being
rude; he hung about until ten o'clock. At eleven o'clock
Miep and Henk Van Santen arrived. Once again, shoes,
stockings, books, and underclothes disappeared into
Miep's bag and Henk's deep pockets, and at eleven-thirty
they too disappeared. I was dog-tired and although I knew
that it would be my last night in my own bed, I fell asleep
immediately and didn't wake up until Mummy called me
at five-thirty the next morning. Luckily it was not so hot
as Sunday; warm rain fell steadily all day. We put on

13

heaps of clothes as if we were going to the North Pole, the sole reason being to take clothes with us. No Jew in our situation would have dreamed of going out with a suitcase full of clothing. I had on two vests, three pairs of pants, a dress, on top of that a skirt, jacket, summer coat, two pairs of stockings, lace-up shoes, woolly cap, scarf, and still more; I was nearly stifled before we started, but no one inquired about that.

Margot filled her satchel with schoolbooks, fetched her bicycle, and rode off behind Miep into the unknown, as far as I was concerned. You see I still didn't know where our secret hiding place was to be. At seven-thirty the door closed behind us. Moortje, my little cat, was the only creature to whom I said farewell. She would have a good home with the neighbors. This was all written in a lettter addressed to Mr. Goudsmit.

There was one pound of meat in the kitchen for the cat, breakfast things lying on the table, stripped beds, all giving the impression that we had left helter-skelter. But we didn't care about impressions, we only wanted to get away, only escape and arrive safely, nothing else. Continued tomorrow.

Yours, Anne

Thursday, 9 July, 1942

Dear Kitty,

So we walked in the pouring rain, Daddy, Mummy, and I, each with a school satchel and shopping bag filled to the brim with all kinds of things thrown together anyhow.

We got sympathetic looks from people on their way to work. You could see by their faces how sorry they were they couldn't offer us a lift; the gaudy yellow star spoke for itself.

Only when we were on the road did Mummy and Daddy begin to tell me bits and pieces about the plan. For months as many of our goods and chattels and necessities of life as possible had been sent away and they were sufficiently ready for us to have gone into hiding of our

14

own accord on July 16. The plan had had to be speeded up ten days because of the call-up, so our quarters would not be so well organized, but we had to make the best of it. The hiding place itself would be in the building where Daddy has his office. It will be hard for outsiders to understand, but I shall explain that later on. Daddy didn't have many people working for him: Mr. Kraler, Koophuis, Miep, and Elli Vossen, a twenty-three-year-old typist who all knew of our arrival. Mr. Vossen, Elli's father, and two boys worked in the warehouse; they had not been told.

I will describe the building: there is a large warehouse on the ground floor which is used as a store. The front door to the house is next to the warehouse door, and inside the front door is a second doorway which leads to a staircase (A). There is another door at the top of the stairs, with a frosted glass window in it, which has "Office" written in black letters across it. That is the large main office, very big, very light, and very full. Elli, Miep, and Mr. Koophuis work there in the daytime. A small dark room containing the safe, a wardrobe, and a large cupboard leads to a small somewhat dark second office. Mr. Kraler and Mr. Van Daan used to sit here, now it is only Mr. Kraler. One can reach Kraler's office from the passage, but only via a glass door which can be opened from the inside, but not easily from the outside.

From Kraler's office a long passage goes past the coal store, up four steps and leads to the showroom of the whole building: the private office. Dark, dignified furniture, linoleum and carpets on the floor, radio, smart lamp, everything first-class. Next door there is a roomy kitchen with a hot-water faucet and a gas stove. Next door the W.C. That is the first floor.

A wooden staircase leads from the downstairs passage to the next floor (B). There is a small landing at the top. There is a door at each end of the landing, the left one leading to a storeroom at the front of the house and to the attics. One of those really steep Dutch staircases runs from the side to the other door opening on to the street (C).

The right-hand door leads to our "Secret Annexe." No

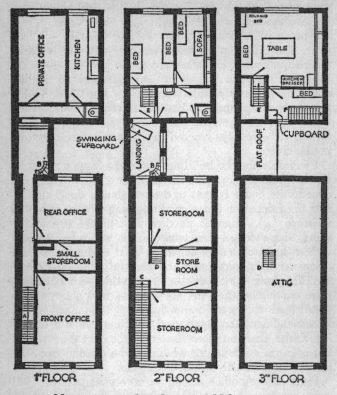

PRIVATE OFFICE   KITCHEN

SWINGING CUPBOARD

REAR OFFICE

SMALL STOREROOM

FRONT OFFICE

1ˢᵗ FLOOR

BED   BED   BED   SOFA

LANDING

STOREROOM

STORE ROOM

STOREROOM

2ⁿᵈ FLOOR

FOLDING BED   TABLE

BED

KITCHEN DRESSER

BED

FLAT ROOF   CUPBOARD

ATTIC

3ʳᵈ FLOOR

one would ever guess that there would be so many rooms
hidden behind that plain gray door. There's a little step
in front of the door and then you are inside.

There is a steep staircase immediately opposite the entrance (D). On the left a tiny passage brings you into a
room which was to become the Frank family's bed-sitting-
room, next door a smaller room, study and bedroom for
the two young ladies of the family. On the right a little
room without windows containing the washbasin and a
small W.C. compartment, with another door leading to
Margot's and my room. If you go up the next flight of
stairs and open the door, you are simply amazed that there
could be such a big light room in such an old house by

16

the canal. There is a gas stove in this room (thanks to the fact that it was used as a laboratory) and a sink. This is now the kitchen for the Van Daan couple, besides being general living room, dining room, and scullery.

A tiny little corridor room will become Peter Van Daan's apartment. Then, just as on the lower landing, there is a large attic. So there you are, I've introduced you to the whole of our beautiful "Secret Annexe."

Yours, Anne

Friday, 10 July, 1942

Dear Kitty,

I expect I have thoroughly bored you with my long-winded descriptions of our dwelling. But still I think you should know where we've landed.

But to continue my story—you see, I've not finished yet—when we arrived at the Prinsengracht, Miep took us quickly upstairs and into the "Secret Annexe." She closed the door behind us and we were alone. Margot was already waiting for us, having come much faster on her bicycle. Our living room and all the other rooms were chock-full of rubbish, indescribably so. All the cardboard boxes which had been sent to the office in the previous months lay piled on the floor and the beds. The little room was filled to the ceiling with bedclothes. We had to start clearing up immediately, if we wished to sleep in decent beds that night. Mummy and Margot were not in a fit state to take part; they were tired and lay down on their beds, they were miserable, and lots more besides. But the two "clearers-up" of the family—Daddy and myself—wanted to start at once.

The whole day long we unpacked boxes, filled cupboards, hammered and tidied, until we were dead beat. We sank into clean beds that night. We hadn't had a bit of anything warm the whole day, but we didn't care; Mummy and Margot were too tired and keyed up to eat, and Daddy and I were too busy.

On Tuesday morning we went on where we left off the

day before. Elli and Miep collected our rations for us, Daddy improved the poor blackout, we scrubbed the kitchen floor, and were on the go the whole day long again. I hardly had time to think about the great change in my life until Wednesday. Then I had a chance, for the first time since our arrival, to tell you all about it, and at the same time to realize myself what had actually happened to me and what was still going to happen.

Yours, Anne

Saturday, 11 July, 1942

Dear Kitty,

Daddy, Mummy, and Margot can't get used to the sound of the Westertoren clock yet, which tells us the time every quarter of an hour. I can. I loved it from the start, and especially in the night it's like a faithful friend. I expect you will be interested to hear what it feels like to "disappear"; well, all I can say is that I don't know myself yet. I don't think I shall ever feel really at home in this house, but that does not mean that I loathe it here, it is more like being on vacation in a very peculiar boardinghouse. Rather a mad idea, perhaps, but that is how it strikes me. The "Secret Annexe" is an ideal hiding place. Although it leans to one side and is damp, you'd never find such a comfortable hiding place anywhere in Amsterdam, no, perhaps not even in the whole of Holland. Our little room looked very bare at first with nothing on the walls; but thanks to Daddy who had brought my film-star collection and picture postcards on beforehand, and with the aid of paste pot and brush, I have transformed the walls into one gigantic picture. This makes it look much more cheerful, and, when the Van Daans come, we'll get some wood from the attic, and make a few little cupboards for the walls and other odds and ends to make it look more lively.

Margot and Mummy are a little bit better now. Mummy felt well enough to cook some soup for the first time yesterday, but then forgot all about it, while she was downstairs

18

talking, so the peas were burned to a cinder and utterly refused to leave the pan. Mr. Koophuis has brought me a book called *Young People's Annual.* The four of us went to the private office yesterday evening and turned on the radio. I was so terribly frightened that someone might hear it that I simply begged Daddy to come upstairs with me. Mummy understood how I felt and came to. We are very nervous in other ways, too, that the neighbors might hear us or see something going on. We made curtains straight away on the first day. Really one can hardly call them curtains, they are just light, loose strips of material, all different shapes, quality, and pattern, which Daddy and I sewed together in a most unprofessional way. These works of art are fixed in position with drawing pins, not to come down until we emerge from here.

There are some large business premises on the right of us, and on the left a furniture workshop; there is no one there after working hours but even so, sounds could travel through the walls. We have forbidden Margot to cough at night, although she has a bad cold, and make her swallow large doses of codeine. I am looking for Tuesday when the Van Daans arrive; it will be much more fun and not so quiet. It is the silence that frightens me so in the evenings and at night. I wish like anything that one of our protectors could sleep here at night. I can't tell you how oppressive it is *never* to be able to go outdoors, also I'm very afraid that we shall be discovered and be shot. That is not exactly a pleasant prospect. We have to whisper and tread lightly during the day, otherwise the people in the warehouse might hear us.

Someone is calling me.

Yours, Anne

Friday, 14 August, 1942

Dear Kitty,

I have deserted you for a whole month, but honestly, there is so little news here that I can't find amusing things to tell you every day. The Van Daans arrived on July 13.

19

We thought they were coming on the fourteenth, but between the thirteenth and sixteenth of July the Germans called up people right and left which created more and more unrest, so they played for safety, better a day too early than a day too late. At nine-thirty in the morning (we were still having breakfast) Peter arrived, the Van Daans' son, not sixteen yet, a rather soft, shy, gawky youth; can't expect much from his company. He brought his cat (Mouschi) with him. Mr. and Mrs. Van Daan arrived half an hour later, and to our great amusement she had a large pottie in her hat box. "I don't feel at home anywhere without my chamber," she declared, so it was the first thing to find its permanent resting place under her divan. Mr. Van Daan did not bring his, but carried a folding tea table under his arm.

From the day they arrived we all had meals cozily together and after three days it was just as if we were one large family. Naturally the Van Daans were able to tell us a lot about the extra week they had spent in the inhabited world. Among other things we were very interested to hear what had happened to our house and to Mr. Goudsmit. Mr. Van Daan told us:

"Mr. Goudsmit phoned at nine o'clock on Monday morning and asked if I could come around. I went immediately and found G. in a state of great agitation. He let me read a letter that the Franks had left behind and wanted to take the cat to the neighbors as indicated in the letter, which pleased me. Mr. G. was afraid that the house would be searched so we went through all the rooms, tidied up a bit, and cleared away the breakfast things. Suddenly I discovered a writing pad on Mrs. Frank's desk with an address in Maastricht written on it. Although I knew that this was done on purpose, I pretended to be very surprised and shocked and urged Mr. G. to tear up this unfortunate little piece of paper without delay.

"I went on pretending that I knew nothing of your disappearance all the time, but after seeing the paper, I got a brain wave. 'Mr. Goudsmit'—I said—'it suddenly dawns on me what this address may refer to. Now it all comes back to me, a high-ranking officer was in the office about six months ago, he appeared to be very friendly with Mr. Frank and offered to help him, should the need arise. He was stationed in Maastricht. I think he must have kept his word and somehow or other managed to get them into Belgium and then on to Switzerland. I should tell this to any friends who may inquire. Don't, of course, mention Maastricht.'

"With these words I left the house. Most of your friends know already, because I've been told myself several times by different people."

We were highly amused at the story and, when Mr. Van Daan gave us further details, laughed still more at the way people can let their imagination run away with them. One family had seen the pair of us pass on bicycles very early in the morning and another lady knew quite definitely that we were fetched by a military car in the middle of the night.

Yours, Anne

Friday, 21 August, 1942

Dear Kitty,

The entrance to our hiding place has now been properly concealed. Mr. Kraler thought it would be better to put a cupboard in front our door (because a lot of houses are being searched for hidden bicycles), but of course it had to be a movable cupboard that can open like a door.

Mr. Vossen made the whole thing. We had already let him into the secret and he can't do enough to help. If we want to go downstairs, we have to first bend down and then jump, because the step has gone. The first three days we were all going about with masses of lumps on our foreheads, because we all knocked ourselves against the low doorway. Now we have nailed a cloth filled with wood wool against the top of the door. Let's see if that helps!

I'm not working much at present; I'm giving myself holidays until September. Then Daddy is going to give me lessons; it's shocking how much I've forgotten already.

21

There is little change in our life here. Mr. Van Daan and I usually manage to upset each other, it's just the opposite with Margot whom he likes very much. Mummy sometimes treats me just like a baby, which I can't bear. Otherwise things are going better. I still don't like Peter any more, he is so boring; he flops lazily on his bed half the time, does a bit of carpentry, and then goes back for another snooze. What a fool!

It is lovely weather and in spite of everything we make the most we can of it by lying on a camp bed in the attic, where the sun shines through an open window.

Yours, Anne

Wednesday, 2 September, 1942

Dear Kitty,

Mr. and Mrs. Van Daan have had a terrific quarrel, I've never seen anything quite like it before. Mummy and Daddy would never dream of shouting at each other. The cause was so trivial that the whole thing was a pure waste of breath. But, still, everyone to his own liking.

Naturally it is very unpleasant for Peter, who has to stand by. No one takes him seriously, he is so frightfully touchy and lazy. Yesterday he was badly upset because he found that his tongue was blue instead of red; this unusual phenomenon of nature disappeared just as quickly as it had come. Today he is going about with a scarf on, as he has a stiff neck; in addition "M'lord" complains of lumbago. Pains around the heart, kidneys, and lungs are not unusual either, he is a real hypochondria (that's the word for such people, isn't it?)! It is not all honey between Mummy and Mrs. Van Daan; there is plenty of cause for unpleasantness. To give a small example, I will tell you that Mrs. Van Daan has taken all three of her sheets out of the common linen cupboard. She takes it for granted that Mummy's sheets will do for all of us. It will be a nasty surprise for her when she finds that Mummy has followed her good example.

Also, she is thoroughly piqued that her dinner service

and not ours is in use. She is always trying to find out where we have actually put our plates; they are closer than she thinks, they are in a cardboard box behind a lot of junk in the attic. Our plates are unget-at-able as long as we are here, and a good thing too. I always have bad luck; I smashed one of Mrs. Van Daan's soup plates into a thousand pieces yesterday. "Oh!" she cried angrily. "Couldn't you be careful for once—that's the last one I've got." Mr. Van Daan is all sugar to me nowadays. Long may it last. Mummy gave me another frightful sermon this morning; I can't bear them. Our ideas are completely opposite. Daddy is a darling, although he can sometimes be angry with me for five minutes on end. Last week we had a little interruption in our monotonous life; it was over a book about women—and Peter. First I must tell you that Margot and Peter are allowed to read nearly all the books that Mr. Koophuis lends us, but the grownups held back this particular book on the subject of women. Peter's curiosity was aroused at once. What was it the two of them were not allowed to read in this book? He got hold of the book on the sly, while his mother was downstairs talking, and disappeared with his booty to the attic. All went well for a few days. His mother knew what he was doing, but didn't tell tales, until Father found out. He was very angry, took the book away, and thought that that would finish the whole business. However, he had not allowed for his son's curiosity, which waxed rather than waned because of his father's attitude. Peter, determined to finish it, thought of a way to get hold of this enthralling book. In the meantime, Mrs. Van Daan had asked Mummy what she thought about it all. Mummy thought this particular book was not suitable for Margot, but she saw no harm in letting her read most books.

"There is a great difference, Mrs. Van Daan," said Mummy, "between Margot and Peter. In the first place, Margot is a girl and girls are always more grownup than boys, secondly, Margot has read quite a lot of serious books, and does not go in search of things that are forbidden her, and thirdly, Margot is far more developed and intelligent, shown by the fact of her being in the fourth

23

form at school." Mrs. Van Daan agreed, but still thought it was wrong in principle to let children read books which were written for grownups.

In the meantime Peter had found a time of the day when no one bothered about him or the book: seven-thirty in the evening—then everyone was in the private office listening to the radio. That was when he took his treasure to the attic again. He should have been downstairs again by eight-thirty, but because the book was so thrilling he forgot the time and was just coming downstairs as his father came into the room. You can imagine the consequences! With a slap and a snatch, the book lay on the table and Peter was in the attic. That's how matters stood as we sat down to table. Peter stayed upstairs—no one bothered about him, and he had to go to bed without any supper. We went on with the meal, chattering gaily, when suddenly we heard a piercing whistle; we all stopped eating and looked with pale changed faces from one to another. Then we heard Peter's voice, calling down the chimney, "I say, I'm not coming down anyway." Mr. Van Daan sprang to his feet, his napkin fell to the floor, and scarlet in the face he shouted, "I've had enough of this." Daddy took his arm, afraid of what might happen, and the two men went together to the attic. After a good deal of resistance and stamping, Peter landed up in his room with the door closed and we went on eating. Mrs. Van Daan wanted to save one slice of bread for the dear boy, but his father stood firm. "If he doesn't apologize soon, he will have to sleep in the attic." Loud protests from the rest of us, as we thought missing supper was quite enough punishment. Besides, Peter might catch cold and we couldn't call a doctor.

Peter did not apologize; he was already in the attic. Mr. Van Daan did nothing more about, but I noticed the next morning that Peter's bed had been slept in. Peter was back in the attic at seven o'clock, but Daddy managed with a few friendly words to persuade him to come down again. Sour faces and obstinate silences for three days and then everything went smoothly once more.

Yours, Anne

Monday, 21 September, 1942

Dear Kitty,

Today I'm going to tell you our general news.

Mrs. Van Daan is unbearable. I get nothing but "blow-ups" from her for my continuous chatter. She is always pestering us in some way or other. This is the latest: she doesn't want to wash up the pans if there is a fragment left; instead of putting it into a glass dish, as we've always done until now, she leaves it in the pan to go bad.

After the next meal Margot sometimes has about seven pans to wash up and then Madame says: "Well, well, Margot, you have got a lot to do!"

I'm busy with Daddy working out his family tree: as we go along he tells me little bits about everyone—it's terribly interesting. Mr. Koophuis brings a few special books for me every other week. I'm thrilled with the *Joop ter Heul* series. I've enjoyed the whole of Cissy van Marxveldt very much. And I've read *Een Zomerzotheid* four times and I still laugh about some of the ludicrous situations that arise.

Term time has begun again, I'm working hard at my French and manage to pump in five irregular verbs per day. Peter sighs and groans over his English. A few schoolbooks have just arrived; we have a good stock of exercise books, pencils, rubbers, and labels, as I brought these with me. I sometimes listen to the Dutch news from London, heard Prince Bernhard recently. He said that Princess Juliana is expecting a baby about next January. I think it is lovely; it surprises the others that I should be so keen on the Royal Family.

I was being discussed and they decided that I'm not completely stupid after all, which had the effect of making me work extra hard the next day. I certainly don't want to still be in the first form when I'm fourteen or fifteen.

Also the fact that I'm hardly allowed to read any decent books was mentioned. Mummy is reading *Heeren,*

Vrouwen en Knechten now, which I'm not allowed (Margot is). First I must be more developed, like my talented sister. Then we talk about my ignorance of philosophy and psychology, about which I know nothing. Perhaps by next year I shall be wiser! (I looked up these difficult words quickly in *Koenen*.)

I have just woken up to the disturbing fact that I have one long-sleeved dress and three cardigans for the winter. I've received permission from Daddy to knit a jumper of white sheep's wool; it's not very nice wool, but as long as it's warm that's all that matters. We have some clothes deposited with friends, but unfortunately we shall not see them until after the war, that is if they are still there then. I had just written something about Mrs. Van Daan when in she came. Slap! I closed the book. "Hey, Anne, can't I just have a look?"

"I'm afraid not."

"Just the last page then?"

"No, I'm sorry."

Naturally it gave me a frightful shock, because there was an unflattering description of her on this particular page.

Yours, Anne

Friday, 25 September, 1942

Dear Kitty,

Yesterday evening I went upstairs and "visited" the Van Daans. I do so occasionally to have a chat. Sometimes it can be quite fun. Then we have some moth biscuits (the biscuit tin is kept in the wardrobe which is full of moth balls) and drink lemonade. We talked about Peter. I told them how Peter often strokes my cheek and that I wished he wouldn't as I don't like being pawed by boys.

In a typical way parents have, they asked if I couldn't get fond of Peter, because he certainly liked me very much. I thought "Oh dear!" and said: "Oh, no!" Imagine it!

26

I did say that I thought Peter rather awkward, but that it was probably shyness, as many boys who haven't had much to do with girls are like that.

I must say that the Refuge Committee of the "Secret Annexe" (male section) is very ingenious. I'll tell you what they've done now to get news of us through to Mr. Van Dijk, Travies' chief representative and a friend who has surreptitiously hidden some of our things for us! They typed a letter to a chemist in South Zeeland, who does business with our firm, in such a way that he has to send the enclosed reply back in an addressed envelope. Daddy addressed the envelope to the office. When this envelope arrives from Zeeland, the enclosed letter is taken out, and is replaced by a message in Daddy's handwriting as a sign of life. Like this, Van Dijk won't become suspicious when he reads the note. They specially chose Zeeland because it is so close to Belgium and the letter could have easily been smuggled over the border, in addition no one is allowed into Zeeland without a special permit; so if they thought we were there, he couldn't try and look us up.

Yours, Anne

Sunday, 27 September, 1942

Dear Kitty,

Just had a big bust-up with Mummy for the umpteenth time; we simply don't get on together these days and Margot and I don't hit it off any too well either. As a rule we don't go in for such outbursts as this in our family. Still, it's by no means always pleasant for me. Margot's and Mummy's natures are completely strange to me. I can understand my friends better than my own mother—too bad!

We often discuss postwar problems, for example, how one ought to address servants.

Mrs. Van Daan had another tantrum. She is terribly moody. She keeps hiding more of her private belongings. Mummy ought to answer each Van Daan "disappearance" with a Frank "disappearance." How some people do adore bringing up other people's children in addition to their own. The Van Daans are that kind. Margot doesn't need it, she is such a goody-goody, perfection itself, but I seem to have enough mischief in me for the two of us put together. You should hear us at mealtimes, with reprimands and cheeky answers flying to and fro. Mummy and Daddy always defend me stoutly. I'd have to give up if it weren't for them. Although they do tell me that I mustn't talk so much, that I must be more retiring and not poke my nose into everything, still I seem doomed to failure. If Daddy wasn't so patient, I'd be afraid I was going to turn out to be a terrific disappointment to my parents and they are plenty lenient with me.

If I take a small helping of some vegetable I detest and make up with potatoes, the Van Daans, and Mevrouw in particular, can't get over it, that any child should be so spoiled.

"Come along, Anne, have a few more vegetables," she says straight away.

"No, thank you, Mrs. Van Daan," I answer, "I have plenty of potatoes."

"Vegetables are good for you, your mother says so too. Have a few more," she says, pressing them on me until Daddy comes to my rescue.

Then we have from Mrs. Van Daan—"You ought to have been in our home, we were properly brought up. It's absurd that Anne's so frightfully spoiled. I wouldn't put up with it if Anne were my daughter."

These are always her first and last words "if Anne were my daughter." Thank heavens I'm not!

But to come back to this "upbringing" business. There was a deadly silence after Mrs. Van Daan had finished speaking yesterday. Then Daddy said, "I think Anne is extremely well brought up; she has learned one thing anyway, and that is to make no reply to your long sermons. As to vegetables, look at your own plate." Mrs. Van Daan was beaten, well and truly beaten. She had taken a minute helping of vegetables herself. But *she* is not spoiled! Oh, no, too many vegetables in the evening make her constipated. Why on earth doesn't she keep her mouth shut about me, then she wouldn't need to make such feeble excuses. It's gorgeous the way Mrs. Van Daan blushes. I don't and that is just what she hates.

Yours, Anne

Monday, 28 September, 1942

Dear Kitty,

I had to stop yesterday, long before I'd finished. I just must tell you about another quarrel, but before I start on that, something else.

Why do grownups quarrel so easily, so much, and over the most idiotic things? Up till now I thought that only children squabbled and that that wore off as you grew up. Of course, there is sometimes a real reason for a quarrel, but this is just plain bickering. I suppose I should get used to it. But I can't nor do I think I shall, as long as I am the subject of nearly every discussion (they use the word "discussion" instead of quarrel). Nothing, I repeat, nothing about me is right; my general appearance, my character, my manners are discussed from A to Z. I'm expected (by order) to simply swallow all the harsh words and shouts in silence and I am not used to this. In fact, I can't! I'm not going to take all these insults lying down, I'll show them that Anne Frank wasn't born yesterday. Then they'll be surprised and perhaps they'll keep their mouths shut when I let them see that I am going to start educating them. Shall I take up that attitude? Plain barbarism! I'm simply amazed again and again over their awful manners and especially . . . stupidity (Mrs. Van Daan's), but as soon as I get used to this—and it won't be long—then I'll give them some of their own back, and no half measures. Then they'll change their tune!

Am I really so bad-mannered, conceited. headstrong, pushing, stupid, lazy, etc., etc., as they all say? Oh, of course not. I have my faults, just like everyone else, I know that, but they thoroughly exaggerate everything.

Kitty, if only you knew how I sometimes boil under so many gibes and jeers. And I don't know how long I shall be able to stifle my rage. I shall just blow up one day.

Still, no more of this, I've bored you long enough with all these quarrels. But I simply must tell you of one highly interesting discussion at table. Somehow or other, we got on to the subject of Pim's (Daddy's nickname) extreme modesty. Even the most stupid people have to admit this about Daddy. Suddenly Mrs. Van Daan says, "I too, have an unassuming nature, more so than my husband."

Did you ever! This sentence in itself shows quite clearly how thoroughly forward and pushing she is! Mr. Van Daan thought he ought to give an explanation regarding the reference to himself. "I don't wish to be modest—in my experience it does not pay." Then to me: "Take my advice, Anne, don't be too unassuming, it doesn't get you anywhere."

Mummy agreed with this too. But Mrs. Van Daan had to add, as always, her ideas on the subject. Her next remark was addressed to Mummy and Daddy. "You have a strange outlook on life. Fancy saying such a thing to Anne; it was very different when I was young. And I feel sure that it still is, except in your modern home." This was a direct hit at the way Mummy brings up her daughters.

Mrs. Van Daan was scarlet by this time. Mummy calm and cool as a cucumber. People who blush get so hot and excited, it is quite a handicap in such a situation. Mummy, still entirely unruffled, but anxious to close the conversation as soon as possible, thought for a second and then said: "I find, too, Mrs. Van Daan, that one gets on better in life if one is not over-modest. My husband, now, and Margot, and Peter are exceptionally modest, whereas your husband, Anne, you, and I, though not exactly the opposite, don't allow ourselves to be completely pushed to one side." Mrs. Van Daan: "But, Mrs. Frank, I don't understand you; I'm so very modest and retiring, how can you think of calling me anything else?" Mummy: "I did not say you were exactly forward, but no one could say you had a retiring disposition." Mrs. Van Daan: "Let us get this matter cleared up, once and for all. I'd like to know in what way I am pushing? I know one thing, if I didn't look after myself, I'd soon be starving."

This absurd remark in self-defense just made Mummy rock with laughter. That irritated Mrs. Van Daan, who added a string of German-Dutch, Dutch-German expressions, until she became completely tongue-tied; then she rose from her chair and was about to leave the room.

Suddenly her eye fell on me. You should have seen her. Unfortunately, at the very moment that she turned round, I was shaking my head sorrowfully—not on purpose, but quite involuntarily, for I had been following the whole conversation so closely.

Mrs. Van Daan turned round and began to reel off a lot of harsh German, common, and ill-mannered, just like a coarse, red-faced fishwife—it was a marvelous sight. If I could draw, I'd have liked to catch her like this; it was a scream, such a stupid, foolish little person!

Anyhow, I've learned one thing now. You only really get to know people when you've had a jolly good row with them. Then and then only can you judge their true characters!

Yours, Anne

Tuesday, 29 September, 1942

Dear Kitty,

Extraordinary things can happen to people who go into hiding. Just imagine, as there is no bath, we use a washtub and because there is hot water in the office (by which I always mean the whole of the lower floor) all seven of us take it in turns to make use of this great luxury.

But because we are all so different and some are more modest than others, each member of the family has found his own place for carrying out the performance. Peter uses the kitchen in spite of its glass door. When he is going to have a bath, he goes to each one of us in turn and

31

tells us that we must not walk past the kitchen for half an hour. He seems to think this is sufficient. Mr. Van Daan goes right upstairs; to him it is worth the bother of carrying hot water all that way, so as to have the seclusion of his own room. Mrs. Van Daan simply doesn't bathe at all at present; she is waiting to see which is the best place. Daddy has his bath in the private office, Mummy behind a fire guard in the kitchen; Margot and I have chosen the front office for our scrub. The curtains there are drawn on Saturday afternoons, so we wash ourselves in semi-darkness.

However, I don't like this place any longer, and since last week I've been on the lookout for more comfortable quarters. Peter gave me an idea and that was to try the large office W.C. There I can sit down, have the light on, lock the door, pour my own bath water away, and I'm safe from prying eyes.

I tried my beautiful bathroom on Sunday for the first time and although it sounds mad, I think it is the best place of all. Last week the plumber was at work downstairs to move the drains and water pipes from the office W.C. to the passage. This change is a precaution against frozen pipes, in case we should have a cold winter. The plumber's visit was far from pleasant for us. Not only were we unable to draw water the whole day, but we could not go to the W.C. either. Now it is rather indecent to tell you what we did to overcome this difficulty, however, I'm not such a prude that I can't talk about these things.

The day we arrived here, Daddy and I improvised a pottie for ourselves; not having a better receptacle, we sacrificed a glass preserving jar for this purpose. During the plumber's visit, nature's offerings were deposited in these jars in the sitting room during the day. I don't think this was nearly as bad as having to sit still and not talk the whole day. You can't imagine what a trial that was for "Miss Quack-Quack." I have to whisper on ordinary days; but not being able to speak or move was ten times worse. After being flattened by three days of con-

32

tinuous sitting, my bottom was very stiff and painful.
Some exercises at bedtime helped.

Yours, Anne

Thursday, 1 October, 1942

Dear Kitty,

I got a terrible shock yesterday. Suddenly at eight
o'clock the bell rang loudly. Of course, I thought that
someone had come; you'll guess who I mean. But I calmed
down a bit when everyone said it must be some urchins
or perhaps the postman.

The days are becoming very quiet here. Lewin, a small
Jewish chemist and dispenser, works for Mr. Kraler in
the kitchen. He knows the whole building well and therefore we are always afraid that he'll take it into his head
to have a peep in the old laboratory. We are as quiet as
mice. Who, three months ago, would ever have guessed
that quicksilver Anne would have to sit still for hours—
and, what's more, could?

The twenty-ninth was Mrs. Van Daan's birthday. Although it could not be celebrated in a big way, we
managed a little party in her honor, with a specially nice
meal, and she received some small presents and flowers.
Red carnations from her husband; that seems to be a
family tradition. To pause for a moment on the subject
of Mrs. Van Daan, I must tell you that her attempts to
flirt with Daddy are a source of continual irritation for
me. She strokes his face and hair, pulls her skirt right up,
and makes so-called witty remarks, trying in this way
to attract Pim's attention. Pim, thank goodness, doesn't
find her either attractive or funny, so he doesn't play ball.
Mummy doesn't behave like that with Mr. Van Daan,
I've said that to Mrs. Van Daan's face.

Now and then Peter comes out of his shell and can be
quite funny. We have one thing in common, from which
everyone usually gets a lot of amusement: we both love
dressing up. He appeared in one of Mrs. Van Daan's very

33

narrow dresses and I put on his suit. He wore a hat and I a cap. The grownups were doubled up with laughter and we enjoyed ourselves as much as they did. Elli has bought new skirts for Margot and me at Bijenkorf's. The material is rotten, just like sacking, and they cost 24.00 florins and 7.50 florins respectively. What a difference compared with before the war!

Another nice thing I've been keeping up my sleeve. Elli has written to some secretarial school or other and ordered a correspondence course in shorthand for Margot, Peter, and me. You wait and see what perfect experts we shall be by next year. In any case it's extremely important to be able to write in a code.

Yours, Anne

Saturday, 3 October, 1942

Dear Kitty,

There was another dust-up yesterday. Mummy kicked up a frightful row and told Daddy just what she thought of me. Then she had an awful fit of tears so, of course, off I went too; and I'd got such an awful headache anyway. Finally I told Daddy that I'm much more fond of him than Mummy, to which he replied that I'd get over that. But I don't believe it. I have to simply force myself to stay calm with her. Daddy wishes that I would sometimes volunteer to help Mummy, when she doesn't feel well or has a headache; but I shan't. I am working hard at my French and am now reading *La Belle Nivernaise*.

Yours, Anne

Friday, 9 October, 1942

Dear Kitty,

I've only got dismal and depressing news for you today. Our many Jewish friends are being taken away by the dozen. These people are treated by the Gestapo without a shred of decency, being loaded into cattle trucks and sent to Westerbork, the big Jewish camp in Drente. Westerbork sounds terrible: only one washing cubicle for à hundred people and not nearly enough lavatories. There is no separate accommodations. Men, women, and children all sleep together. One hears of frightful immorality because of this; and a lot of the women, and even girls, who stay there any length of time are expecting babies.

It is impossible to escape; most of the people in the camp are branded as inmates by their shaven heads and many also by their Jewish appearance.

If it is as bad as this in Holland whatever will it be like in the distant and barbarous regions they are sent to? We assume that most of them are murdered. The English radio speaks of their being gassed.

Perhaps that is the quickest way to die. I feel terribly upset. I couldn't tear myself away while Miep told these dreadful stories; and she herself was equally wound up for that matter. Just recently for instance, a poor old crippled Jewess was sitting on her doorstep; she had been told to wait there by the Gestapo, who had gone to fetch a car to take her away. The poor old thing was terrified by the guns that were shooting at English planes overhead, and by the glaring beams of the searchlights. But Miep did not dare take her in; no one would undergo such a risk. The Germans strike without the slightest mercy. Elli too is very quiet: her boy friend has got to go to Germany. She is afraid that the airmen who fly over her home will drop their bombs, often weighing a million kilos, on Dirk's head. Jokes such as "he's not likely to get a million" and "it only takes one bomb" are in rather bad taste. Dirk is certainly not the only one who has to go: trainloads of boys leave daily. If they stop at a small station en route, sometimes some of them manage to get out unnoticed and escape; perhaps a few manage it. This, however, is not the end of my bad news. Have you ever heard of hostages? That's the latest thing in penalties for sabotage. Can you imagine anything so dreadful?

Prominent citizens—innocent people—are thrown into prison to await their fate. If the saboteur can't be traced,

35

the Gestapo simply puts about five hostages against the wall. Announcements of their deaths appear in the papers frequently. These outrages are described as "fatal accidents." Nice people, the Germans! To think that I was once one of them too! No, Hitler took away our nationality long ago. In fact, Germans and Jews are the greatest enemies in the world.

Yours, Anne

Friday, 16 October, 1942

Dear Kitty,

I'm terribly busy. I've just translated a chapter out of *La Belle Nivernaise* and made notes of new words. Then a perfectly foul math problem and three pages of French grammar. I flatly refuse to do these math problems every day. Daddy agrees that they're vile. I'm almost better at them than he is, though neither of us are much good and we often have to fetch Margot. I'm the furthest on of the three of us in shorthand.

Yesterday I finished *The Assault*. It's quite amusing, but doesn't touch *Joop ter Heul*. As a matter of fact, I think Cissy van Marxveldt is a first-rate writer. I shall definitely let my children read her books. Mummy, Margot, and I are as thick as thieves again. It's really much better. Margot and I got in the same bed together last evening, it was a frightful squash, but that was just the fun of it. She asked if she could read my diary. I said "Yes—at least, bits of it"; and then I asked if I could read hers and she said "Yes." Then we got on to the subject of the future. I asked her what she wanted to be. But she wouldn't say and made a great secret of it. I gathered something about teaching; I'm not sure if I'm right, but I think so. Really, I shouldn't be so curious!

This morning I was lying on Peter's bed, having chased him off at first. He was furious with me, not that I cared very much. He might be a bit more friendly with me for once; after all I did give him an apple yesterday.

I asked Margot if she thought I was very ugly. She

said that I was quite attractive and that I had nice eyes. Rather vague, don't you think?

Till next time,

Yours, Anne

Tuesday, 20 October, 1942

Dear Kitty,

My hand still shakes, although it's two hours since we had the shock. I should explain that there are five fire extinguishers in the house. We knew that someone was coming to fill them, but no one had warned us when the carpenter, or whatever you call him, was coming.

The result was that we weren't making any attempt to keep quiet, until I heard hammering outside on the landing opposite our cupboard door. I thought of the carpenter at once and warned Elli, who was having a meal with us, that she shouldn't go downstairs. Daddy and I posted ourselves at the door so as to hear when the man left. After he'd been working for a quarter of an hour, he laid his hammer and tools down on top of our cupboard (as we thought) and knocked at our door. We turned absolutely white. Perhaps he had heard something after all and wanted to investigate our secret den. It seemed like it. The knocking, pulling, pushing, and wrenching went on. I nearly fainted at the thought that this utter stranger might discover our beautiful secret hiding place. And just as I thought my last hour was at hand, I heard Mr. Koophuis say, "Open the door, it's only me." We opened it immediately. The hook that holds the cupboard, which can be undone by people who know the secret, had got jammed. That was why no one had been able to warn us about the carpenter. The man had now gone downstairs and Koophuis wanted to fetch Elli, but couldn't open the cupboard again. It was a great relief to me, I can tell you. In my imagination the man who I thought was trying to get in had been growing and growing in size until in the end he appeared to be a giant and the greatest fascist that ever walked the earth.

Well! Well! Luckily everything was okay this time. Meanwhile we had great fun on Monday. Miep and Henk spent the night here. Margot and I went in Mummy and Daddy's room for the night, so that the Van Santens could have our room. The meal tasted divine. There was one small interruption. Daddy's lamp blew a fuse, and all of a sudden we were sitting in darkness. What was to be done? There was some fuse wire in the house, but the fuse box is right at the very back of the dark storeroom—not such a nice job after dark. Still the men ventured forth and after ten minutes we were able to put the candles away again.

I got up early this morning. Henk had to leave at half past eight. After a cozy breakfast Miep went downstairs. It was pouring and she was glad not to have to cycle to the office. Next week Elli is coming to stay for a night.

Yours, Anne

Thursday, 29 October, 1942

Dear Kitty,

I am awfully worried, Daddy is ill. He has a high temperature and a red rash, it looks like measles. Think of it, we can't even call a doctor! Mummy is letting him have a good sweat. Perhaps that will send his temperature down.

This morning Miep told us that all the furniture has been removed from the Van Daans' home. We haven't told Mrs. Van Daan yet. She's such a bundle of nerves already, and we don't feel like listening to another moan over all the lovely china and beautiful chairs that she left at home. *We* had to leave almost all our nice things behind; so what's the good of grumbling about it now?

I'm allowed to read more grown-up books lately. I'm now reading *Eva's Youth* by Nico van Suchtelen. I can't see much difference between this and the schoolgirl love stories. It is true there are bits about women selling themselves to unknown men in back streets. They ask a packet of money for it. I'd die of shame if anything like that happened to me. Also it says that Eva has a monthly period. Oh, I'm so longing to have it too; it seems so important.

Daddy has brought the plays of Goethe and Schiller from the big cupboard. He is going to read to me every evening. We've started with *Don Carlos*.

Following Daddy's good example, Mummy has pressed her prayer book into my hand. For decency's sake I read some of the prayers in German; they are certainly beautiful but they don't convey much to me. Why does she force me to be pious, just to oblige her?

Tomorrow we are going to light the fire for the first time. I expect we shall be suffocated with smoke. The chimney hasn't been swept for ages, let's hope the thing draws.

Yours, Anne

Saturday, 7 November, 1942

Dear Kitty,

Mummy is frightfully irritable and that always seems to herald unpleasantness for me. Is it just a chance that Daddy and Mummy never rebuke Margot and that they always drop on me for everything? Yesterday evening, for instance: Margot was reading a book with lovely drawings in it; she got up and went upstairs, put the book down ready to go on with it later. I wasn't doing anything, so picked up the book and started looking at the pictures. Margot came back, saw "her" book in my hands, wrinkled her forehead and asked for the book back. Just because I wanted to look a little further on, Margot got more and more angry. Then Mummy joined in: "Give the book to Margot; she was reading it," she said. Daddy came into the room. He didn't even know what it was all about, but saw the injured look on Margot's face and promptly dropped on me: "I'd like to see what you'd say if Margot ever started looking at one of your books!" I gave way at once, laid the book down, and left the

39

room—offended, as they thought. It so happened I was neither offended nor cross, just miserable. It wasn't right of Daddy to judge without knowing what the squabble was about. I would have given Margot the book myself, and much more quickly, if Mummy and Daddy hadn't interfered. They took Margot's part at once, as though she were the victim of some great injustice.

It's obvious that Mummy would stick up for Margot; she and Margot always do back each other up. I'm so used to that that I'm utterly indifferent to both Mummy's jawing and Margot's moods.

I love them; but only because they are Mummy and Margot. With Daddy it's different. If he holds Margot up as an example, approves of what she does, praises and caresses her, then something gnaws at me inside, because I adore Daddy. He is the one I look up to. I don't love anyone in the world but him. He doesn't notice that he treats Margot differently from me. Now Margot is just the prettiest, sweetest, most beautiful girl in the world. But all the same I feel I have some right to be taken seriously too. I have always been the dunce, the ne'er-do-well of the family, I've always had to pay double for my deeds, first with the scolding and then again because of the way my feelings are hurt. Now I'm not satisfied with this apparent favoritism any more. I want something from Daddy that he is not able to give me.

I'm not jealous of Margot, never have been. I don't envy her good looks or her beauty. It is only that I long for Daddy's real love: not only as his child, but for me—Anne, myself.

I cling to Daddy because it is only through him that I am able to retain the remnant of family feeling. Daddy doesn't understand that I need to give vent to my feelings over Mummy sometimes. He doesn't want to talk about it; he simply avoids anything which might lead to remarks about Mummy's failings. Just the same, Mummy and her failings are something I find harder to bear than anything else. I don't know how to keep it all to myself. I can't always be drawing attention to her untidiness, her sarcasm, and her lack of sweetness, neither can I believe that I'm always in the wrong.

We are exact opposites in everything; so naturally we are bound to run up against each other. I don't pronounce judgment on Mummy's character, for that is something I can't judge. I only look at her as a mother, and she just doesn't succeed in being that to me; I have to be my own mother. I've drawn myself apart from them all; I am my own skipper and later on I shall see where I come to land. All this comes about particularly because I have in my mind's eye an image of what a perfect mother and wife should be; and in her whom I must call "Mother" I find no trace of that image.

I am always making resolutions not to notice Mummy's bad example. I want to see only the good side of her and to seek in myself what I cannot find in her. But it doesn't work; and the worst of it is neither Daddy nor Mummy understands this gap in my life, and I blame them for it. I wonder if anyone can ever succeed in making their children absolutely content.

Sometimes I believe that God wants to try me, both now and later on; I must become good through my own efforts, without examples and without good advice. Then later on I shall be all the stronger. Who besides me will ever read these letters? From whom but myself shall I get comfort? As I need comforting often, I frequently feel weak, and dissatisfied with myself; my shortcomings are too great. I know this, and every day I try to improve myself, again and again.

My treatment varies so much. One day Anne is so sensible and is allowed to know everything; and the next day I hear that Anne is just a silly little goat who doesn't know anything at all and imagines that she's learned a wonderful lot from books. I'm not a baby or a spoiled darling any more, to be laughed at, whatever she does. I have my own views, plans, and ideas, though I can't put them into words yet. Oh, so many things bubble up inside me as I lie in bed, having to put up with people I'm fed up with, who always misinterpret my intentions. That's why in the end I always come back to my diary. That is

41

where I start and finish, because Kitty is always patient. I'll promise her that I shall persevere, in spite of everything, and find my own way through it all, and swallow my tears. I only wish I could see the results already or occasionally receive encouragement from someone who loves me.

Don't condemn me; remember rather that sometimes I too can reach the bursting point.

Yours, Anne

Monday, 9 November, 1942

Dear Kitty,

Yesterday was Peter's birthday, he was sixteen. He had some nice presents. Among other things a game of Monopoly, a razor, and a lighter. Not that he smokes much; it's really just for show.

The biggest surprise came from Mr. Van Daan when, at one o'clock, he announced that the British had landed in Tunis, Algiers, Casablanca, and Oran. "This is the beginning of the end," everyone was saying, but Churchill, the British Prime Minister, who had probably heard the same thing in England, said: "This is not the end. It is not even the beginning of the end. But it is, perhaps, the end of the beginning." Do you see the difference? There is certainly reason for optimism. Stalingrad, the Russian town which they've already been defending for three months, still hasn't fallen into German hands.

But to return to affairs in our secret den. I must tell you something about our food supply. As you know, we have some real greedy pigs on the top floor. We get our bread from a nice baker, a friend of Koophuis. We don't get so much as we used to at home, naturally. But it's sufficient. Four ration cards have also been bought illegally. Their price is going up all the time; it has now gone up from twenty-seven florins to thirty-three. And all that for a little slip of printed paper! In order to have something in the house that will keep, apart from our 150 tins of vegetables, we have bought 270 pounds of dried peas and beans. They are not all for us, some are for the office people. They are in sacks which hang on hooks in our little passage (inside the hidden door). Owing to the weight of the contents, a few stitches in the sacks burst open. So we decided it would be better to put our winter store in the attic and Peter was given the job of dragging it all up there.

He had managed to get five of the six sacks upstairs intact, and he was just busy pulling up number six, when the bottom seam of the sack split and a shower—no, a positive hailstorm of brown beans came pouring down and rattled down the stairs. There were about fifty pounds in the sack and the noise was enough to waken the dead. Downstairs they thought the old house with all its contents was coming down on them. (Thank God there were no strangers in the house.) It gave Peter a moment's fright. But he was soon roaring with laughter, especially when he saw me standing at the bottom of the stairs, like a little island in the middle of a sea of beans! I was entirely surrounded up to my ankles in beans. Quickly we started to pick them up. But beans are so slippery and small that they seemed to roll into all the possible and impossible corners and holes. Now, every time anyone goes downstairs they bend down once or twice, in order to be able to present Mrs. Van Daan with a handful of beans.

I'd almost forgotten to mention that Daddy is quite better again.

Yours, Anne

P.S. The news has just come over the radio that Algiers has fallen. Morocco, Casablanca, and Oran have been in British hands for several days. Now we're waiting for Tunis.

Tuesday, 10 November, 1942

Dear Kitty,

Great news—we want to take in an eighth person. Yes, really! We've always thought that there was quite enough room and food for one more. We were only afraid of giving Koophuis and Kraler more trouble. But now that the appalling stories we hear about Jews are getting even worse, Daddy got hold of the two people who had to decide, and they thought it was an excellent plan. "It is just as dangerous for seven as for eight," they said, and quite rightly. When this was settled, we ran through our circle of friends, trying to think of a single person who would fit in well with our "family." It wasn't difficult to hit on someone. After Daddy had refused all members of the Van Daan family, we chose a dentist called Albert Dussel, whose wife was fortunate enough to be out of the country when war broke out. He is known to be quiet, and so far as we and Mr. Van Daan can judge from a superficial acquaintance, both families think he is a congenial person. Miep knows him too, so she will be able to make arrangements for him to join us. If he comes, he will have to sleep in my room instead of Margot, who will use the camp bed.

Yours, Anne

Thursday, 12 November, 1942

Dear Kitty,

Dussel was awfully pleased when Miep told him that she had got a hiding place for him. She urged him to come as soon as possible. Preferably Saturday. He thought that this was rather doubtful, since he had to bring his card index up to date first, see to a couple of patients, and settle his accounts. Miep came to us with this news this morning. We thought it was unwise of him to put it off. All these preparations entail explanations to a number of people, whom we would rather keep out of it. Miep is going to ask if he can't manage to come on Saturday after all.

Dussel said no; now he is coming on Monday. I must say I think it's pretty crazy that he doesn't jump at the proposal—whatever it is. If he were to get picked up outside, would he still be able to do his card index, settle his finances, and see to his patients? Why delay then?

I think it's stupid of Daddy to have given in. No other news—

Yours, Anne

Tuesday, 17 November, 1942

Dear Kitty,

Dussel has arrived. All went well. Miep had told him that he must be at a special place in front of the Post Office at eleven o'clock, where a man would meet him. Dussel was standing at the rendezvous dead on time. Mr. Koophuis, who knows Dussel too, went up to him and told him that the said gentleman could not come, but asked whether he would just go to Miep at the office. Koophuis got into a tram and went back to the office, while Dussel walked in the same direction. At twenty past eleven Dussel tapped at the office door. Miep helped him off with his coat, so that the yellow star would not be seen, and took him to the private office, where Koophuis engaged him in conversation until the charwoman had gone. Then Miep went upstairs with Dussel under the pretext that the private office was needed for something, opened the swinging cupboard, and stepped inside before the eyes of the dumfounded Dussel.

We all sat around the table upstairs, waiting with coffee and cognac to greet the newcomer. Miep showed him into our sitting room first. He recognized our furniture at once, and had not the remotest idea that we were there, above his head. When Miep told him he nearly passed out with surprise. But luckily Miep didn't give him much time and took him straight upstairs.

Dussel sank into a chair, speechless, and looked at us all for a while, as if he had to really take it all in first. After a while he stuttered "But . . . *aber, sind* you not in Belgium then? *Ist der Militär nicht* come, *das Auto,* the escape is *sie nicht* successful?"

We explained everything to him, that we had spread the story about the soldiers and the car on purpose to put

45

people, and especially the Germans, on the wrong track, should they try to find us.

Dussel was again struck dumb by such ingenuity and, when he had explored further our superpractical exquisite little "Secret Annexe," he could do nothing but gaze about him in astonishment.

We all had lunch together. Then he had a little nap and joined us for tea, tidied up his things a bit (Miep had brought them beforehand), and began to feel more at home. Especially when he received the following typed "Secret Annexe Rules" (Van Daan product).

PROSPECTUS AND GUIDE TO THE "SECRET ANNEXE"

Special institution as temporary residence for Jews and suchlike.

Open all the year round. Beautiful, quiet, free from woodland surroundings, in the heart of Amsterdam. Can be reached by trams 13 and 17, also by car or bicycle. In special cases also on foot, if the Germans prevent the use of transport.

Board and lodging: Free.

Special fat-free diet.

Running water in the bathroom (alas, no bath) and down various inside and outside walls.

Ample storage room for all types of goods.

Own radio center, direct communication with London, New York, Tel Aviv, and numerous other stations. This appliance is only for residents' use after six o'clock in the evening. No stations are forbidden, on the understanding that German stations are only listened to in special cases, such as classical music and the like.

Rest hours: 10 o'clock in the evening until 7:30 in the morning. 10:15 on Sundays. Residents may rest during the day, conditions permitting, as the directors indicate. For reasons of public security rest hours must be strictly observed!!

Holidays (outside the home): postponed indefinitely.

Use of language: Speak softly at all times, by order! All civilized languages are permitted, therefore no German!

Lessons: One written shorthand lesson per week. English, French, Mathematics, and History at all times.

46

Small Pets—Special Department (permit is necessary): Good treatment available (vermin excepted).

Mealtimes: breakfast, every day except Sunday and Bank Holidays, 9 A.M. Sundays and Bank Holidays, 11:30 A.M. approximately.

Lunch: (not very big): 1:15 P.M. to 1:45 P.M.

Dinner: cold and/or hot: no fixed time (depending on the news broadcast).

Duties: Residents must always be ready to help with office work.

Baths: The washtub is available for all residents from 9 A.M. on Sundays. The W.C. kitchen, private office or main office, whichever preferred, are available.

Alcoholic Beverages: only with doctor's prescription.

END

Yours, Anne

Thursday, 19 November, 1942

Dear Kitty,

Dussel is a very nice man, just as we had all imagined. Of course he thought it was all right to share my little room.

Quite honestly I'm not so keen that a stranger should use my things, but one must be prepared to make some sacrifices for a good cause, so I shall make my little offering with a good will. "If we can save someone, then everything else is of secondary importance," says Daddy, and he's absolutely right.

The first day that Dussel was here, he immediately asked me all sorts of questions: When does the charwoman come? When can one use the bathroom? When is one allowed to use the lavatory? You may laugh, but these things are not so simple in a hiding place. During the day we mustn't make any noise that might be heard downstairs; and if there is some stranger—such as the charwoman for example—then we have to be extra careful. I explained all this carefully to Dussel. But one thing amazed me: he is very slow on the uptake. He asks

47

everything twice over and still doesn't seem to remember. Perhaps that will wear off in time, and it's only that he's thoroughly upset by the sudden change.

Apart from that, all goes well. Dussel has told us a lot about the outside world, which we have missed for so long now. He had very sad news. Countless friends and acquaintances have gone to a terrible fate. Evening after evening the green and gray army lorries trundle past. The Germans ring at every front door to inquire if there are any Jews living in the house. If there are, then the whole family has to go at once. If they don't find any, they go on to the next house. No one has a chance of evading them unless one goes into hiding. Often they go around with lists, and only ring when they know they can get a good haul. Sometimes they let them off for cash—so much per head. It seems like the slave hunts of olden times. But it's certainly no joke; it's much too tragic for that. In the evenings when it's dark, I often see rows of good, innocent people accompanied by crying children, walking on and on, in charge of a couple of these chaps, bullied and knocked about until they almost drop. No one is spared—old people, babies, expectant mothers, the sick—each and all join in the march of death.

How fortunate we are here, so well cared for and undisturbed. We wouldn't have to worry about all this misery were it not that we are so anxious about all those dear to us whom we can no longer help.

I feel wicked sleeping in a warm bed, while my dearest friends have been knocked down or have fallen into a gutter somewhere out in the cold night. I get frightened when I think of close friends who have now been delivered into the hands of the cruelest brutes that walk the earth. And all because they are Jews!

Yours, Anne

Dear Kitty,

None of us really knows how to take it all. The news about the Jews had not really penetrated through to us until now, and we thought it best to remain as cheerful as possible. Every now and then, when Miep lets out something about what has happened to a friend, Mummy and Mrs. Van Daan always begin to cry, so Miep thinks it better not to tell us any more. But Dussel was immediately plied with questions from all sides, and the stories he told us were so gruesome and dreadful that one can't get them out of one's mind.

Yet we shall have our jokes and tease each other, when these horrors have faded a bit in our minds. It won't do us any good, or help those outside, to go on being as gloomy as we are at the moment. And what would be the object of making our "Secret Annexe" into a "Secret Annexe of Gloom"? Must I keep thinking about those other people, whatever I am doing? And if I want to laugh about something, should I stop myself quickly and feel ashamed that I am cheerful? Ought I then to cry the whole day long? No, that I can't do. Besides, in time this gloom will wear off.

Added to this misery there is another, but of a purely personal kind; and it pales into insignificance beside all the wretchedness I've just told you about. Still, I can't refrain from telling you that lately I have begun to feel deserted. I am surrounded by too great a void. I never used to feel like this, my fun and amusements, and my girl friends, completely filled my thoughts. Now I either think about unhappy things, or about myself. And at long last I have made the discovery that Daddy, although he's such a darling, still cannot take the place of my entire little world of bygone days. But why do I bother you with such foolish things? I'm very ungrateful, Kitty; I know that. But it often makes my head swim if I'm jumped

upon too much, and then on top of that have to think
about all those other miseries!

Yours, Anne

Saturday, 28 November, 1942

Dear Kitty,
We have used too much electricity, more than our
ration. Result: the utmost economy and the prospect of
having it cut off. No light for a fortnight; a pleasant
thought, that, but who knows, perhaps it won't happen
after all! It's too dark to read in the afternoons after four
or half past. We pass the time in all sorts of crazy ways:
asking riddles, physical training in the dark, talking
English and French, criticizing books. But it all begins
to pall in the end. Yesterday evening I discovered something new: to peer through a powerful pair of field glasses
into the lighted rooms of the houses at the back. In the
daytime we can't allow even as much as a centimeter's
chink to appear between our curtains, but it can't do any
harm after dark. I never knew before that neighbors
could be such interesting people. At any rate, ours are. I
found one couple having a meal, one family was in the
act of taking a home movie; and the dentist opposite was
just attending to an old lady, who was awfully scared.

It was always said about Mr. Dussel that he could get
on wonderfully with children and that he loved them all.
Now he shows himself in his true colors; a stodgy, old-
fashioned disciplinarian, and preacher of long, drawn-out
sermons on manners.

As I have unusual good fortune (!) to share my bedroom—alas, a small one—with His Lordship, and as I'm
generally considered to be the most badly behaved of
the three young people, I have a lot to put up with and
have to pretend to be deaf in order to escape the old,
much-repeated tickings-off and warnings. All this wouldn't
be too bad, if he wasn't such a frightful sneak and he
didn't pick on Mummy of all people to sneak to every
time. When I've already just had a dose from him,

Mummy goes over it all again, so I get a gale aft as well as fore. Then, if I'm really lucky, I'm called on to give an account of myself to Mrs. Van Daan and then I get a veritable hurricane!

Honestly, you needn't think it's easy to be the "badly brought-up" central figure of a hypercritical family in hiding. When I lie in bed at night and think over the many sins and shortcomings attributed to me, I get so confused by it all that I either laugh or cry: it depends what sort of mood I am in.

Then I fall asleep with a stupid feeling of wishing to be different from what I am or from what I want to be; perhaps to behave differently from the way I want to behave, or do behave. Oh, heavens above, now I'm getting you in a muddle too. Forgive me, but I don't like crossing things out, and in these days of paper shortage we are not allowed to throw paper away. Therefore I can only advise you not to read the last sentence again, and certainly not to try to understand it, because you won't succeed anyhow!

Yours, Anne

Monday, 7 December, 1942

Dear Kitty,

Chanuka and St. Nicholas Day came almost together this year—just one day's difference. We didn't make much fuss about Chanuka: we just gave each other a few little presents and then we had the candles. Because of the shortage of candles we only had them alight for ten minutes, but it is all right as long as you have the song. Mr. Van Daan has made a wooden candlestick, so that too was all properly arranged.

Saturday, the evening of St. Nicholas Day, was much more fun. Miep and Elli had made us very inquisitive by whispering all the time with Daddy, so naturally we guessed that something was on.

And so it was. At eight o'clock we all filed down the wooden staircase through the passage in pitch-darkness (it made me shudder and wish that I was safely upstairs again) into the little dark room. There, as there are no windows, we were able to turn on a light. When that was done, Daddy opened the big cupboard. "Oh! how lovely," we all cried. A large basket decorated with St. Nicholas paper stood in the corner and on top there was a mask of Black Peter.

We quickly took the basket upstairs with us. There was a nice little present for everyone, with a suitable poem attached. I got a doll, whose skirt is a bag for odds and ends; Daddy got book ends, and so on. In any case it was a nice idea and as none of us had ever celebrated St. Nicholas, it was a good way of starting.

Yours, Anne

Thursday, 10 December, 1942

Dear Kitty,

Mr. Van Daan used to be in the meat, sausage, and spice business. It was because of his knowledge of this trade that he was taken on in Daddy's business. Now he is showing the sausagy side of himself, which, for us, is by no means disagreeable.

We had ordered a lot of meat (under the counter, of course) for preserving in case we should come upon hard times. It was fun to watch, first the way the pieces of meat went through the mincer, two or three times, then how all the accompanying ingredients were mixed with the minced meat, and then how the intestine was filled by means of a spout, to make the sausages. We fried the sausage meat and ate it with sauerkraut for supper that evening, but the Gelderland sausages had to be thoroughly dried first, so we hung them over a stick tied to the ceiling with string. Everyone who came into the room began to laugh when they caught a glimpse of the row of sausages on show. They looked terribly funny!

The room was in a glorious mess. Mr. Van Daan was wearing one of his wife's aprons swathed round his substantial person (he looked fatter than he is!) and was busy with the meat. Hands smothered in blood, red face, and the soiled apron, made him look like a butcher. Mrs. Van Daan was trying to do everything at once, learning Dutch from a book, stirring the soup, watching the meat being done, sighing and complaining about her injured rib. That's what happens to elderly ladies (!) who do such idiotic exercises to reduce their large behinds!

Dussel had inflammation in one eye and was bathing it with camomile tea by the fire. Pim, who was sitting on a chair in a beam of sunlight that shone through the window, kept being pushed from one side to the other. In addition, I think his rheumatism was bothering him, because he sat rather hunched up with a miserable look on his face, watching Mr. Van Daan at work. He looked exactly like some shriveled-up old man from an old people's home. Peter was doing acrobatics round the room with his cat. Mummy, Margot, and I were peeling potatoes; and, of course, all of us were doing everything wrong because we were so busy watching Mr. Van Daan.

Dussel has opened his dental practice. For the fun of it, I must tell you about his first patient. Mummy was ironing; and Mrs. Van Daan was the first to face the ordeal. She went and sat on a chair in the middle of the room. Dussel began to unpack his case in an awfully important way, asked for some eau de cologne as a disinfectant and vaseline to take the place of wax.

He looked in Mrs. Van Daan's mouth and found two teeth which, when touched, just made her crumple up as if she was going to pass out, uttering incoherent cries of pain. After a lengthy examination (in Mrs. Van Daan's case, lasting in actual fact not more than two minutes) Dussel began to scrape away at one of the holes. But, no fear—it was out of the question—the patient flung her arms and legs about wildly in all directions until at one point Dussel let go of the scraper—that remained stuck in Mrs. Van Daan's tooth.

Then the fat was really in the fire! She cried (as far as it was possible with such an instrument in one's mouth), tried to pull the thing out of her mouth, and only succeeded in pushing it further in. Mr. Dussel stood with his hands against his sides calmly watching the little comedy. The rest of the audience lost all control and roared with laughter. It was rotten of us, because I for one am quite sure that I should have screamed even louder. After much turning, kicking, screaming, and calling out, she got the instrument free at last and Mr. Dussel went on with his work, as if nothing had happened!

This he did so quickly that Mrs. Van Daan didn't have time to start any fresh tricks. But he'd never had so much help in all his life before. Two assistants are pretty useful: Van Daan and I performed our duties well. The whole scene looked like a picture from the Middle Ages entitled "A Quack at Work." In the meantime, however, the patient hadn't much patience; she had to keep an eye on "her" soup and "her" meal. One thing is certain. Mrs. Van Daan won't be in such a hurry to allow herself to be treated again!

Yours, Anne

Sunday, 13 December, 1942

Dear Kitty,

I'm sitting cozily in the main office, looking outside through a slit in the curtain. It is dusk but still just light enough to write to you.

It is a very queer sight, as I watch the people walking by; it looks just as if they are all in a terrible hurry and nearly trip over their own toes. With cyclists, now, one simply can't keep pace with their speed. I can't even see what sort of person is riding on the machine.

The people in this neighborhood don't look very attractive. The children especially are so dirty you wouldn't want to touch them with a barge pole. Real slum kids with running noses. I can hardly understand a word they say.

Yesterday afternoon Margot and I were having a bath here and I said, "Supposing we were to take the children who are walking past, one by one, hoist them up with a fishing rod, give them each a bath, wash and mend their clothes, and then let them go again, then . . ." Margot interrupted me, "By tomorrow they would look just as filthy and ragged as before."

But I'm just talking nonsense; besides, there are other things to see—cars, boats, and rain. I like particularly the screech of the trams as they go by.

There is no more variety in our thoughts than there is for ourselves. They go round and round like a roundabout—from Jews to food and from food to politics. By the way, talking of Jews, I saw two Jews through the curtain yesterday. I could hardly believe my eyes; it was a horrible feeling, just as if I'd betrayed them and was now watching them in their misery. There is a houseboat immediately opposite, where a bargeman lives with his family. He has a small yapping dog. We only know the little dog by his bark and his tail, which we can see when he runs round the deck. Ugh! Now it's started to rain and most of the people are hidden under umbrellas. I see nothing but raincoats and occasionally the back of someone's hat. Really I don't need to see more. I'm gradually getting to know all the women at a glance, blown out with potatoes, wearing a red or a green coat, trodden-down heels and with a bag under their arms. Their faces either look grim or kind—depending on their husbands' dispositions.

Yours, Anne

Tuesday, 22 December, 1942

Dear Kitty,

The "Secret Annexe" has heard the joyful news that each person will receive an extra quarter of a pound of butter for Christmas. It says half a pound in the newspapers, but that's only for the lucky mortals who get their ration books from the government, not for Jews who have gone into hiding, who can only afford to buy four illegal ration books, instead of eight.

We are all going to bake something with our butter.

I made some biscuits and two cakes this morning. Everyone is very busy upstairs and Mummy has told me I must not go there to work or read, until the household jobs are done.

Mrs. Van Daan is in bed with her bruised rib, complains the whole day long, allows herself to be given fresh dressings all the time, and isn't satisfied with anything. I shall be glad when she's on her feet again and tidies up her own things, because I must say this for her: she's exceptionally industrious and tidy, all the while she is healthy in mind and body. She is cheerful too.

Just as if I didn't hear enough "ssh-ssh" during the day, for making too much noise, my gentleman bedroom companion now repeatedly calls out "ssh-ssh" to me at night too. According to him, I am not even allowed to turn over! I refuse to take the slightest notice of him, and shall go "ssh-ssh" back at him the next time.

He makes me furious, on Sundays especially, when he turns the light on early to do his exercises. It seems to take simply hours, while I, poor tormented creature, feel the chairs, which are placed at the head of my bed to lengthen it, slide backwards and forwards continually under my sleepy head. When he has ended with a couple of violent arm-waving exercises to loosen his muscles, His Lordship begins his toilet. His pants are hanging up, so to and fro he must go to collect them. But he forgets his tie, which is lying on the table. Therefore once more he pushes and bumps the chairs to get it.

But I won't bore you any longer on the subject of old men. It won't make things any better and all my plans of revenge (such as disconnecting the lamp, shutting the door, hiding his clothes) must be abandoned in order to keep the peace. Oh, I'm becoming so sensible! One must apply one's reason to everything here, learning to obey, to hold your tongue, to help, to be good, to give in, and I don't know what else. I'm afraid I shall use up all my brains too quickly, and I haven't got so very many. Then I shall not have any left for when the war is over.

Yours, Anne

Wednesday, 13 January, 1943

Dear Kitty,

Everything has upset me again this morning, so I wasn't able to finish a single thing properly.

It is terrible outside. Day and night more of those poor miserable people are being dragged off, with nothing but a rucksack and a little money. On the way they are deprived even of these possessions. Families are torn apart, the men, women, and children all being separated. Children coming home from school find that their parents have disappeared. Women return from shopping to find their homes shut up and their families gone.

The Dutch people are anxious too, their sons are being sent to Germany. Everyone is afraid.

And every night hundreds of planes fly over Holland and go to German towns, where the earth is so plowed up by their bombs, and every hour hundreds and thousands of people are killed in Russia and Africa. No one is able to keep out of it, the whole globe is waging war and although it is going better for the Allies, the end is not yet in sight.

And as for us, we are fortunate. Yes, we are luckier than millions of people. It is quiet and safe here, and we are, so to speak, living on capital. We are even so selfish as to talk about "after the war," brighten up at the thought of having new clothes and new shoes, whereas we really ought to save every penny, to help other people, and save what is left from the wreckage after the war.

The children here run about in just a thin blouse and clogs; no coat, no hat, no stockings, and no one helps them. Their tummies are empty, they chew an old carrot to stay the pangs, go from their cold homes out into the cold street and, when they get to school, find themselves in an even colder classroom. Yes, it has even got so bad in Holland that countless children stop the passers-by and beg for a piece of bread. I could go on for hours about all the suffering the war has brought, but then I would only make myself more dejected. There is nothing we can do but wait as calmly as we can till the misery comes to an end. Jews and Christians wait, the whole earth waits; and there are many who wait for death.

Yours, Anne

Saturday, 30 January, 1943

Dear Kitty,

I'm boiling with rage, and yet I mustn't show it. I'd like to stamp my feet, scream, give Mummy a good shaking, cry, and I don't know what else, because of the horrible words, mocking looks, and accusations which are leveled at me repeatedly every day, and find their mark, like shafts from a tightly strung bow, and which are just as hard to draw from my body.

I would like to shout to Margot, Van Daan, Dussel—and Daddy too—"Leave me in peace, let me sleep one night at least without my pillow being wet with tears, my eyes burning and my head throbbing. Let me get away from it all, preferably away from the world!" But I can't do that, they mustn't know my despair, I couldn't bear their sympathy and their kindhearted jokes, it would only make me want to scream all the more. If I talk, everyone thinks I'm showing off; when I'm silent they think I'm ridiculous; rude if I answer, sly if I get a good idea, lazy if I'm tired, selfish if I eat a mouthful more than I should, stupid, cowardly, crafty, etc., etc. The whole day long I hear nothing else but that I am an insufferable baby, and although I laugh about it and pretend not to take any notice, I *do* mind. I would like to ask God to give me a different nature, so that I didn't put everyone's back up. But that can't be done. I've got the nature that has been given to me and I'm sure it can't be bad. I do my very best to please everybody, far more than they'd ever guess. I try to laugh it all off, because I don't want to let them see my trouble. More than once, after a whole string of undeserved rebukes, I have flared up at Mummy:

"I don't care what you say anyhow. Leave me alone: I'm a hopeless case anyway." Naturally, I was then told I was rude and was virtually ignored for two days; and then, all at once, it was quite forgotten, and I was treated like everyone else again. It is impossible for me to be all sugar one day and spit venom the next. I'd rather choose the golden mean (which is not so golden), keep my thoughts to myself, and try for *once* to be just as disdainful to them as they are to me. Oh, if only I could!

Yours, Anne

Friday, 5 February, 1943

Dear Kitty,

Although I haven't written anything about our rows for a long time, there still isn't any change. The discord, long accepted by us, struck Mr. Dussel as a calamity at first. But he is getting used to it now and tries not to think about it. Margot and Peter aren't a bit what you would call "young," they are both so staid and quiet. I show up terribly against them and am always hearing, "You don't find Margot and Peter doing that—why don't you follow their example?" I simply loathe it. I might tell you I don't want to be in the least like Margot. She is much too soft and passive for my liking and allows everyone to talk her around, and gives in about everything. I want to be a stronger character! But I keep such ideas to myself: they would only laugh at me, if I came along with this as an explanation of my attitude. The atmosphere at table is usually strained, though luckily the outbursts are sometimes checked by "the soup eaters"! The "soup eaters" are the people from the office who come in and are served with a cup of soup. This afternoon Mr. Van Daan was talking about Margot eating so little again. "I suppose you do it to keep slim," he added, teasing her. Mummy, who always defends Margot, said loudly: "I can't bear your stupid chatter any longer." Mr. Van Daan turned scarlet, looked straight in front of him, and said nothing. We often laugh about things; just recently Mrs. Van

Daan came out with some perfect nonsense. She was recalling the past, how well she and her father got on together and what a flirt she was. "And do you know," she went on, "if a man gets a bit aggressive, my father used to say, then you must say to him, 'Mr. So and So, remember I am a lady!' and he will know what you mean." We thought that was a good joke and burst out laughing. Peter too, although usually so quiet, sometimes gives cause for mirth. He is blessed with a passion for foreign words, although he does not always know their meaning. One afternoon we couldn't go to the lavatory because there were visitors in the office; however, Peter had to pay an urgent call. So he didn't pull the plug. He put a notice upon the lavatory door to warn us, with "S.V.P. gas" on it. Of course he meant to put "Beware of gas"; but he thought the other looked more genteel. He hadn't got the faintest notion it meant "if you please."

Yours, Anne

Saturday, 27 February, 1943

Dear Kitty,

Pim is expecting the invasion any day. Churchill has had pneumonia, but is improving slowly. The freedom-loving Gandhi of India is holding his umpteenth fast. Mrs. Van Daan claims to be fatalistic. But who is the most scared when the guns go off? No one else but Petronella.

Henk brought a copy of the bishop's letter to church-goers for us to read. It was very fine and inspiring. "Do not rest, people of the Netherlands, everyone is fighting with his own weapons to free the country, the people, and their religion." "Give help, be generous, and do not dismay!" is what they cry from the pulpit, just like that. Will it help? It won't help the people of our religion.

You'd never guess what has happened to us now. The owner of these premises has sold the house without informing Kraler and Koophuis. One morning the new owner arrived with an architect to have a look at the house. Luckily, Mr. Koophuis was present and showed the gentlemen everything except the "Secret Annexe." He professed to have forgotten the key of the communicating door. The new owner didn't question any further. It will be all right as long as he doesn't come back and want to see the "Secret Annexe," because then it won't look too good for us.

Daddy has emptied a card index box for Margot and me, and put cards in it. It is to be a book card system; then we both write down which books we have read, who they are by, etc. I have procured another little notebook for foreign words.

Lately Mummy and I have been getting on better together, but we still *never* confide in each other. Margot is more catty than ever and Daddy has got something he is keeping to himself, but he remains the same darling.

New butter and margarine rationing at table! Each person has their little bit of fat put on their plate. In my opinion the Van Daans don't divide it at all fairly. However, my parents are much too afraid of a row to say anything about it. Pity, I think you should always give people like them tit for tat.

Yours, Anne

Wednesday, 10 March, 1943

Dear Kitty,

We had a short circuit last evening, and on top of that the guns kept banging away all the time. I still haven't got over my fear of everything connected with shooting and planes, and I creep into Daddy's bed nearly every night for comfort. I know it's very childish but you don't know what it is like. The A.A. guns roar so loudly that you can't hear yourself speak. Mrs. Van Daan, the fatalist, was nearly crying, and said in a very timid little voice, "Oh, it is so unpleasant! Oh, they are shooting so hard," by which she really means "I'm so frightened."

It didn't seem nearly so bad by candlelight as in the dark. I was shivering, just as if I had a temperature, and begged Daddy to light the candle again. He was relentless, the light remained off. Suddenly there was a burst of machine-gun fire, and that is ten times worse than guns. Mummy jumped out of bed and, to Pim's annoyance, lit the candle. When he complained her answer was firm: "After all, Anne's not exactly a veteran soldier." And that was the end of it.

Have I already told you about Mrs. Van Daan's other fears? I don't think so. If I am to keep you informed of all that happens in the "Secret Annexe," you must know about this too. One night Mrs. Van Daan thought she heard burglars in the attic; she heard loud footsteps and was so frightened that she woke her husband. Just at that moment the burglars disappeared and the only sounds that Mr. Van Daan could hear were the heartbeats of the frightened fatalist herself. "Oh, Putti [Mr. Van Daan's nickname], they are sure to have taken the sausages and all our peas and beans. And Peter, I wonder if he is still safely in bed?" "They certainly won't have stolen Peter. Listen, don't worry and let me go to sleep." But nothing came of that. A few nights after that the whole Van Daan family was woken by ghostly sounds. Peter went up to the attic with a torch—and scamper—scamper! What do you think it was running away? A swarm of enormous rats! When we knew who the thieves were, we let Mouschi sleep in the attic and the uninvited guests didn't come back again; at least not during the night.

Peter went up to the loft a couple of evenings ago to fetch some old newspapers. He had to hold the trap door firmly to get down the steps. He put his hand down without looking . . . and went tumbling down the ladder from the sudden shock and pain. Without knowing it he had put his hand on a large rat, and it had bitten him hard. By the time he reached us, as white as a sheet and with his knees knocking, the blood had soaked through his pajamas. And no wonder; it's not very pleasant to stroke a large rat; and to get bitten into the bargain is really dreadful.

Yours, Anne

Friday, 12 March, 1943

Dear Kitty,

May I introduce someone to you: Mama Frank, champion of youth! Extra butter for the young; the problems of modern youth; Mummy defends youth in everything and after a certain amount of squabbling she always gets her way. A bottle of preserved sole has gone bad; gala dinner for Mouschi and Boche. You haven't met Boche yet, although she was here before we went into hiding. She is the warehouse and office cat and keeps down the rats in the storerooms. Her odd political name requires an explanation. For some time the firm had two cats; one for the warehouse and one for the attic. Now it occasionally happened that the two cats met; and the result was always a terrific fight. The aggressor was always the warehouse cat; yet it was always the attic cat who managed to win—just like among nations. So the storehouse cat was named the German or "Boche" and the attic cat the English or "Tommy." Tommy was got rid of later; we are all entertained by Boche when we go downstairs.

We have eaten so many kidney beans and haricot beans that I can't bear the sight of them any more. The mere thought of them makes me feel quite sick. Bread is no longer served in the evenings now. Daddy has just said that he doesn't feel in a good mood. His eyes look so sad again—poor soul!

I can't drag myself away from a book called *The Knock at the Door* by Ina Boudier-Bakker. The story of the family is exceptionally well written. Apart from that, it is about war, writers, the emancipation of women; and quite honestly I'm not awfully interested.

Horrible air raids on Germany. Mr. Van Daan is in a bad mood; the cause—cigarette shortage. Discussions over the question of whether we should, or should not, use our canned vegetables ended in our favor.

I can't get into a single pair of shoes any more, except ski boots, which are not much use about the house. A pair of rush sandals costing 6.50 florins lasted me just one week, after which they were out of action. Perhaps Miep will scrounge something under the counter. I must cut Daddy's hair. Pim maintains that he will never have another barber after the war, as I do the job so well. If only I didn't snip his ear so often!

Yours, Anne

Thursday, 18 March, 1943

Dear Kitty,
Turkey is in the war. Great excitement. Waiting in suspense for the news.

Yours, Anne

Friday, 19 March, 1943

Dear Kitty,
An hour later joy was followed by disappointment. Turkey is not in the war yet. It was only a cabinet minister talking about them soon giving up their neutrality. A newspaper in the Dam[1] was crying, "Turkey on England's side." The newspapers were torn out of his hands. This is how the joyful news reached us too; 500- and 1000-guilder notes have been declared no longer valid. It is a trap for black marketeers and suchlike, but even for people who have got other kinds of "black" money, and for people in hiding. If you wish to hand in a 1000-guilder note you must be able to declare, and prove, exactly how you got it. They may still be used to pay taxes, but only until next week. Dussel has received an old-fashioned foot-operated dentist's drill, I expect he'll soon give me a thorough check-over. The "Führer aller Germanen" has been talking to wounded soldiers. Listening-in to it was

[1] A square in front of the Royal Palace.

pitiful. Question and answer went something like this:
"My name is Heinrich Scheppel."
"Wounded where?"
"Near Stalingrad."
"What kind of wound?"
"Two feet frozen off and a broken joint in the left arm."
This is exactly what the frightful puppet show on the radio was like. The wounded seemed to be proud of their wounds—the more the better. One of them felt so moved at being able to shake hands with the Führer (that is, if he still had a hand!) that he could hardly get the words out of his mouth.

Yours, Anne

Thursday, 25 March, 1943

Dear Kitty,
Yesterday Mummy, Daddy, Margot, and I were sitting pleasantly together when suddenly Peter came in and whispered something in Daddy's ear. I heard something about "a barrel fallen over in the warehouse" and "someone fumbling about at the door." Margot had heard it too; but when Daddy and Peter went off immediately, she tried to calm me down a bit, because I was naturally as white as a sheet and very jittery.

The three of us waited in suspense. A minute or two later Mrs. Van Daan came upstairs; she'd been listening to the wireless in the private office. She told us that Pim had asked her to turn off the wireless and go softly upstairs. But you know what that's like, if you want to be extra quiet, then each step of the old stairs creaks twice as loudly. Five minutes later Pim and Peter appeared again, white to the roots of their hair, and told us their experience.

They had hidden themselves under the stairs and waited, with no result at first. But suddenly, yes, I must tell you, they heard two loud bumps, just as if two doors were banged here in the house. Pim was upstairs in one leap. Peter warned Dussel first, who finally landed upstairs with a lot of fuss and noise. Then we all went up in stockinged feet to the Van Daans on the next floor. Mr. Van Daan had a bad cold and had already gone to bed, so we all drew up closely around his bed and whispered our suspicions to him.

Each time Mr. Van Daan coughed loudly, Mrs. Van Daan and I were so scared that we thought we were going to have a fit. That went on until one of us got the bright idea of giving him some codeine, which soothed the cough at once. Again we waited and waited, but we heard no more and finally we all came to the conclusion that the thieves had taken to their heels when they heard footsteps in the house, which was otherwise so silent.

Now it was unfortunate that the wireless downstairs was still tuned to England, and that the chairs were neatly arranged round it. If the door had been forced, and the air-raid wardens had noticed and warned the police, then the results might have been very unpleasant. So Mr. Van Daan got up and put on his coat and hat and followed Daddy cautiously downstairs, Peter took up the rear, armed with a large hammer in case of emergencies. The ladies upstairs (including Margot and me) waited in suspense, until the gentlemen reappeared five minutes later and told us that all was quiet in the house.

We arranged that we would not draw any water or pull the plug in the lavatory. But as the excitement had affected most of our tummies, you can imagine what the atmosphere was like when we had each paid a visit in succession.

When something like that happens, heaps of other things seem to come at the same time, as now. Number One was that the clock at the Westertoren, which I always find so reassuring, did not strike. Number Two was that Mr. Vossen having left earlier than usual the previous evening, we didn't know definitely whether Elli had been able to get hold of the key, and had perhaps forgotten to shut the door. It was still evening and we were still in a state of uncertainty, although we certainly did feel a bit reassured by the fact that from about eight o'clock, when the burglar had alarmed the house, until half past ten we had not heard a sound. On further reflection it also seemed very unlikely to us that a thief would have forced open a door so early in the evening, while there were still people about in the street. Moreover, one of us got the idea that it was possible that the caretaker of the warehouse next door was still at work since, in the excitement, and with the thin walls, one can easily make a mistake, and what's more, one's imagination can play a big part at such critical moments.

So we all went to bed; but none of us could get to sleep. Daddy as well as Mummy and Mr. Dussel were awake, and without much exaggeration I can say that I hardly slept a wink. This morning the men went downstairs to see whether the outside door was still shut, and everything turned out to be quite safe. We gave everyone a detailed description of the nerve-racking event. They all made fun of it, but it is easy to laugh at such things afterwards. Elli was the only one who took us seriously.

Yours, Anne

Saturday, 27 March, 1943

Dear Kitty,

We have finished our shorthand course; now we are beginning to practice speed. Aren't we getting clever? I must tell you more about my time-killing subjects (I call them such, because we have got nothing else to do but make the days go by as quickly as possible, so that the end of our time here comes more quickly); I'm mad on Mythology and especially the Gods of Greece and Rome. They think here that it is just a passing craze, they've never heard of an adolescent kid of my age being interested in Mythology. Well, then, I shall be the first!

Mr. Van Daan has a cold, or rather he has a little tickle in his throat. He makes a tremendous fuss about it. Gargling with camomile tea, painting his throat with tincture of myrrh, rubbing eucalyptus all over his chest, nose, teeth, and tongue; and then getting into an evil mood on top of it all.

Rauter, one of the German big shots, has made a speech. "All Jews must be out of the German-occupied countries before July 1. Between April 1 and May 1 the province of Utrecht must be cleaned out [as if the Jews were cockroaches]. Between May 1 and June 1 the provinces of North and South Holland." These wretched people are sent to filthy slaughterhouses like a herd of sick, neglected cattle. But I won't talk about it, I only get nightmares from such thoughts.

One good little piece of news is that the German department of the Labor Exchange has been set on fire by saboteurs. A few days after, the Registrar's Office went the same way. Men in German police uniforms gagged the guards and managed to destroy important papers.

Yours, Anne

Thursday, 1 April, 1943

Dear Kitty,

I'm really not April-fooling (see the date), but the opposite; today I can easily quote the saying: "Misfortunes never come singly." To begin with, Mr. Koophuis, the one who always cheers us up, has had hemorrhage of the stomach and has got to stay in bed for at least three weeks. Secondly, Elli has flu. Thirdly, Mr. Vossen is going to the hospital next week. He has probably got an abdominal ulcer. And fourthly, some important business conferences, the main points of which Daddy had discussed in detail with Mr. Koophuis, were due to be held, but now there isn't time to explain everything thoroughly to Mr. Kraler.

The gentlemen who had been expected duly arrived; even before they came Daddy was trembling with anxiety as to how the talks would go. "If only I could be there, if only I was downstairs" he cried. "Why don't you go and lie with one ear pressed against the floor, then you'll be able to hear everything." Daddy's face cleared, and at half past ten yesterday morning Margot and Pim (two ears are better than one!) took up their positions on the floor.

68

The talks were not finished in the morning, but by the afternoon Daddy was not in a fit state to continue the listening campaign. He was half paralyzed from remaining in so unusual and uncomfortable a position. I took his place at half past two, as soon as we heard voices in the passage. Margot kept me company. The talk at times was so long-winded and boring that quite suddenly I fell asleep on the cold hard linoleum floor. Margot did not dare to touch me for fear they might hear us, and talking was out of the question. I slept for a good half hour and then woke with a shock, having forgotten every word of the important discussions. Luckily Margot had paid more attention.

Yours, Anne

Friday, 2 April, 1943

Dear Kitty,

Oh dear: I've got another terrible black mark against my name. I was lying in bed yesterday evening waiting for Daddy to come and say my prayers with me, and wish me good night, when Mummy came into my room, sat on my bed, and asked very nicely, "Anne, Daddy can't come yet, shall I say your prayers with you tonight?" "No, Mummy," I answered.

Mummy got up, paused by my bed for a moment, and walked slowly towards the door. Suddenly she turned around, and with a distorted look on her face said, "I don't want to be cross, love cannot be forced." There were tears in her eyes as she left the room.

I lay still in bed, feeling at once that I had been horrible to push her away so rudely. But I knew too that I couldn't have answered differently. It simply wouldn't work. I felt sorry for Mummy; very, very sorry, because I had seen for the first time in my life that she minds my coldness. I saw the look of sorrow on her face when she spoke of love not being forced. It is hard to speak the truth, and yet it is the truth: she herself has pushed me away, her tactless remarks and her crude jokes, which I don't find

69

at all funny, have now made me insensitive to any love from her side. Just as I shrink at her hard words, so did her heart when she realized that the love between us was gone. She cried half the night and hardly slept at all. Daddy doesn't look at me and if he does for a second, then I read in his eyes the words: "How can you be so unkind, how can you bring yourself to cause your mother such sorrow?"

They expect me to apologize; but this is something I can't apologize for because I spoke the truth and Mummy will have to know it sooner or later anyway. I seem, and indeed am, indifferent both to Mummy's tears and Daddy's looks, because for the first time they are both aware of something which I have always felt. I can only feel sorry for Mummy, who has now had to discover that I have adopted her own attitude. For myself, I remain silent and aloof; and I shall not shrink from the truth any longer, because the longer it is put off, the more difficult it will be for them when they do hear it.

Yours, Anne

Tuesday, 27 April, 1943

Dear Kitty,

Such quarrels that the whole house thunders! Mummy and I, the Van Daans and Daddy, Mummy and Mrs. Van Daan, everyone is angry with everyone else. Nice atmosphere, isn't it? Anne's usual list of failings has been brought out again and fully ventilated.

Mr. Vossen is already in the Binnengasthuis hospital. Mr. Koophuis is up again, the hemorrhage having stopped sooner than usual. He told us that the Registrar's Office received additional damage from the Fire Service who, instead of just quenching the flames, soaked the whole place with water. I'm glad!

The Carlton Hotel is smashed to bits. Two British planes loaded with incendiary bombs fell right on top of the "Offiziersheim." [1] The whole Vijzelstraat-Singel corner

[1] German Officers' Club.

70

is burned down. The air raids on German towns are growing in strength every day. We don't have a single quiet night. I've got dark rings under my eyes from lack of sleep. Our food is miserable. Dry bread and coffee substitute for breakfast. Dinner: spinach or lettuce for a fortnight on end. Potatoes twenty centimeters long and tasting sweet and rotten. Whoever wants to follow a slimming course should stay in the "Secret Annexe"! They complain bitterly upstairs, but we don't regard it as such a tragedy. All the men who fought in 1940 or were mobilized have been called up to work for "der Führer" as prisoners of war. Suppose they're doing that as a precaution against invasion.

Yours, Anne

Saturday, 1 May, 1943

Dear Kitty,
If I just think of how we live here, I usually come to the conclusion that it is a paradise compared with how other Jews who are not in hiding must be living. Even so, later on, when everything is normal again, I shall be amazed to think that we, who were so spick and span at home, should have sunk to such a low level. By this I mean that our manners have declined. For instance, ever since we have been here, we have had one oilcloth on our table which, owing to so much use, is not one of the cleanest. Admittedly I often try to clean it with a dirty dishcloth, which is more hole than cloth. The table doesn't do us much credit either, in spite of hard scrubbing. The Van Daans have been sleeping on the same flannelette sheet the whole winter; one can't wash it here because the soap powder we get on the ration isn't sufficient, and besides it's not good enough. Daddy goes about in frayed trousers and his tie is beginning to show signs of wear too. Mummy's corsets have split today and are too old to be repaired, while Margot goes about in a brassiere two sizes too small for her.

Mummy and Margot have managed the whole winter with three vests between them, and mine are so small that they don't even reach my tummy.

Certainly, these are all things which can be overcome. Still, I sometimes realize with a shock: "How are we, now going about in worn-out things, from my pants down to Daddy's shaving brush, ever going to get back to our prewar standards?"

They were banging away so much last night that four times I gathered all my belongings together. Today I have packed a suitcase with the most necessary things for an escape. But Mummy quite rightly says: "Where will you escape to?" The whole of Holland is being punished for the strikes which have been going on in many parts of the country. Therefore a state of siege has been declared and everyone gets one butter coupon less. What naughty little children!

Yours, Anne

Tuesday, 18 May, 1943

Dear Kitty,

I witnessed a terrific air battle between German and British planes. Unfortunately a couple of the Allies had to jump from burning machines. Our milkman, who lives in Halfweg, saw four Canadians sitting by the roadside, one of them spoke fluent Dutch. He asked the milkman to give him a light for his cigarette and told him that the crew had consisted of six men. The pilot was burned to death, and their fifth man had hidden himself somewhere. The German police came and fetched the four perfectly fit men. I wonder how they managed to have such clear brains after that terrifying parachute trip.

Although it is fairly warm, we have to light our fires every other day, in order to burn vegetable peelings and refuse. We can't put anything in the garbage pails, because we must always think of the warehouse boy. How easily one could be betrayed by being a little careless!

All students who wish either to get their degrees this

year, or continue their studies, are compelled to sign that they are in sympathy with the Germans and approve of the New Order. Eighty per cent have refused to go against their consciences. Naturally they had to bear the consequences. All the students who do not sign have to go to a labor camp in Germany. What will be left of the youth of the country if they have all got to do hard labor in Germany? Mummy shut the window last night because of all the banging; I was in Pim's bed. Suddenly Mrs. Van Daan jumped out of bed above us, just as if Mouschi had bitten her. A loud clap followed immediately. It sounded just as if an incendiary bomb had fallen beside my bed. I shrieked out, "Light, light!" Pim turned on the lamp. I expected nothing less than to see the room ablaze within a few minutes. Nothing happened. We all hurried upstairs to see what was going on. Mr. and Mrs. Van Daan had seen a red glow through the open window. He thought that there was a fire in the neighborhood and she thought that our house had caught fire. When the clap came Mrs. Van Daan was already on her feet with her knees knocking. But nothing more happened and we all crept back into our beds.

Before a quarter of an hour had passed the shooting started up again. Mrs. Van Daan sat bolt upright at once and then went downstairs to Mr. Dussel's room, seeking there the rest which she could not find with her spouse. Dussel received her with the words, "Come into my bed, my child!" which sent us off into uncontrollable laughter. The gunfire troubled us no longer, our fears was banished!

Yours, Anne

Sunday, 13 June, 1943

Dear Kitty,

My birthday poem from Daddy is too good to keep from you. As Pim usually writes verses in German, Margot volunteered to translate it. Judge for yourself whether Margot didn't do it brilliantly. After the usual summary of the events of the year, this is how it ran:

73

Though youngest here, you are no longer small,
But life is very hard, since one and all
Aspire to be your teacher, thus and thus:
"We have experience, take a tip from us."
"We know because we did it long ago."
"Elders are always better, you must know."
At least that's been the rule since life began!
Our personal faults are much too small to scan
This makes it easier to criticize
The faults of others, which seem double size.
Please bear with us, your parents, for we try
To judge you fairly and with sympathy.
Correction sometimes take against your will,
Though it's like swallowing a bitter pill,
Which must be done if we're to keep the peace,
While time goes by till all this suffering cease.
You read and study nearly all the day,
Who might have lived in such a different way.
You're never bored and bring us all fresh air.
Your only moan is this: "What can I wear?
I have no knickers, all my clothes are small,
My vest might be a loincloth, that is all!
To put on shoes would mean to cut off toes,
Oh dear, I'm worried by so many woes!"

There was also a bit about food that Margot could
not translate into rhyme, so I shall leave it out. Don't
you think my birthday poem is good? I have been thoroughly spoiled in other ways and received a lot of lovely
things. Among other things a fat book on my pet subject
—the mythology of Greece and Rome. I can't complain
of a shortage of sweets either—everyone has broken into
their last reserves. As the Benjamin of the family in hiding,
I am really more honored than I deserve.

Yours, Anne

Tuesday, 15 June, 1943

Dear Kitty,

Lots of things have happened, but I often think that
all my uninteresting chatter bores you very much and that

74

you are glad not to receive too many letters. So I shall give you the news in brief.

Mr. Vossen has not been operated on for his duodenal ulcer. When he was on the operating table and they had opened him up, the doctors saw that he had cancer, which was far too advanced to operate. So they stitched him up again, kept him in bed for three weeks and gave him good food, and finally sent him home again. I do pity him terribly and think it is rotten that we can't go out, otherwise I should certainly visit him frequently to cheer him up. It is a disaster for us that good old Vossen won't be able to keep us in touch with all that goes on, and all he hears in the warehouse. He was our best helper and security adviser; we miss him very much indeed.

It will be our turn to hand in our radio next month. Koophuis has a clandestine baby set at home that he will let us have to take the place of our big Phillips. It certainly is a shame to have to hand in our lovely set, but in a house where people are hiding, one daren't, under any circumstances, take wanton risks and so draw the attention of the authorities. We shall have the little radio upstairs. On top of hidden Jews, clandestine money and clandestine buying, we can add a clandestine radio. Everyone is trying to get hold of an old set and to hand that in instead of their "source of courage." It is really true that as the news from outside gets worse, so the radio with its miraculous voice helps us to keep up our morale and to say again, "Chins up, stick it out, better times will come!"

Yours, Anne

Sunday, 11 July, 1943

Dear Kitty,

To return to the "upbringing" theme for the umpteenth time, I must tell you that I really am trying to be helpful, friendly, and good, and to do everything I can so that the rain of rebukes dies down to a light summer drizzle. It is mighty difficult to be on such model behavior with people you can't bear, especially when you don't mean a word of it. But I do really see that I get on better by shamming a bit, instead of my old habit of telling everyone exactly what I think (although no one ever asked my opinion or attached the slightest importance to it).

I often lose my cue and simply can't swallow my rage at some injustice, so that for four long weeks we hear nothing but an everlasting chatter about the cheekiest and most shameless girl on earth. Don't you think that sometimes I've cause for complaint? It's a good thing I'm not a grouser, because then I might get sour and bad-tempered.

I have decided to let my shorthand go a bit, firstly to give me more time for my other subjects and secondly because of my eyes. I'm so miserable and wretched as I've become very shortsighted and ought to have had glasses for a long time already (phew, what an owl I shall look!) but you know, of course, in hiding one cannot. Yesterday everyone talked of nothing but Anne's eyes, because Mummy had suggested sending me to the oculist with Mrs. Koophuis. I shook in my shoes somewhat at this announcement, for it is no small thing to do. Go out of doors, imagine it, in the street—doesn't bear thinking about! I was petrified at first, then glad. But it doesn't go as easily as that, because all the people who would have to approve such a step could not reach an agreement quickly. All the difficulties and risks had first to be carefully weighed, although Miep would have gone with me straight away.

In the meantime I got out my gray coat from the cupboard, but it was so small that it looked as if it belonged to my younger sister.

I am really curious to know what will come of it all, but I don't think the plan will come off because the British have landed in Sicily now and Daddy is once again hoping for a "quick finish."

Elli gives Margot and me a lot of office work; it makes us both feel quite important and is a great help to her. Anyone can file away correspondence and write in the sales book, but we take special pains.

Miep is just like a pack mule, she fetches and carries

so much. Almost every day she manages to get hold of some vegetables for us and brings everything in shopping bags on her bicycle. We always long for Saturdays when our books come. Just like little children receiving a present.

Ordinary people simply don't know what books mean to us, shut up here. Reading, learning, and the radio are our amusements.

Yours, Anne

Tuesday, 13 July, 1943

Dear Kitty,

Yesterday afternoon, with Daddy's permission, I asked Dussel whether he would please be so good (being really very polite) as to allow me to use the little table in our room twice a week in the afternoons, from four o'clock till half past five. I sit there every day from half past two till four, while Dussel sleeps, but otherwise the room plus table are out of bounds. Inside, in our common room, there is much too much going on; it is impossible to work there, and besides, Daddy likes to sit at the writing table and work too sometimes.

So it was quite a reasonable request, and the question was put very politely. Now honestly what do you think the very learned Dussel replied: "No." Just plain "No!" I was indignant and refused to be put off like that, so I asked him the reason for his "No." But I was sent away with a flea in my ear. This was the barrage which followed:

"I have to work too, and if I can't work in the afternoons, then there is no time left for me at all. I must finish my task, otherwise I've started it all for nothing. Anyway, you don't work seriously at anything. Your mythology, now just what kind of work is that; knitting and reading are not work either. I am at the table and shall stay there."

My reply was:

"Mr. Dussel, I do work seriously and there is nowhere else for me to work in the afternoons. I beg of you to kindly reconsider my request!"

With these words the offended Anne turned her back on the very learned doctor, ignoring him completely. I was seething with rage, and thought Dussel frightfully rude (which he certainly was) and myself very friendly. In the evening when I could get hold of Pim, I told him how it had gone off and discussed what I should do next, because I was not going to give in, and preferred to clear it up myself. Pim told me how I ought to tackle the problem, but warned me that it would be better to leave it till the next day, as I was so het up. I let this advice go to the winds, and waited for Dussel after the dishes were done. Pim sat in the room next to us, which had a calming influence on me. I began: "Mr. Dussel, I don't suppose you see any point in discussing the matter any more, but I must ask you to do so." Dussel then remarked with his sweetest smile: "I am always, and at all times, prepared to discuss this matter, but it has already been settled."

I went on talking, though continually interrupted by Dussel. "When you first came here we arranged that this room should be for both of us; if we were to divide it fairly, you would have the morning and I all the afternoon! But I don't even ask that much, and I think that my two afternoons are really perfectly reasonable." At this Dussel jumped up as if someone had stuck a needle into him. "You can't talk about your rights here at all. And where am I to go, then? I shall ask Mr. Van Daan whether he will build a little compartment in the attic, then I can go and sit there. I simply can't work anywhere. With you one always gets trouble. If your sister Margot, who after all has more reason to ask such a thing, would have come to me with the same questions, I should not think of refusing, but you . . ." Then followed the business about the mythology and the knitting, and Anne was insulted again. However, she did not show it and let Dussel finish speaking: "But you, one simply can't talk to you. You are so outrageously selfish, as long as you can get what you want, you don't mind pushing everyone else to one side, I've never seen such a child. But after all, I suppose I shall be obliged to give you your own way, because otherwise I shall be told later on that Anne Frank failed her exam because Mr. Dussel would not give up the table for her."

It went on and on and finally it was such a torrent I could hardly keep pace with it. At one moment I thought, "In a minute I'll give him such a smack in the face that he'll fly up to the ceiling together with his lies," but the next moment I said to myself, "Keep calm! Such a fellow isn't worth getting worked up about."

After giving final vent to his fury, Master Dussel left the room with an expression of mixed wrath and triumph, his coat stuffed with food. I dashed to Daddy and told him all that he had not already heard of the story. Pim decided to talk to Dussel the same evening, which he did. They talked for over half an hour. The theme of the conversation was something like this: first of all they talked about whether Anne should sit at the table, yes or no. Daddy said that he and Dussel had already discussed the subject once before, when he had professed to agree with Dussel, in order not to put him in the wrong in front of the young. But Daddy had not thought it fair then. Dussel thought that I should not speak as if he was an intruder who tried to monopolize everything, but Daddy stuck up for me firmly over that, because he had heard for himself that I had not breathed a word of such a thing.

To and fro it went, Daddy defending my selfishness and my "trifling" work, Dussel grumbling continually.

Finally, Dussel had to give in after all, and I had the opportunity of working undisturbed until five o'clock for two afternoons a week. Dussel looked down his nose very much, didn't speak to me for two days and still had to go and sit at the table from five till half past—frightfully childish.

A person of fifty-four who is still so pedantic and small-minded must be so by nature, and will never improve.

Yours, Anne

Dear Kitty,

Burglars again, but real this time! This morning Peter went to the warehouse at seven o'clock as usual, and at once noticed that both the warehouse door and the door opening on to the street were ajar. He told Pim, who tuned the radio in the private office to Germany and locked the door. Then they went upstairs together.

The standing orders for such times were observed as usual: no taps to be turned on; therefore, no washing, silence, everything to be finished by eight o'clock and no lavatory. We were all very glad that we had slept so well and not heard anything. Not until half past eleven did we learn from Mr. Koophuis that the burglars had pushed in the outer door with a crowbar and had forced the warehouse door. However, they did not find much to steal, so they tried their luck upstairs. They stole two cashboxes containing forty florins, postal orders and checkbooks and then, worst of all, all the coupons for 150 kilos of sugar.

Mr. Koophuis thinks that they belonged to the same gang as the ones who tried all three doors six weeks ago. They were unsuccessful then.

It has caused rather a stir in the building, but the "Secret Annexe" can't seem to go on without sensations like this. We were very glad that the typewriters and money in our wardrobe, where they are brought upstairs every evening, were safe.

Yours, Anne

Monday, 19 July, 1943

Dear Kitty,

North Amsterdam was very heavily bombed on Sunday. The destruction seems to be terrible. Whole streets lie in ruins, and it will take a long time before all the people are dug out. Up till now there are two hundred dead and countless wounded; the hospitals are crammed. You hear of children lost in the smoldering ruins, looking for their parents. I shudder when I recall the dull droning rumble in the distance, which for us marked the approaching destruction.

Yours, Anne

Friday, 23 July, 1943

Dear Kitty,

Just for fun I'm going to tell you each person's first wish, when we are allowed to go outside again. Margot and Mr. Van Daan long more than anything for a hot bath filled to overflowing and want to stay in it for half an hour. Mrs. Van Daan wants most to go and eat cream cakes immediately. Dussel thinks of nothing but seeing Lotje, his wife; Mummy of her cup of coffee; Daddy is going to visit Mr. Vossen first; Peter the town and a cinema, while I should find it so blissful, I shouldn't know where to start! But most of all, I long for a home of our own, to be able to move freely and to have some help with my work again at last, in other words—school.

Elli has offered to get us some fruit. It costs next to nothing—grapes f.5.00 per kilo, gooseberries f.0.70 per pound, *one* peach f.0.50, one kilo melon f.1.50.[1] Then you see in the newspapers every evening in bold letters, "Play fair and keep prices down!"

Yours, Anne

Monday, 26 July, 1943

Dear Kitty,

Nothing but tumult and uproar yesterday, we are still very het up about it all. You might really ask, does a day go by without some excitement?

We had the first warning siren while we were at

[1] Equivalent prices, in order, would be approximately $1.40, twenty-one cents, fourteen cents, and forty-two cents.

breakfast, but we don't give a hoot about that, it only means that the planes are crossing the coast.

After breakfast I went and lay down for an hour as I had a bad headache, then I went downstairs. It was about two o'clock. Margot had finished her office work at half past two: she had not packed her things together when the sirens began to wail, so upstairs I went again with her. It was high time, for we had not been upstairs five minutes when they began shooting hard, so much so that we went and stood in the passage. And yes, the house rumbled and shook, and down came the bombs.

I clasped my "escape bag" close to me, more because I wanted to have something to hold than with an idea of escaping, because there's nowhere we can go. If ever we come to the extremity of fleeing from here, the street would be just as dangerous as an air raid. This one subsided after half an hour, but the activity in the house increased. Peter came down from his lookout post in the attic, Dussel was in the main office, Mrs. Van Daan felt safe in the private office, Mr. Van Daan had been watching from the loft, and we on the little landing dispersed ourselves too: I went upstairs to see rising above the harbor the columns of smoke Mr. Van Daan had told us about. Before long you could smell burning, and outside it looked as if a thick mist hung everywhere. Although such a big fire is not a pleasant sight, luckily for us it was all over, and we went about our respective tasks. That evening at dinner: another air raid alarm! It was a nice meal, but my hunger vanished, simply at the sound of the alarm. Nothing happened and three quarters of an hour later it was all clear. The dishes were stacked ready to be done: air-raid warning, ack-ack fire, an awful lot of planes. "Oh, dear me, twice in one day, that's too much," we all thought, but that didn't help at all; once again the bombs rained down, the other side this time, on Schiphol,[1] according to the British. The planes dived and climbed, we heard the hum of their engines and it was very gruesome. Each moment I thought: "One's falling now. Here it comes."

[1] Amsterdam airport.

I can assure you that when I went to bed at nine o'clock I couldn't hold my legs still. I woke up at the stroke of twelve: planes. Dussel was undressing. I didn't let that put me off, and at the first shot, I leaped out of bed, wide awake. Two hours with Daddy and still they kept coming. Then they ceased firing and I was able to go to bed. I fell asleep at half past two.

Seven o'clock. I sat up in bed with a start. Mr. Van Daan was with Daddy. Burglars was my first thought. I heard Mr. Van Daan say "everything." I thought that everything had been stolen. But no, this time it was wonderful news, such as we have not heard for months, perhaps in all the war years. "Mussolini has resigned, the King of Italy has taken over the government." We jumped for joy. After the terrible day yesterday, at last something good again and—hope. Hope for it to end, hope for peace.

Kraler called in and told us that Fokkers has been badly damaged. Meanwhile we had another air-raid alarm with planes overhead and one more warning siren. I'm just about choked with alarms, very tired and don't feel a bit like work. But now the suspense over Italy will awaken the hope that it will soon end, perhaps even this year.

Yours, Anne

Thursday, 29 July, 1943

Dear Kitty,

Mrs. Van Daan, Dussel, and I were doing the dishes and I was extraordinarily quiet, which hardly ever happens, so they would have been sure to notice.

In order to avoid questions I quickly sought a fairly neutral topic, and thought that the book *Henry from the Other Side* would meet the need. But I had made a mistake. If Mrs. Van Daan doesn't pounce on me, then Mr. Dussel does. This was what it came to: Mr. Dussel had specially recommended us this book as being excellent. Margot and I thought it was anything but excellent. The boy's character was certainly well drawn, but the rest—

I had better gloss over that. I said something to that effect while we were washing the dishes, but that brought me a packet of trouble.

"How can you understand the psychology of a man! Of a child is not so difficult (!). You are much too young for a book like that; why, even a man of twenty would not be able to grasp it." (Why did he so especially recommend this book to Margot and me?) Now Dussel and Mrs. Van Daan continued together: "You know much too much about things that are unsuitable for you, you've been brought up all wrong. Later on, when you are older, you won't enjoy anything, then you'll say: 'I read that in books twenty years ago.' You had better make haste, if you want to get a husband or fall in love—or everything is sure to be a disappointment to you. You are already proficient in the theory, it's only the practice that you still lack!"

I suppose it's their idea of a good upbringing to always try to set me against my parents, because that is what they often do. And to tell a girl of my age nothing about "grown-up" subjects is an equally fine method! I see the results of that kind of upbringing frequently and all too clearly.

I could have slapped both their faces at that moment as they stood there making a fool of me. I was beside myself with rage and I'm just counting the days until I'm rid of "those" people.

Mrs. Van Daan is a nice one! She sets a fine example . . . she certainly sets one—a bad one. She is well known as being very pushing, selfish, cunning, calculating, and is never content. I can also add vanity and coquetry to the list. There is no question about it, she is an unspeakably disagreeable person. I could write whole chapters about Madame, and who knows, perhaps I will someday. Anyone can put on a fine coat of varnish outside. Mrs. Van Daan is friendly to strangers and especially men, so it is easy to make a mistake when you have only known her for a short time. Mummy thinks she is too stupid to waste words over, Margot too unimportant, Pim too ugly (literally and figuratively), and I, after long observation—

for I was never prejudiced from the start—have come to the conclusion that she is all three and a lot more! She has so many bad qualities, why should I even begin about one of them?

Yours, Anne

P.S.—Will the reader take into consideration that when this story was written the writer had not cooled down from her fury!

Tuesday, 3 August, 1943

Dear Kitty,

Political news excellent. In Italy the Fascist party has been banned. The people are fighting the Fascists in many places—even the army is actually taking part in the battle. Can a country like that wage war against England?

We've just had a third air raid; I clenched my teeth together to make myself feel courageous. Mrs. Van Daan, who has always said, "A terrible end is better than no end at all," is the greatest coward of us all now. She was shaking like a leaf this morning and even burst into tears. When her husband, with whom she has just made it up after a week's squabbling, comforted her, the expression on her face alone almost made me feel sentimental.

Mouschi has proved that keeping cats has disadvantages as well as advantages. The whole house is full of fleas, and the plague gets worse every day. Mr. Koophuis has scattered yellow powder in every nook and corner, but the fleas don't seem to mind a bit. It's making us all quite nervous; one keeps imagining an itch on one's arms, legs, and various parts of the body, which is why quite a lot of us are doing gymnastics, so as to be able to look at the back of our necks or legs while standing up. Now we're being paid back for not being more supple—we're too stiff to even turn our heads properly. We gave up real gymnastics long ago.

Yours, Anne

Wednesday, 4 August, 1943

Dear Kitty,

Now that we have been in the "Secret Annexe" for over a year, you know something of our lives, but some of it is quite indescribable. There is so much to tell, everything is so different from ordinary times and from ordinary people's lives. But still, to give you a closer look into our lives, now and again I intend to give you a description of an ordinary day. Today I'm beginning with the evening and night.

Nine o'clock in the evening. The bustle of going to bed in the "Secret Annexe" begins and it is always really quite a business. Chairs are shoved about, beds are pulled down, blankets unfolded, nothing remains where it is during the day. I sleep on the little divan, which is not more than one and a half meters long. So chairs have to be used to lengthen it. An eiderdown, sheets, pillows, blankets, are all fetched from Dussel's bed where they remain during the day. One hears terrible creaking in the next room: Margot's concertina-bed being pulled out. Again, divan, blankets, and pillows, everything is done to make the wooden slats a bit more comfortable. It sounds like thunder above, but it is only Mrs. Van Daan's bed. This is shifted to the window, you see, in order to give Her Majesty in the pink bed jacket fresh air to tickle her dainty nostrils!

After Peter's finished, I step into the washing cubicle, where I give myself a thorough wash and general toilet; it occasionally happens (only in the hot weeks or months) that there is a tiny flea floating in the water. Then teeth cleaning, hair curling, manicure, and my cotton-wool pads with hydrogen peroxide (to bleach black mustache hairs)—all this under half an hour.

Half past nine. Quickly into dressing gown, soap in one hand, pottie, hairpins, pants, curlers, and cotton wool in the other, I hurry out of the bathroom; but usually I'm called back once for the various hairs which decorate the washbasin in graceful curves, but which are not approved of by the next person.

Ten o'clock. Put up the blackout. Good night! For at least a quarter of an hour there is creaking of beds and a sighing of broken springs, then all is quiet, at least that is if our neighbors upstairs don't quarrel in bed.

Half past eleven. The bathroom door creaks. A narrow strip of light falls into the room. A squeak of shoes, a large coat, even larger than the man inside it—Dussel returns from his night work in Kraler's office. Shuffling on the floor for ten minutes, crackle of paper (that is the food which has to be stowed away), and a bed is made. Then the form disappears again and one only hears suspicious noises from the lavatory from time to time.

Three o'clock. I have to get up for a little job in the metal pot under my bed, which is on a rubber mat for safety's sake in case of leakage. When this has to take place, I always hold my breath, as it clatters into the tin like a brook from a mountain. Then the pot is returned to its place and the figure in the white nightgown, which evokes the same cry from Margot every evening: "Oh, that indecent nightdress!" steps back into bed.

Then a certain person lies awake for about a quarter of an hour, listening to the sounds of the night. Firstly, to whether there might not be a burglar downstairs, then to the various beds, above, next door, and in my room, from which one is usually able to make out how the various members of the household are sleeping, or how they pass the night in wakefulness.

The latter is certainly not pleasant, especially when it concerns a member of the family by the name of Dussel. First, I hear a sound like a fish gasping for breath, this is repeated nine of ten times, then with much ado and interchanged with little smacking sounds, the lips are moistened, followed by a lengthy twisting and turning in bed and rearranging of pillows. Five minutes' perfect peace and then the same sequence of events unfolds itself at least three times more, after the doctor has soothed himself to sleep again for a little while. It can also happen

87

that we get a bit of shooting in the night, varying between one o'clock and four. I never really realize it, until from habit I am already standing at my bedside. Sometimes I'm so busy dreaming that I'm thinking about French irregular verbs or a quarrel upstairs. It is some time before I begin to realize that guns are firing and that I am still in the room. But it usually happens as described above. I quickly grab a pillow and handerchief, put on my dressing gown and slippers, and scamper to Daddy, like Margot wrote in this birthday poem:

> *The first shot sounds at dead of night.*
> *Hush, look! A door creaks open wide,*
> *A little girl glides into sight,*
> *Clasping a pillow to her side.*

Once landed in the big bed, the worst is over, except if the firing gets very bad.

Quarter to seven. Trrrrr—the alarm clock that raises its voice at any hour of the day (if one asks for it and sometimes when one doesn't). Crack—ping—Mrs. Van Daan has turned it off. Creak—Mr. Van Daan gets up. Puts on water and then full speed to the bathroom.

Quarter past seven. The door creaks again. Dussel can go to the bathroom. Once alone, I take down the blackout—and a new day in the "Secret Annexe" has begun.

Yours, Anne

Thursday, 5 August, 1943

Dear Kitty,

Today I am going to take lunchtime.

It is half past twelve. The whole mixed crowd breathes again. The warehouse boys have gone home now. Above one can hear the noise of Mrs. Van Daan's vacuum cleaner on her beautiful, and only, carpet. Margot goes with a few books under her arm for her Dutch lesson "for children who make no progress," because that's Dussel's attitude. Pim goes into a corner with his inseparable Dickens to try and find peace somewhere. Mummy hurries upstairs to help the industrious housewife, and I go to the bathroom to tidy it up a bit, and myself at the same time.

Quarter to one. The place is filling up. First Mr. Van Santen, then Koophuis or Kraler, Elli and sometimes Miep as well.

One o'clock. We're all sitting listening to the B.B.C., seated around the baby wireless; these are the only times when the members of the "Secret Annexe" do not interrupt each other, because now someone is speaking whom even Mr. Van Daan can't interrupt.

Quarter past one. The great share-out. Everyone from below gets a cup of soup and if there is ever a pudding, some of that as well. Mr. Van Santen is happy and goes to sit on the divan or lean against the writing table. Newspaper, cup, and usually the cat, beside him. If one of the three is missing he's sure to protest. Koophuis tells us the latest news from town, he is certainly an excellent source of information. Kraler comes helter-skelter upstairs—a short, firm knock on the door and in he comes rubbing his hands, according to his mood, in a good temper and talkative, or bad-tempered and quiet.

Quarter to two. Everyone rises from the table and goes about his own business. Margot and Mummy to the dishes. Mr. and Mrs. Van Daan to their divan. Peter up to the attic. Daddy to the divan downstairs. Dussel to his bed and Anne to her work. Then follows the most peaceful hour; everyone is asleep, no one is disturbed. Dussel dreams of lovely food—the expression on his face gives this away, but I don't look long because the time goes so fast and at four o'clock the pedantic doctor is standing, clock in hand, because I'm one minute late in clearing the table for him.

Yours, Anne

Monday, 9 August, 1943

Dear Kitty,
    To continue the "Secret Annexe" daily timetable. I shall now describe the evening meal:

Mr. Van Daan begins. He is first to be served, takes a lot of everything if it is what he likes. Usually talks at the same time, always gives his opinion as the only one worth listening to, and once he has spoken it is irrevocable. Because if anyone *dares* to question it, then he flares up at once. Oh, he can spit like a cat—I'd rather not argue, I can tell you—if you've *once* tried, you don't try again. He has the best opinion, he knows the most about everything. All right then, he has got brains, but "self-satisfaction" has reached a high grade with this gentleman.

Madame. Really, I should remain silent. Some days, especially if there is a bad mood coming on, you can't look at her face. On closer examination, she is the guilty one in all the arguments. Not the subject! Oh, no, everyone prefers to remain aloof over that, but one could perhaps call her the "kindler." Stirring up trouble, that's fun. Mrs. Frank against Anne; Margot against Daddy doesn't go quite so easily.

But now at table, Mrs. Van Daan doesn't go short, although she thinks so at times. The tiniest potatoes, the sweetest mouthful, the best of everything; picking over is her system. The others will get their turn, as long as I have the best. Then talking. Whether anyone is interested, whether they are listening or not, that doesn't seem to matter. I suppose she thinks: "Everyone is interested in what Mrs. Van Daan says." Coquettish smiles, behaving as if one knew everything, giving everyone a bit of advice and encouragement, that's *sure* to make a good impression. But if you look longer, then the good soon wears off.

One, she is industrious, two, gay, three, a coquette—and, occasionally, pretty. This is Petronella Van Daan.

The third table companion. One doesn't hear much from him. Young Mr. Van Daan is very quiet and doesn't draw much attention to himself. As for appetite: a Danaïdean vessel, which is never full and after the heartiest meal declares quite calmly that he could have eaten double.

Number four—Margot. Eats like a little mouse and doesn't talk at all. The only things that go down are vegetables and fruit. "Spoiled" is the Van Daan's judgment; "not enough fresh air and games" our opinion.

Beside her—Mummy. Good appetite, very talkative. No one has the impression, as Mrs. Van Daan: this is the housewife. What is the difference? Well, Mrs. Van Daan does the cooking, and Mummy washes up and polishes.

Numbers six and seven. I won't say much about Daddy and me. The former is the most unassuming of all at table. He looks first to see if everyone else has something. He needs nothing himself, for the best things are for the children. He is the perfect example, and sitting beside him, the "Secret Annexe's" "bundle of nerves."

Dr. Dussel. Helps himself, never looks up, eats and doesn't talk. And if one must talk, then for heaven's sake let it be about food. You don't quarrel about it, you only brag. Enormous helpings go down and the word "No" is never heard, never when the food is good, and not often when it's bad. Trousers wrapping his chest, red coat, black bedroom slippers, and horn-rimmed spectacles. That is how one sees him at the little table, always working, alternated only by his afternoon nap, food, and—his favorite spot—the lavatory. Three, four, five times a day someone stands impatiently in front of the door and wriggles, hopping from one foot to the other, hardly able to contain himself. Does it disturb him? Not a bit! From quarter past seven till half past, from half past twelve till one o'clock, from two till quarter past, from four till quarter past, from six till quarter past, and from half past eleven until twelve. One can make a note of it—these are the regular "sitting times." He won't come off or pay any heed to an imploring voice at the door, giving warning of approaching disaster!

Number nine isn't a member of the "Secret Annexe" family, but rather a companion in the house and at table. Elli has a healthy appetite. Leaves nothing on her plate and is not picky-and-choosy. She is easy to please and that is just what gives us pleasure. Cheerful and good-tempered, willing and good-natured, these are her characteristics.

Yours, Anne

Tuesday, 10 August, 1943

Dear Kitty,

New idea. I talk more to myself than to the others at mealtimes, which is to be recommended for two reasons. Firstly, because everyone is happy if I don't chatter the whole time, and secondly, I needn't get annoyed about other people's opinions. I don't think my opinions are stupid and the others do; so it is better to keep them to myself. I do just the same if I have to eat something that I simply can't stand. I put my plate in front of me, pretend that it is something delicious, look at it as little as possible, and before I know where I am, it is gone. When I get up in the morning, also a very unpleasant process, I jump out of bed thinking to myself: "You'll be back in a second," go to the window, take down the blackout, sniff at the crack of the window until I feel a bit of fresh air, and I'm awake. The bed is turned down as quickly as possible and then the temptation is removed. Do you know what Mummy calls this sort of thing? "The Art of Living"—that's an odd expression. For the last week we've all been in a bit of a muddle about time, because our dear and beloved Westertoren clock bell has apparently been taken away for war purposes, so that neither by day nor night do we ever know the exact time. I still have some hope that they will think up a substitute (tin, copper or some such thing) to remind the neighborhood of the clock.

Whether I'm upstairs or down, or wherever I am, my feet are the admiration of all, glittering in a pair of (for these days) exceptionally fine shoes. Miep managed to get hold of them secondhand for 27.50 florins, wine-colored suede leather with fairly high wedge heels. I feel as if I'm on stilts and look much taller than I am.

Dussel has indirectly endangered our lives. He actually let Miep bring a forbidden book for him, one which abuses Mussolini and Hitler. On the way she happened

92

to be run into by an S.S. car. She lost her temper, shouted, "Miserable wretches," and rode on. It is better not to think of what might have happened if she had had to go to their headquarters.

Yours, Anne

Wednesday, 18 August, 1943

Dear Kitty,

The title for this piece is: "The communal task of the day: potato peeling!"

One person fetches the newspapers, another the knives (keeping the best for himself, of course), a third potatoes, and the fourth a pan of water.

Mr. Dussel begins, does not always scrape well, but scrapes incessantly, glancing right and left. Does everyone do it the way he does? No! "Anne, look here; I take the knife in my hand like this, scrape from the top downwards! No, not like that—like this!"

"I get on better like *this*, Mr. Dussel," I remark timidly.

"But still this is the best way. But *du kannst* take *dies* from me. Naturally I don't care a bit, *aber du* must know for yourself." We scrape on. I look slyly once in my neighbor's direction. He shakes his head thoughtfully once more (over me, I suppose) but is silent.

I scrape on again. Now I look to the other side, where Daddy is sitting; for him scraping potatoes is not just a little odd job, but a piece of precision work. When he reads, he has a deep wrinkle at the back of his head, but if he helps prepare potatoes, beans, or any other vegetables, then it seems as if nothing else penetrates. Then he has on his "potato face," and he would never hand over an imperfectly scraped potato; it's out of the question when he makes that face!

I work on again and then just look up for a second; I know it already. Mrs. Van Daan is trying to attract Dussel's attention. First she looks in his direction and Dussel appears not to notice anything. Then she winks an eye; Dussel works on. Then she laughs, Dussel doesn't look up. Then Mummy laughs too; Dussel takes no notice. Mrs. Van Daan has not achieved anything, so she has to think of something else. A pause and then: "Putti, do put on an apron! Tomorrow I shall have to get all the spots out of your suit!"

"I'm not getting myself dirty!"

Another moment's silence.

"Putti, why don't you sit down?"

"I'm comfortable standing up and prefer it!" Pause.

"Putti, look, *du spatst schon!*" ("You are making a mess!")

"Yes, Mammy, I'm being careful."

Mrs. Van Daan searches for another subject. "I say, Putti, why aren't there any English air raids now?"

"Because the weather is bad, Kerli."

"But it was lovely yesterday, and they didn't fly then either."

"Let's not talk about it."

"Why, surely one can talk about it, or give one's opinion?"

"No."

"Why ever not?"

"Do be quiet, mammi'chen."

"Mr. Frank always answers his wife, doesn't he?"

Mr. Van Daan wrestles with himself. This is his tender spot, it's something he can't take and Mrs. Van Daan begins again: "The invasion seems as if it will never come!"

Mr. Van Daan goes white; when Mrs. Van Daan sees this, she turns red, but goes on again: "The British do nothing!" The bomb explodes!

"And now hold your tongue, *donnerwetter-noch-einmal!*"

Mummy can hardly hold back her laughter. I look straight in front of me.

This sort of thing happens nearly every day, unless they have just had a very bad quarrel, because then they both keep their mouths shut.

I have to go up to the attic to fetch some potatoes. Peter is busy there delousing the cat. He looks up, the cat notices—pop—he has disappeared through the open window into the gutter. Peter swears. I laugh and disappear.

Yours, Anne

Friday, 20 August, 1943

Dear Kitty,
The men in the warehouse go home sharp at half past five and then we are free.

Half past five. Elli comes to give us our evening freedom. Immediately we begin to make some headway with our work. First, I go upstairs with Elli, where she usually begins by having a bite from our second course.

Before Elli is seated, Mrs. Van Daan begins thinking of things she wants. It soon comes out: "Oh, Elli, I have only one little wish. . . ." Elli winks at me; whoever comes upstairs, Mrs. Van Daan never misses a single opportunity of letting them know what she wants. That must be one of the reasons why none of them like coming upstairs.

Quarter to six. Elli departs. I go two floors down to have a look around. First to the kitchen, then to the private office, after that the coalhole, to open the trap door for Mouschi. After a long tour of inspection I land up in Kraler's room. Van Daan is looking in all the drawers and portfolios to find the day's post. Peter is fetching the warehouse key and Boche; Pim is hauling the typewriters upstairs; Margot is looking for a quiet spot to do her office work; Mrs. Van Daan puts a kettle on the gas ring; Mummy is coming downstairs with a pan of potatoes; each one knows his own job.

Peter soon returns from the warehouse. The first question is—bread. This is always put in the kitchen cupboard by the Ladies; but it is not there. Forgotten? Peter offers to look in the main office. He crouches in front of the door to make himself as small as possible and crawls toward the steel lockers on hands and knees, so as not to be seen from outside, gets the bread, which had been put there, and disappears; at least, he wants to disappear, but before

95

he quite realizes what has happened, Mouschi has jumped over him and gone and sat right under the writing table.

Peter looks all around—aha, he sees him there, he crawls into the office again and pulls the animal by its tail. Mouschi spits, Peter sighs. What has he achieved? Now Mouschi is sitting right up by the window cleaning himself, very pleased to have escaped Peter. Now Peter is holding a piece of bread under the cat's nose as a last decoy. Mouschi will not be tempted and the door closes. I stood and watched it all through the crack of the door. We work on. Rat, tat, tat. Three taps means a meal!

Yours, Anne

Monday, 23 August, 1943

Dear Kitty,

Continuation of the "Secret Annexe" daily timetable. As the clock strikes half past eight in the morning, Margot and Mummy are jittery: "Ssh . . . Daddy, quiet, Otto, ssh . . . Pim." "It is half past eight, come back here, you can't run any more water; walk quietly!" These are the various cries to Daddy in the bathroom. As the clock strikes half past eight, he has to be in the living room. Not a drop of water, no lavatory, no walking about, everything quiet. As long as none of the office staff are there, everything can be heard in the warehouse. The door is opened upstairs at twenty minutes past eight and shortly after there are three taps on the floor: Anne's porridge. I climb upstairs and fetch my "puppy-dog" plate. Down in my room again, everything goes at terrific speed: do my hair, put away my noisy tin pottie, bed in place. Hush, the clock strikes! Upstairs Mrs. Van Daan has changed her shoes and is shuffling about in bedroom slippers. Mr. Van Daan, too; all is quiet.

Now we have a little bit of real family life. I want to read or work, Margot as well, also Daddy and Mummy. Daddy is sitting (with Dickens and the dictionary, naturally) on the edge of the sagging, squeaky bed, where there aren't even any decent mattresses: two bolsters on top of each other will also serve the purpose, then he thinks: "Mustn't have them, then I'll manage without!"

Once he is reading he doesn't look up, or about him, laughs every now and then, takes awful trouble to get Mummy interested in a little story. Answer: "I haven't got time now." Looks disappointed for just a second, then reads on again; a little later, when he comes to something extra amusing, he tries it again. "You must read this, Mummy!" Mummy sits on the "Opklap" [1] bed, reads, sews, knits, or works, whatever she feels like. She suddenly thinks of something. Just says it quickly: "Anne, do you know . . . Margot, just jot down . . . !" After a while peace returns once more.

Margot closes her book with a clap. Daddy raises his eyebrows into a funny curve, his reading wrinkle deepens again, and he is lost in his book once more; Mummy begins to chatter with Margot, I become curious and listen too! Pim is drawn into the discussion . . . nine o'clock! Breakfast!

Yours, Anne

Friday, 10 September, 1943

Dear Kitty,

Every time I write to you something special seems to have happened, but they are more often unpleasant than pleasant things. However, now there is something wonderful going on. Last Wednesday evening, 8 September, we sat around listening to the seven o'clock news and the first thing we heard was: "Here follows the best news of the whole war. Italy has capitulated!" Italy's unconditional surrender! The Dutch program from England began at quarter past eight. "Listeners, an hour ago, I had just finished writing the chronicle of the day when the wonderful news of Italy's capitulation came in. I can tell you that I have never deposited my notes in the wastepaper basket with such joy!" "God Save the King," the American na-

---

[1] Dutch type of bed, which folds against the wall to look like a bookcase with curtains hanging before it.

tional anthem, and the "Internationale" were played. As
always, the Dutch program was uplifting, but not too
optimistic.

Still we have troubles, too; it's about Mr. Koophuis. As
you know, we are all very fond of him, he is always
cheerful and amazingly brave, although he is never well,
has a lot of pain, and is not allowed to eat much or do
much walking. "When Mr. Koophuis enters, the sun
begins to shine," Mummy said just recently, and she is
quite right. Now he has had to go into the hospital for a
very unpleasant abdominal operation and will have to
stay there for at least four weeks. You really ought to
have seen how he said good-by to us just as usual—he
might have simply been going out to do a bit of shopping.

Yours, Anne

Thursday, 16 September, 1943

Dear Kitty,

Relations between us here are getting worse all the
time. At mealtimes, no one dares to open their mouths
(except to allow a mouthful of food to slip in) because
whatever is said you either annoy someone or it is misunderstood. I swallow Valerian pills every day against worry
and depression, but it doesn't prevent me from being even
more miserable the next day. A good hearty laugh would
help more than ten Valerian pills, but we've almost
forgotten how to laugh. I feel afraid sometimes that from
having to be so serious I'll grow a long face and my
mouth will droop at the corners. The others don't get
any better either, everyone looks with fear and misgivings
towards that great terror, winter. Another thing that does
not cheer us up is the fact that the warehouseman, V.M.,
is becoming suspicious about the "Secret Annexe." We
really wouldn't mind what V.M. thought of the situation
if he wasn't so exceptionally inquisitive, difficult to fob
off, and, moreover, not to be trusted. One day Kraler
wanted to be extra careful, put on his coat at ten minutes
to one, and went to the chemist round the corner. He was

back in less than five minutes, and sneaked like a thief up the steep stairs that lead straight to us. At a quarter past one he wanted to go again, but Elli came to warn him that V.M. was in the office. He did a right-about turn and sat with us until half past one. Then he took off his shoes and went in stockinged feet to the front attic door, went downstairs step by step, and, after balancing there for a quarter of an hour to avoid creaking, he landed safely in the office, having entered from the outside. Elli had been freed of V.M. in the meantime, and came up to us to fetch Kraler, but he had already been gone a long time; he was still on the staircase with his shoes off. Whatever would the people in the street have thought if they had seen the Manager putting on his shoes outside? Gosh! the Manager in his socks!

Yours, Anne

Wednesday, 29 September, 1943

Dear Kitty,

It is Mrs. Van Daan's birthday. We gave her a pot of jam, as well as coupons for cheese, meat, and bread. From her husband, Dussel, and our protectors she received things to eat and flowers. Such are the times we live in!

Elli had a fit of nerves this week; she had been sent out so often; time and again she had been asked to go and fetch something quickly, which meant yet another errand or made her feel that she had done something wrong. If you just think that she still has to finish her office work downstairs, that Koophuis is ill, Miep at home with a cold, and **that** she herself has a sprained ankle, love worries, and a grumbling father, then it's no wonder she's at her wit's end. We comforted her and said that if she puts her foot down once or twice and says she has no time, then the shopping lists will automatically get shorter.

There is something wrong with Mr. Van Daan again, I can see it coming on already! Daddy is very angry for some reason or other. Oh, what kind of explosion is hanging over us now? If only I wasn't mixed up so much with all these rows! If I could only get away! They'll drive us crazy before long!

Yours, Anne

Sunday, 17 October, 1943

Dear Kitty,

Koophuis is back again, thank goodness! He still looks rather pale, but in spite of this sets out cheerfully to sell clothes for Van Daan. It is an unpleasant fact that the Van Daans have run right out of money. Mrs. Van Daan won't part with a thing from her pile of coats, dresses, and shoes. Mr. Van Daan's suit isn't easily disposed of, because he wants too much for it. The end of the story is not yet in sight. Mrs. Daan will certainly have to part with her fur coat. They've had a terrific row upstairs about it, and now the reconciliation period of "oh, darling Putti" and "precious Kerli" has set in.

I am dazed by all the abusive exchanges that have taken place in this virtuous house during the past month. Daddy goes about with his lips tightly pursed; when anyone speaks to him, he looks up startled, as if he is afraid he will have to patch up some tricky relationship again. Mummy has red patches on her cheeks from excitement. Margot complains of headaches. Dussel can't sleep. Mrs. Van Daan grouses the whole day and I'm going completely crazy! Quite honestly, I sometimes forget who we are quarreling with and with whom we've made it up.

The only way to take one's mind off it all is to study, and I do a lot of that.

Yours, Anne

Friday, 29 October, 1943

Dear Kitty,

There have been resounding rows again between Mr. and Mrs. Van Daan. It came about like this: as I have already told you, the Van Daans are at the end of their money. One day, some time ago now, Koophuis spoke about a furrier with whom he was on good terms; this gave Van Daan the idea of selling his wife's fur coat. It's a fur coat made from rabbit skins, and she has worn it seventeen years. He got 325 florins for it—an enormous sum. However, Mrs. Van Daan wanted to keep the money to buy new clothes after the war, and it took some doing before Mr. Van Daan made it clear to her that the money was urgently needed for the household.

The yells and screams, stamping and abuse—you can't possibly imagine it! It was frightening. My family stood at the bottom of the stairs, holding their breath, ready if necessary to drag them apart! All this shouting and weeping and nervous tension are so unsettling and such a strain, that in the evening I drop into my bed crying, thanking heaven that I sometimes have half an hour to myself.

Mr. Koophuis is away again; his stomach gives him no peace. He doesn't even know whether it has stopped bleeding yet. For the first time, he was very down when he told us that he didn't feel well and was going home.

All goes well with me on the whole, except that I have no appetite. I keep being told: "You don't look at all well." I must say that they are doing their very best to keep me up to the mark. Grape sugar, cod-liver oil, yeast tablets, and calcium have all been lined up.

My nerves often get the better of me: it is especially on Sundays that I feel rotten. The atmosphere is so oppressive, and sleepy and as heavy as lead. You don't hear a single bird singing outside, and a deadly close silence hangs everywhere, catching hold of me as if it will drag me down deep into an underworld.

At such times Daddy, Mummy, and Margot leave me cold. I wander from one room to another, downstairs and up again, feeling like a songbird whose wings have been clipped and who is hurling himself in utter darkness against the bars of his cage. "Go outside, laugh, and take a breath of fresh air," a voice cries within me, but I don't even feel a response any more; I go and lie on the divan and sleep, to make the time pass more quickly, and the stillness and the terrible fear, because there is no way of killing them.

Yours, Anne

Wednesday, 3 November, 1943

Dear Kitty,

In order to give us something to do, which is also educational, Daddy applied for a prospectus from the Teachers' Institute in Leiden. Margot nosed through the thick book at least three times without finding anything to her liking or to suit her purse. Daddy was quicker, and wants a letter written to the Institute asking for a trial lesson in "Elementary Latin."

To give me something new to begin as well, Daddy asked Koophuis for a children's Bible so that I could find out something about the New Testament at last. "Do you want to give Anne a Bible for Chanuka?" asked Margot, somewhat perturbed. "Yes—er, I think St. Nicholas Day is a better occasion," answered Daddy; "Jesus just doesn't go with Chanuka." [1]

Yours, Anne

[1] See entry for 7 December, 1942.

102

Dear Kitty,

If you were to read my pile of letters one after another, you would certainly be struck by the many different moods in which they are written. It annoys me that I am so dependent on the atmosphere here, but I'm certainly not the only one—we all find it the same. If I read a book that impresses me, I have to take myself firmly in hand, before I mix with other people; otherwise they would think my mind rather queer. At the moment, as you've probably noticed, I'm going through a spell of being depressed. I really couldn't tell you why it is, but I believe it's just because I'm a coward, and that's what I keep bumping up against.

This evening, while Elli was still here, there was a long, loud, penetrating ring at the door. I turned white at once, got a tummy-ache and heart palpitations, all from fear. At night, when I'm in bed, I see myself alone in a dungeon, without Mummy and Daddy. Sometimes I wander by the roadside or our "Secret Annexe" is on fire, or they come and take us away at night. I see everything as if it is actually taking place, and this gives me the feeling that it may all happen to me very soon! Miep often says she envies us for possessing such tranquillity here. That may be true, but she is not thinking about all our fears. I simply can't imagine that the world will ever be normal for us again. I do talk about "after the war," but then it is only a castle in the air, something that will never really happen. If I think back to our old house, my girl friends, the fun at school, it is just as if another person lived it all, not me.

I see the eight of us with our "Secret Annexe" as if we were a little piece of blue heaven, surrounded by heavy black rain clouds. The round, clearly defined spot where we stand is still safe, but the clouds gather more closely about us and the circle which separates us from the approaching danger closes more and more tightly. Now we are so surrounded by danger and darkness that we bump against each other, as we search desperately for a means of escape. We all look down below, where people are fighting each other, we look above, where it is quiet and beautiful, and meanwhile we are cut off by the great dark mass, which will not let us go upwards, but which stands before us as an impenetrable wall; it tries to crush us, but cannot do so yet. I can only cry and implore: "Oh, if only the black circle could recede and open the way for us!"

Yours, Anne

Thursday, 11 November, 1943

Dear Kitty,
I have a good title for this chapter:

ODE TO MY FOUNTAIN PEN
IN MEMORIAM

My fountain pen has always been one of my most priceless possessions; I value it highly, especially for its thick nib, for I can only really write neatly with a thick nib. My fountain pen has had a very long and interesting pen-life, which I will briefly tell you about.

When I was nine, my fountain pen arrived in a packet (wrapped in cotton wool) as "sample without value" all the way from Aachen, where my Grandmother, the kind donor, used to live. I was in bed with flu, while February winds howled round the house. The glorious fountain pen had a red leather case and was at once shown around to all my friends. I, Anne Frank, the proud owner of a fountain pen! When I was ten I was allowed to take the pen to school and the mistress went so far as to permit me to write with it.

When I was eleven, however, my treasure had to be put away again, because the mistress in the sixth form only allowed us to use school pens and inkpots.

When I was twelve and went to the Jewish Lyceum,[1]

---

[1] A type of secondary school specializing in the classics, common in most continental countries.

my fountain pen received a new case in honor of the great occasion; it could take a pencil as well, and as it closed with a zipper looked much more impressive.

At thirteen the fountain pen came with us to the "Secret Annexe," where it has raced through countless diaries and compositions for me.

Now I am fourteen, we have spent our last year together.

It was on a Friday afternoon after five o'clock. I had come out of my room and wanted to go and sit at the table to write, when I was roughly pushed on one side and had to make room for Margot and Daddy, who wanted to practice their "Latin." The fountain pen remained on the table unused while, with a sigh, its owner contented herself with a tiny little corner of the table, and starting rubbing beans. "Bean rubbing" is making moldy beans decent again. I swept the floor at a quarter to six and threw the dirt, together with the bad beans, into a newspaper and into the stove. A terrific flame leaped out and I thought it was grand that the fire should burn up so well when it was practically out. All was quiet again, the "Latinites" had finished, and I went and sat at the table to clear up my writing things, but look as I might, my fountain pen received a new case in honor of the great Margot looked, but there was not a trace of the thing. "Perhaps it fell into the stove together with the beans," Margot suggested. "Oh, no, of course not!" I answered. When my fountain pen didn't turn up that evening, however, we all took it that it had been burned, all the more as celluloid is terribly inflammable.

And so it was, our unhappy fears were confirmed; when Daddy did the stove the following morning the clip used for fastening was found among the ashes. Not a trace of the gold nib was found. "Must have melted and stuck to some stone or other," Daddy thought.

I have one consolation, although a slender one: my fountain pen has been cremated, just what I want later!

Yours, Anne

Dear Kitty,

Shattering things are happening. Diphtheria reigns in Elli's home, so she is not allowed to come into contact with us for six weeks. It makes it very awkward over food and shopping, not to mention missing her companionship. Koophuis is still in bed and has had nothing but porridge and milk for three weeks. Kraler is frantically busy.

The Latin lessons Margot sends in are corrected by a teacher and returned, Margot writing in Elli's name. The teacher is very nice, and witty, too. I expect he is glad to have such a clever pupil.

Dussel is very put out, none of us knows why. It began by his keeping his mouth closed upstairs; he didn't utter a word to either Mr. or Mrs. Van Daan. Everyone was struck by it, and when it lasted a couple of days, Mummy took the opportunity of warning him about Mrs. Van Daan, who, if he went on like this, could make things very disagreeable for him.

Dussel said that Mr. Van Daan started the silence, so he was not going to be the one to break it.

Now I must tell you that yesterday was the sixteenth of November, the day he had been exactly one year in the "Secret Annexe." Mummy received a plant in honor of the occasion, but Mrs. Van Daan, who for weeks beforehand had made no bones about the fact that she thought Dussel should treat us to something, received nothing.

Instead of expressing, for the first time, his thanks for our unselfishness in taking him in, he didn't say a word. And when I asked him, on the morning of the sixteenth, whether I should congratulate or condole, he answered that it didn't matter to him. Mummy, who wanted to act as peacemaker, didn't get one step further, and finally the situation remained as it was.

> *Der Man hat einen grossen Geist*
> *Und ist so klein von Taten!* [1]

Yours, Anne

[1] (The spirit of the man is great,
How puny are his deeds!)

Saturday, 27 November, 1943

Dear Kitty,

Yesterday evening, before I fell asleep, who should suddenly appear before my eyes but Lies!

I saw her in front of me, clothed in rags, her face thin and worn. Her eyes were very big and she looked so sadly and reproachfully at me that I could read in her eyes: "Oh, Anne, why have you deserted me? Help, oh, help me, rescue me from this hell!"

And I cannot help her, I can only look on, how others suffer and die, and can only pray to God to send her back to us.

I just saw Lies, no one else, and now I understand. I misjudged her and was too young to understand her difficulties. She was attached to a new girl friend, and to her it seemed as though I wanted to take her away. What the poor girl must have felt like, I know; I know the feeling so well myself!

Sometimes, in a flash, I saw something of her life, but a moment later I was selfishly absorbed again in my own pleasures and problems. It was horrid of me to treat her as I did, and now she looked at me, oh so helplessly, with her pale face and imploring eyes. If only I could help her!

Oh, God, that I should have all I could wish for and that she should be seized by such a terrible fate. I am not more virtuous than she; she, too, wanted to do what was right, why should I be chosen to live and she probably to die? What was the difference between us? Why are we so far from each other now?

Quite honestly, I haven't thought about her for months, yes, almost a year. Not completely forgotten her, but still I had never thought about her like this, until I saw her before me in all her misery.

Oh, Lies, I hope that, if you live until the end of the war, you will come back to us and that I shall be able to take you in and do something to make up for the wrong I did you.

But when I am able to help her again, then she will not need my help so badly as now. I wonder if she ever thinks of me; if so, what would she feel?

Good Lord, defend her, so that at least she is not alone. Oh, if only You could tell her that I think lovingly of her and with sympathy, perhaps that would give her greater endurance.

I must not go on thinking about it, because I don't get any further. I only keep seeing her great big eyes, and cannot free myself from them. I wonder if Lies has real faith in herself, and not only what has been thrust upon her?

I don't even know, I never took the trouble to ask her! Lies, Lies, if only I could take you away, if only I could let you share all the things I enjoy. It is too late now, I can't help, or repair the wrong I have done. But I shall never forget her again, and I shall always pray for her.

Yours, Anne

Monday, 6 December, 1943

Dear Kitty,

When St. Nicholas' Day approached, none of us could help thinking of the prettily decorated basket we had last year and I, especially, thought it would be very dull to do nothing at all this year. I thought a long time about it, until I invented something, something funny.

I consulted Pim, and a week ago we started composing a little poem for each person.

On Sunday evening at a quarter to eight we appeared upstairs with the large laundry basket between us, decorated with little figures, and bows of pink and blue carbon copy paper. The basket was covered with a large piece of brown paper, on which a letter was pinned. Everyone was rather astonished at the size of the surprise package.

I took the letter from the paper and read:

> *"Santa Claus has come once more,*
> *Though not quite as he came before;*
> *We can't celebrate his day*
> *In last year's fine and pleasant way.*
> *For then our hopes were high and bright,*
> *All the optimists seemed right,*
> *None supposing that this year*
> *We would welcome Santa here.*
> *Still, we'll make his spirit live,*
> *And since we've nothing left to give,*
> *We've thought of something else to do*
> *Each please look inside his shoe."*

As each owner took his shoe from the basket there was a resounding peal of laughter. A little paper package lay in each shoe with the address of the shoe's owner on it.

Yours, Anne

Wednesday, 22 December, 1943

Dear Kitty,

A bad attack of flu has prevented me from writing to you until today. It's wretched to be ill here. When I wanted to cough—one, two, three—I crawled under the blankets and tried to stifle the noise. Usually the only result was that the tickle wouldn't go away at all; and milk and honey, sugar or lozenges had to be brought into operation. It makes me dizzy to think of all the cures that were tried on me. Sweating, compresses, wet cloths on my chest, dry cloths on my chest, hot drinks, gargling, throat painting, lying still, cushion for extra warmth, hot-water bottles, lemon squashes, and, in addition, the thermometer every two hours!

Can anyone really get better like this? The worst moment of all was certainly when Mr. Dussel thought he'd play doctor, and came and lay on my naked chest with his greasy head, in order to listen to the sounds within. Not only did his hair tickle unbearably, but I was embarrassed, in spite of the fact that he once, thirty years ago, studied medicine and has the title of Doctor. Why should the fellow come and lie on my heart? He's not my lover, after all. For that matter, he wouldn't hear whether it's healthy or unhealthy inside me anyway; his ears need syringing first, as he's becoming alarmingly hard of hearing.

But that is enough about illness. I'm as fit as a fiddle again, one centimeter taller, two pounds heavier, pale, and with a real appetite for learning.

There is not much news to tell you. We are all getting on well together for a change! There's no quarreling—we haven't had such peace in the home for at least half a year. Elli is still parted from us.

We received extra oil for Christmas, sweets and syrup; the "chief present" is a brooch, made out of a two-and-a-half-cent piece, and shining beautifully. Anyway, lovely, but indescribable. Mr. Dussel gave Mummy and Mrs. Van Daan a lovely cake which he had asked Miep to bake for him. With all her work, she has to do that as well! I have also something for Miep and Elli. For at least two months I have saved the sugar from my porridge, you see, and with Mr. Koophuis's help, I'll have it made into fondants.

It is drizzly weather, the stove smells, the food lies heavily on everybody's tummy, causing thunderous noises on all sides! The war at a standstill, morale rotten.

Yours, Anne

Friday, 24 December, 1943

Dear Kitty,

I have previously written about how much we are affected by atmospheres here, and I think that in my own case this trouble is getting much worse lately.

"Himmelhoch jauchzend und zum Tode betrübt" [1] certainly fits here. I am *"Himmelhoch jauchzend"* if I only think how lucky we are here compared with other Jewish children, and *"zum Tode betrübt"* comes over me when, as happened today, for example, Mrs. Koophuis comes and tells us about her daughter Corry's hockey club, canoe

---

[1] A famous line from Goëthe: "On top of the world, or in the depths of despair."

trips, theatrical performances, and friends. I don't think I'm jealous of Corry, but I couldn't help feeling a great longing to have lots of fun myself for once, and to laugh until my tummy ached. Especially at this time of the year with all the holidays for Christmas and the New Year, and we are stuck here like outcasts. Still, I really ought not to write this, because it seems ungrateful and I've certainly been exaggerating. But still, whatever you think of me, I can't keep everything to myself, so I'll remind you of my opening words—"Paper is patient."

When someone comes in from outside, with the wind in their clothes and the cold on their faces, then I could bury my head in the blankets to stop myself thinking: "When will we be granted the privilege of smelling fresh air?" And because I must not bury my head in the blankets, but the reverse—I must keep my head high and be brave, the thoughts will come, not once, but oh, countless times. Believe me, if you have been shut up for a year and a half, it can get too much for you some days. In spite of all justice and thankfulness, you can't crush your feelings. Cycling, dancing, whistling, looking out into the world, feeling young, to know that I'm free— that's what I long for; still, I mustn't show it, because I sometimes think if all eight of us began to pity ourselves, or went about with discontented faces, where would it lead us? I sometimes ask myself, "Would anyone, either Jew or non-Jew, understand this about me, that I am simply a young girl badly in need of some rollicking fun?" I don't know, and I couldn't talk about it to anyone, because then I know I should cry. Crying can bring such relief.

In spite of all my theories, and however much trouble I take, each day I miss having a real mother who understands me. That is why with everything I do and write I think of the "Mumsie" that I want to be for my children later on. The "Mumsie" who doesn't take everything that is said in general conversation so seriously, but who does take what *I* say seriously. I have noticed, though I can't explain how, that the word "Mumsie" tells you everything.

Do you know what I've found? To give me the feeling of calling Mummy something which sounds like "Mumsie" I often call her "Mum"; then from that comes "Mums"; the incomplete "Mumsie," as it were, whom I would so love to honor with the extra "ie" and yet who does not realize it. It's a good thing, because it would only make her unhappy.

That's enough about that, writing has made my *"zum Tode betrübt"* go off a bit.

Yours, Anne

Saturday, 25 December, 1943

Dear Kitty,

During these days, now that Christmas is here, I find myself thinking all the time about Pim, and what he told me about the love of his youth. Last year I didn't understand the meaning of his words as well as I do now. If he'd only talk about it again, perhaps I would be able to show him that I understand.

I believe that Pim talked about it because he who "knows the secrets of so many other hearts" had to express his own feelings for once; because otherwise Pim never says a word about himself, and I don't think Margot has any idea of all Pim has had to go through. Poor Pim, he can't make *me* think that he has forgotten everything. He will never forget this. He has become very tolerant. I hope that I shall grow a bit like him, without having to go through all that.

Yours, Anne

Monday, 27 December, 1943

Dear Kitty,

On Friday evening for the first time in my life I received something for Christmas. Koophuis, Kraler and the girls had prepared a lovely surprise again. Miep has made a lovely Christmas cake, on which was written "Peace 1944."

Elli had provided a pound of sweet biscuits of prewar quality. For Peter, Margot, and me a bottle of yoghourt, and a bottle of beer for each of the grownups. Everything was so nicely done up, and there were pictures stuck on the different packages. Otherwise Christmas passed by quickly for us.

Yours, Anne

Wednesday, 29 December, 1943

Dear Kitty,

I was very unhappy again last evening. Granny and Lies came into my mind. Granny, oh, darling Granny, how little we understood of what she suffered, or how sweet she was. And besides all this, she knew a terrible secret which she carefully kept to herself the whole time.[1] How faithful and good Granny always was; she would never have let one of us down. Whatever it was, however naughty I had been, Granny always stuck up for me.

Granny, did you love me or didn't you understand me either? I don't know. No one ever talked about themselves to Granny. How lonely Granny must have been, how lonely in spite of us! A person can be lonely even if he is loved by many people, because he is still not the "One and Only" to anyone.

And Lies, is she still alive? What is she doing? Oh, God, protect her and bring her back to us. Lies, I see in you all the time what my lot might have been, I keep seeing myself in your place. Why then should I often be unhappy over what happens here? Shouldn't I always be glad, contented, and happy, except when I think about her and her companions in distress? I am selfish and cowardly. Why do I always dream and think of the most terrible things—my fear makes me want to scream out loud sometimes. Because still, in spite of everything, I have not enough faith in God. He has given me so much—which I certainly do not deserve—and I still do so much

[1] A severe internal disease.

that is wrong every day. If you think of your fellow creatures, then you only want to cry, you could really cry the whole day long. The only thing to do is to pray that God will perform a miracle and save some of them. And I hope that I am doing that enough.

Yours, Anne

Sunday, 2 January, 1944

Dear Kitty,

This morning when I had nothing to do I turned over some of the pages of my diary and several times I came across letters dealing with the subject "Mummy" in such a hotheaded way that I was quite shocked, and asked myself: "Anne, is it really you who mentioned hate? Oh, Anne, how could you!" I remained sitting with the open page in my hand, and thought about it and how it came about that I should have been so brimful of rage and really so filled with such a thing as hate that I had to confide it all in you. I have been trying to understand the Anne of a year ago and to excuse her, because my conscience isn't clear as long as I leave you with these accusations, without being able to explain, on looking back, how it happened.

I suffer now—and suffered then—from moods which kept my head under water (so to speak) and only allowed me to see the things subjectively without enabling me to consider quietly the words of the other side, and to answer them as the words of one whom I, with my hotheaded temperament, had offended or made unhappy.

I hid myself within myself, I only considered myself and quietly wrote down all my joys, sorrows, and contempt in my diary. This diary is of great value to me, because it has become a book of memoirs in many places, but on a good many pages I could certainly put "past and done with."

I used to be furious with Mummy, and still am sometimes. It's true that she doesn't understand me, but I

114

don't understand her either. She did love me very much and she was tender, but as she landed in so many unpleasant situations through me, and was nervous and irritable because of other worries and difficulties, it is certainly understandable that she snapped at me.

I took it much too seriously, was offended, and was rude and aggravating to Mummy, which, in turn, made her unhappy. So it was really a matter of unpleasantness and misery rebounding all the time. It wasn't nice for either of us, but it is passing.

I just didn't want to see all this, and pitied myself very much; but that, too, is understandable. Those violent outbursts on paper were only giving vent to anger which in a normal life could have been worked off by stamping my feet a couple of times in a locked room, or calling Mummy names behind her back.

The period when I caused Mummy to shed tears is over. I have grown wiser and Mummy's nerves are not so much on edge. I usually keep my mouth shut if I get annoyed, and so does she, so we appear to get on much better together. I can't really love Mummy in a dependent childlike way—I just don't have that feeling.

I soothe my conscience now with the thought that it is better for hard words to be on paper than that Mummy should carry them in her heart.

Yours, Anne

Wednesday, 5 January, 1944

Dear Kitty,

I have two things to confess to you today, which will take a long time. But I must tell someone and you are the best one to tell, as I know that, come what may, you always keep a secret.

The first is about Mummy. You know that I've grumbled a lot about Mummy, yet still tried to be nice to her again. Now it is suddenly clear to me what she lacks. Mummy herself has told us that she looked upon us more as her friends than her daughters. Now that is all very fine, but still, a friend can't take a mother's place. I need my mother as an example which I can follow, I want to be able to respect her. I have the feeling that Margot thinks differently about these things and would never be able to understand what I've just told you. And Daddy avoids all arguments about Mummy.

I imagine a mother as a woman who, in the first place, shows great tact, especially towards her children when they reach our age, and who does not laugh at me if I cry about something—not pain, but other things—like "Mums" does.

One thing, which perhaps may seem rather fatuous, I have never forgiven her. It was on a day that I had to go to the dentist. Mummy and Margot were going to come with me, and agreed that I should take my bicycle. When we had finished at the dentist, and were outside again, Margot and Mummy told me that they were going into the town to look at something or buy something—I don't remember exactly what. I wanted to go, too, but was not allowed to, as I had my bicycle with me. Tears of rage sprang into my eyes, and Mummy and Margot began laughing at me. Then I became so furious that I stuck my tongue out at them in the street just as an old woman happened to pass by, who looked very shocked! I rode home on my bicycle, and I know I cried for a long time.

It is queer that the wound that Mummy made then still burns, when I think of how angry I was that afternoon.

The second is something that is very difficult to tell you, because it is about myself.

Yesterday I read an article about blushing by Sis Heyster. This article might have been addressed to me personally. Although I don't blush very easily, the other things in it certainly all fit me. She writes roughly something like this—that a girl in the years of puberty becomes quiet within and begins to think about the wonders that are happening to her body.

I experience that, too, and that is why I get the feeling lately of being embarrassed about Margot, Mummy, and

Reader's Supplement

to

ANNE FRANK:
THE DIARY OF A YOUNG GIRL

ANNE AND HER FATHER, OTTO FRANK

BIOGRAPHICAL BACKGROUND

Ordinarily, when the events of an author's life are reviewed, the problem is to decide what to eliminate so that the telling will not be too lengthy. Here we have a writer whose total existence was tragically cut short three months before her sixteenth birthday. What there is to tell, therefore, must be pieced together from the pages of a remarkable diary found in a trash heap on the floor of an abandoned apartment on the Prinsengracht, one of the canals in Amsterdam, Holland.

Anne Frank tells us that her parents came from very wealthy stock (p. 205M). Her father had been a "real little rich boy" and her mother had known "engagement parties of two hundred and fifty people, private balls and dinners." The family fortunes of Anne's grandparents had apparently been lost in the inflationary periods that followed World War I, but when we first meet the Franks they are leading comparatively prosperous middle-class lives.

Mr. Frank was eleven years older than his wife when they were married, and their first child was Margot, born in Frankfort Am Main, Germany, in 1926. Three years later Anne came along. She was but a tiny tot of four when the family had to get out of Germany because, in 1933, Hitler's gangs had already begun to roam the streets, looking to victimize the national scapegoats, the Jews.

When Mr. Frank brought his family to Holland, he became Managing Director of an established firm and for seven years did rather well. But on May 10, 1940, on the pretext that they were protecting the Dutch from attack by France and Great Britain, the Nazi armies invaded the Netherlands. In four days all resistance was crushed and the difficult period for the Frank family began. They, among thousands of others, were prime targets for the anti-Jewish laws that followed almost before the dust of battle had settled.

For six years Anne, a carefree little girl, had been quite acceptable to the Montessori School, which she had entered as a kindergartner shortly after her arrival from Germany. Now she suddenly had to become aware that she was somehow different, could not be taught by her sixth-form teacher, and would henceforth have to attend schools reserved for the wearers of the yellow Star of David.

Although restricted on every side by racial regulations, the Franks courageously pretended to live normal lives for two more years. Each day, however, the vise closed tighter and it was only a matter of time before a decision would have to be made—submit to arrest and eventual gas chambers, or hide. Mr. Frank had long planned the "disappearance" of his family when the critical hour arrived. Early in July, 1942, when it would have been sheer suicide to wait any longer, the Franks, together with the Van Daans, went through a door above a warehouse and virtually vanished.

The rest of Anne's "biography," covering two years in the hiding place, you will be privileged to read in the fascinating pages that follow. You may laugh now and then, sigh often, and perhaps be moved to tears—but out of this emotional experience will come a realization that Anne Frank was destined to live many years more than are counted by dates and birthdays.

On this theme, George Stevens, producer of the Cinema-Scope motion picture, *The Diary of Anne Frank,* wrote:

> Of all the many remarkable things about Anne Frank, I believe the most important is the fact of her survival—a survival contained between the covers of a small red-checkered cloth-covered diary book.

Within this diary exists a young girl touched with a perceptive genius on one hand and an almost consuming sensitivity on the other. And combined with these is a most exquisite sense of feeling and knowledge of life at its finest. "I believe in the good of man," said Anne, with her quiet smile. "My mission is to destroy and exterminate," hoarsely shouted the leader of the great forces of Nazi Germany.

In 1943, this seemed quite a hopeless and unequal contest. All the communications machinery of a powerful nation was projecting the voice of its Fuehrer, and his words were heard around the world. At the same time, Anne was quietly penning her words in the little diary seen only by herself.

Today, the shouting voice is no longer heard, but daily more and more people of many tongues are repeating and reflecting on what Anne Frank had to say.

This destiny to survive was illustrated dramatically in a conversation I had with Mr. Otto Frank in 1957. We were sitting in a cramped attic in Amsterdam and I was holding in my hand a printed edition of *The Diary of a Young Girl*. It was in this building that Mr. Frank had sheltered his little group while they hid from the Nazis. After serious hesitation, I asked Mr. Frank a question to which I felt I must have the answer—"Can you tell me something about what occurred when the Gestapo broke into this room? Their mission was to destroy—how was it they did not find and destroy the diary?"

While Mr. Frank bravely described what happened on that fateful day, I looked at the little volume in my hand and realized that Anne's persistent belief in the triumph of the good in human nature was best exemplified by the very survival of her writing.

On that day in August, 1944, Sergeant Silverbauer,

of the Green Police, and four subordinates were executing just another phase of what Hitler and Goebbels had conceived as the "final solution of the Jewish problem." Their mission was to remove the Jews from Holland. While so doing, they were to loot and to plunder and, most importantly, they were to leave no record or documentation of this work.

While searching the attic, the sergeant picked up Mr. Frank's brief case. He asked if there were any jewels. Mr. Frank said there was nothing but papers. The sergeant opened it. Disappointed, he threw the papers and the diary to the floor and put the silverware and the Hanukkah candlestick into the brief case. The little group which had spent the last twenty-five months in this attic was led away. The room was left in disarray.

However, there remained on the floor the diary of a young girl. The Nazi soldiers had failed in their mission. They had left behind a statement to the world. They had left behind a comment on their work. They had left behind a story of a girl in adolescence, her troubles with her parents, and her young love.

HISTORICAL BACKGROUND

Anne Frank's diary is a work utterly complete in itself, and its eloquence requires no further comment. But the experiences Anne described become perhaps even more meaningful when seen in their immediate historical context. It is the purpose here to provide at least the outlines of that context and to bring Anne's own story to its conclusion.

I

The German Empire, which since the beginning of the twentieth century had been the strongest power in Europe, collapsed in 1918 as a result of its defeat in World War I. The Emperor, or Kaiser, fled to Holland and a group of democratic politicians in Berlin proclaimed the establishment of a German republic.

The leaders of the new republic sued for peace, and in April, 1919, sent a delegation to the Versailles Peace Conference. Contrary to their expectations, the German representatives were not permitted to help frame the Treaty of Versailles, by which peace was restored to Europe. Instead, the victorious Allies—among them Great Britain, France, Italy, and the United States—submitted the finished treaty to the German delegates who were told that if they did not sign, Germany would be invaded. The treaty placed upon Germany sole responsibility for the war. It stripped Germany of its overseas colonies and of valuable territories in Europe. It virtually disarmed the once great military power, and it demanded that Germany pay the cost of all civilian damage caused by the war. The leaders of the German republic had no choice but to accept these terms.

Within Germany, the Treaty of Versailles was the subject of widespread indignation. Many Germans thought that their nation was no more responsible for causing the war than any other and that Germany had been unfairly singled out for blame. Nationalists spread the false belief that republican politicians had administered a "stab in the back" to the undefeated German army in November, 1918, and branded these politicians the "November criminals." To many Germans this theory proved a comforting rationalization for their country's defeat.

The new German government, which became known as the Weimar republic because its constitution was drawn up at Weimar, faced a number of serious problems. One of these problems was its identification with the unpopular Treaty of Versailles. Another was the fact that no political party was able to achieve a majority in the Reichstag, or parliament, so that the government was always a combination of several parties.

Opposition to the republic came from many quarters. Middle-class Germans who had lost everything in the inflation of the early 1920s blamed the republican government for their distress. Unemployed workers, impatient with the conservative republic, looked for solutions to their problems in radical movements of both the left and right. Industrialists, landowners, and army officers longed to replace the republic with a regime more in keeping with the autocratic and militaristic traditions of the old empire.

Although there were also many in Germany who hoped that the experiment in democratic government would succeed, the years immediately following the war saw the establishment of a number of political parties dedicated to the destruction of the republic and the reversal of the Treaty of Versailles. One of these was the National Socialist German Workers—or Nazi—Party. Like other extremist groups, the Nazis appealed to all sorts of discontented people—to demobilized soldiers and youthful idealists, to unemployed workingmen hostile to "the interests," and to businessmen and property owners fearful of a Communist revolution, to cranks and criminals and outcasts of every kind. The Nazi program combined the strong appeals of nationalism and socialism. It promised to restore Germany's power through the establishment of a totalitarian state; it also promised to redistribute the national wealth and to provide jobs for everyone.

The man who became leader, or Führer, of the Nazi Party in 1921 was an Austrian-born former house painter named Adolf Hitler. Shrewd, fanatical, never hesitating to use lies or brute force to achieve his ends, Hitler had the ability to rouse an audience to hysterical enthusiasm. Hitler and the Nazis blamed the decline in Germany's power on Jews and radicals and preached the supremacy of the so-called German, or Aryan, race. The Germans, Hitler declared, were the "master race," creators of all civilization, and fitted by nature to rule the world. To provide ample living space for this race, Hitler planned to expand Germany's frontiers in the east, carving out a great empire in Poland and Russia at the expense of the Slavic inhabitants of those lands. The Slavs, he said, were a subhuman people fit only to be slaves. In Hitler's New Order, they would either serve the "master race" or be exterminated.

During the 1920s the Nazis were prominent only in the southern German state of Bavaria. In the increasingly prosperous years between 1924 and 1929 most Germans regarded them as ruffians and clowns of no great importance. But with the onset of the world-wide depression in 1929, ever greater numbers of Germans began to listen to Hitler. His simplifications of complex issues satisfied them. His promise of a glorious national future appealed to their pride. His willingness to assume total responsibility if given total power relieved them of the unaccustomed burdens of citizenship in a democracy. In the elections of 1930 and 1932, the Nazis became the largest party in the Reichstag.

Hitler's most violent racial attacks were directed against the Jews. Despite the many distinguished contributions Jews had made to German life over the centuries, Hitler's propaganda described them as an alien, inferior race. Not only were they non-Aryan, he said, but they were the originators of all those doctrines hostile to Nazi aims—Communism, pacifism, internationalism, Christianity. In Hitler's view, as long as Jews remained in Germany, they were a constant source of ideological infection and a threat to German racial purity.

The racial theories Hitler adopted, like his nationalism, had deep roots in the German past and appealed strongly to many Germans. After 1930, the thousand-year-old Jewish community in Germany, numbering half a million people, watched the rapid rise of the Nazis with mixed disbelief and foreboding.

On January 30, 1933, the aged president of the republic, Field Marshal Paul von Hindenburg, appointed Hitler Chancellor of Germany. Hitler proceeded to bring the republic to an end and to establish in Germany a totalitarian regime. Shortly after becoming Chancellor, Hitler demanded that the Reichstag grant him emergency powers for four years. On March 23 the Reichstag gave in to his demands, and then dissolved itself. Thereafter Hitler ruled by decree. All political parties but the Nazis were outlawed. Churches, labor unions, youth organizations became organs of the state. Every medium of communication—radio, newspapers, motion pictures, books—was used to manipulate public opinion. The majority of Germans supported Hitler or acquiesced in his government, though many were disturbed by his methods. Those who did not support him were suppressed by Storm Troopers or by the dreaded secret police, the Gestapo. Midnight arrests, beatings and torture at the hands of the Gestapo, imprisonment without trial in concentration camps soon silenced most of Hitler's opponents, or drove them underground.

Hitler did not long delay putting into effect his anti-Jewish program. Jews were promptly dismissed from public office and the civil service. They were not allowed to teach in schools or universities or to work in journalism, radio, the movies, or the theater. Later they were barred from practicing law or medicine or engaging in business. Even private employment was increasingly denied them, so that many lost all means of livelihood. Both by law and by unofficial police terror, Jews were segregated from their Aryan neighbors. Jewish children could not attend school with Aryans. Jews were forbidden to marry or employ Aryans. Many stores and shops refused to serve Jews or hotels to accommodate them. Emigration, which had been relatively easy for Jews at first, was made increasingly difficult. Many of those who managed to escape from Germany in later years were compelled to leave all their possessions behind.

In September, 1939, Hitler launched in the east the war for which he had been preparing since soon after becoming Chancellor. Convinced at last that appeasement of the German dictator would lead only to further aggression, England and France declared war and prepared for the inevitable attack in the west. In eighteen days the German army, spearheaded by tanks and dive bombers, conquered Poland. In April, 1940, the Germans seized Denmark and invaded Norway. On May 10 Hitler struck in the west. Within a few days his armies had crushed neutral Holland and Belgium and were pouring into France. Unable to withstand the highly mobilized German assault, France surrendered on June 22. The British miraculously rescued their badly mauled expeditionary force from the beaches at Dunkirk and made preparations for the expected German invasion of England. Hitler was now master of most of Europe, and in June, 1941, after unsuccessfully attempting to bomb Britain into submission, Germany attacked the Soviet Union despite the non-aggression pact that Hitler had signed with Stalin in 1939.

Nazi-dominated Europe was a virtual slave empire. On farms and in factories, hungry populations toiled for their Nazi overlords. Thousands of men and women were taken to Germany as slave laborers. The Germans dealt ruthlessly with resistance. The shooting of a German soldier or policeman was avenged by the slaughter of hostages. Captured partisans were tortured and killed in Gestapo prisons. Listening to British broadcasts or possession of anti-German literature were made crimes punishable by imprisonment and death.

Everywhere in conquered Europe the German occupation forces vigorously implemented Hitler's racial policies. For the "Jewish question," as he called it, Hitler adopted the "final solution"—extermination. Special S.S. (Elite Guard) units following in the wake of the German army in Russia killed hundreds of thousands of Jews. To deal with the Jews of occupied Europe, the Germans created an efficient apparatus that rounded up Jews and transported them to special extermination camps, many of them in Poland. There the prisoners were worked to exhaustion before being shot or gassed. To Treblinka, Belsen, Sibibor, Chelmo, but especially to Auschwitz, the long, slow trains began to move in 1941, carrying their wretched human freight to destruction. Before the Nazi nightmare had passed, an estimated six million Jews—men, women, and children—had been systematically murdered. Millions of non-Jews in Poland, Czechoslovakia, Russia, and elsewhere, most of them Slavs, were also victims of the Nazis.

II

Anne Frank was born on June 12, 1929, in the historic

German city of Frankfurt. Frankfurt owed much of its commercial and cultural preeminence to its Jewish community, of which the Franks were members; the founders of the great Jewish banking family, the Rothschilds, had been natives of Frankfurt. Anne's father, Otto Frank, a respected businessman, could trace his family in the city's archives back to the seventeenth century. For Anne and her older sister Margot, the world of early childhood was a secure place inhabited by loving parents, relatives, and nurses.

Beyond the nursery, beyond the comfortable five-room flat on Ganghoferstrasse, the world was not so pleasant. Otto Frank did not wait for the full force of Nazi persecution to make itself felt. In the summer of 1933 the Franks left Frankfurt. Mrs. Frank with the two girls joined her mother in Aachen, near the Belgian border. Otto Frank went directly to Holland, where he established himself in a food products business. For centuries Holland had provided a refuge for the persecuted. In the 1930s it received many German Jews as it had welcomed French Huguenots in the sixteenth century and English Puritans in the seventeenth. By the spring of 1934, the Franks were reunited and settled in Amsterdam.

During the next few years, while crisis followed crisis and the threat of a second world war increased, Anne Frank lived happily in Amsterdam like any Dutch girl. She attended the Montessori School, had a host of friends, and discovered with delight that boys liked her.

But all of this began to change once the Germans invaded Holland in 1940. Shortly after the invasion Queen Wilhelmina and her cabinet escaped to England, where they formed a government in exile to cooperate with the Allies. Occupied Holland was ruled by a German high commissioner, Arthur Seyss-Inquart, who would one day be hanged as a major war criminal. The Germans terrorized and exploited Holland as they did other conquered countries. They banned listening to Allied broadcasts, muzzled the press, and suppressed political parties and trade unions. They closed the universities and imprisoned the country's political, military, and intellectual leaders. Thousands of persons were sent to Germany as slave laborers. As the resistance movement grew stronger, the Germans exacted savage reprisals. In Holland as elsewhere, they imposed harsh anti-Jewish measures. Despite strikes and protests by the brave Dutch, the roundup and deportation of Jews to extermination camps began.

For Anne Frank, life under the German occupation was at first not greatly different from what it had been before. She was compelled to leave the Montessori School and to attend the Jewish Lyceum. But she still had her family and friends, and she was absorbed in the experiences of everyday life. The growing number of anti-Jewish decrees did not weigh heavily upon her.

Her father, however, perceived the direction of events clearly enough. In February, 1941, the Nazis launched their first roundup of Jews in Amsterdam. Those arrested were taken to reception camps at Westerbork and Vught and from there shipped eastward into Germany. As the roundups continued, Otto Frank made plans for his family's safety. He had been forced by a German decree to leave his business, but his Dutch associates and employees remained loyal friends. Secretly, a group of rooms at the top and back of a building on the Prinsengracht Canal, that served as a warehouse and office for the business, was prepared as a hiding place. On July 5, 1942, the Germans summoned 16-year-old Margot to report for deportation. The following morning the Franks slipped away from their home and went into hiding in the "secret annexe." They were soon joined there by a business associate of Otto Frank, Mr. Van Daan, and by the latter's wife and 15-year-old son Peter. Later, they invited an elderly dentist, Albert Dussel, to share their refuge.

The eight Jews in the "secret annexe" remained quiet during the day while business was conducted as usual in the lower part of the building. They stirred only at night when the building was deserted. Their friends in the office below—Mr. Koophuis and Mr. Kraler, Miep van Santen and Elli Vossen—kept their secret, brought food and even gifts, provided what news they could of events in the city. That news, in the fall of 1942, was terrifying. The roundup and deportation of Jews from Holland was proceeding according to plan.

When the Franks went into hiding, Germany was at the height of its conquests. Hitler's empire extended from the English Channel deep into Russia, from the Arctic Circle to North Africa. Gradually, the tide began to turn. In the fall of 1942, the German advance into Russia was checked at Stalingrad. At the same time, in North Africa, the British drove the Germans back from Egypt and, with their French and American allies—the United States having entered the war in December, 1941—landed in Morocco and Algeria behind the German forces. While the Russians counterattacked along the eastern front in 1943, the western Allies cleared Africa of Hitler's *Afrika Korps,* conquered Sicily, and invaded Italy, toppling Hitler's Fascist partner, Benito Mussolini. Daily, Allied air raids over Europe grew in intensity. In June, 1944, came the long awaited Allied invasion of France. For two long years the little group in the "secret annexe" followed these events over their illegal radio. Joyfully, they looked forward to the day when the Germans would be driven from Holland and they could emerge from hiding.

But on August 4, 1944, following information provided by a Dutch informer, the Gestapo penetrated into the Franks' hiding place. The eight Jews, together with Mr. Koophuis and Mr. Kraler, were taken to Gestapo headquarters in Amsterdam. After a few weeks' imprisonment, Mr. Koophuis was released for medical care. Mr. Kraler spent eight months in a forced labor camp. The Franks, the Van Daans, and Mr. Dussel were sent to Westerbork.

On September 3, the day the Allies captured Brussels, these eight were among the last shipment of a thousand Jews to leave Holland. The prisoners were herded aboard a freight train, seventy-five people to a car. The cars, each with only a small, barred window high on one side, were sealed. For three days and nights the train wandered eastward across Germany, often stopping, backing, detouring. On the third night it reached Auschwitz in Poland. In the glare of searchlights, watched by black-uniformed S.S. men tightly reining their police dogs, the Jews left the train. On the platform men and women were separated. It was the last Otto Frank saw of his family.

At Auschwitz the healthier prisoners, their heads shaved, worked twelve hours a day digging sod, driven relentlessly by the sadistic *Kapos,* criminals who served the S S. as labor overseers. At night they were locked into crowded barracks Outside the windows they could see the sky glow red above the crematories.

Through the research of Ernst Schnabel, a German writer whose book *Anne Frank, A Portrait in Courage,* was published in 1958, some of the events of the last few months of Anne's life have been reconstructed. Auschwitz, a former inmate told Mr. Schnabel, was " 'fantastically well-organized, spick-and-span hell. The food was bad, but it was distributed regularly. We kept our barracks so clean that you could have eaten off the floor. Anyone who died in the barracks was taken away first thing in the morning. Anyone who fell ill disappeared also. Those who were gassed did not scream. They just were no longer there. The crematories smoked, but we received our rations and had roll calls. The S.S. harassed us at roll call and kept guard with machine guns from the watchtowers, and the camp fences were charged with high-tension electricity, but we could wash every day and sometimes even take showers. If you could forget the gas chambers, you could manage to live.' "

The prisoners moved like sleep walkers, half dead, protected somehow from seeing anything, from feeling anything. " 'But Anne had no such protection,' " another survivor recalled. " 'I can still see her standing at the door and looking down the camp street as a herd of naked gypsy girls was driven by to the crematory, and Anne watched them go and cried. And she cried also when we marched past the Hungarian children who had already been waiting half a day in the rain in front of the gas chambers because it was not yet their turn. And Anne nudged me and said: "Look, look. Their eyes. . . ." ' "

In October, 1944, Anne, Margot, and Mrs. Van Daan were among a group of the youngest and strongest women selected to be moved to Belsen in Germany. Left alone, refusing to eat, her mind wandering, Mrs. Frank died in the infirmary barracks at Auschwitz on January 6, 1945. Otto Frank, in the men's camp, saw Mr. Van Daan taken off to be gassed. Mr. Dussel was sent back to Germany and died in the Neuengamme camp. When the S.S. abandoned Auschwitz in February, 1945, to escape the advancing Russians, they took Peter Van Daan with them on the winter march to the west; he was never heard from again. Otto Frank survived to be liberated by the Russians.

Belsen, Anne discovered, was different from Auschwitz. There was no organization, no roll call, no food or water, only the barren, frozen heath and the starving people looking like ghosts. By January, 1945, the Allies had reached the Rhine, but at Belsen typhus raged and hope was dead.

At Belsen, Anne found her school friend, Lies Goosens. " 'I waited shivering in the darkness,' " Lies related of the night when Anne was brought to her. " 'It took a long time. But suddenly I heard a voice: "Lies, Lies? Where are you?"

" 'It was Anne, and I ran in the direction of the voice, and then I saw her beyond the barbed wire. She was in rags. I saw her emaciated, sunken face in the darkness. Her eyes were very large. We cried and cried, for now there was only the barbed wire between us, nothing more. And no longer any difference in our fates.

" 'I told Anne that my mother had died and my father was dying, and Anne told me that she knew nothing about her father, but that her mother had stayed behind in Auschwitz. Only Margot was still with her, but she was already very sick. They had seen Mrs. Van Daan again only after their arrival here in Belsen.' "

Mrs. Van Daan died at Belsen, but no witness marked the date. Margot died at the end of February or beginning of March, 1945. " 'Anne, who was already sick at the time,' " recalled a survivor, " 'was not informed of her sister's death; but after a few days she sensed it, and soon afterwards she died, peacefully, feeling that nothing bad was happening to her.' " She was not yet 16.

III

In May, 1945, the war ended. Months later, Otto Frank returned to Amsterdam by way of Odessa and Marseilles. Miep and Elli gave him the notebooks and papers in Anne's handwriting that they had found strewn over the floor of the "secret annexe" after the Gestapo had gone. These were Anne's diary, stories, and sketches. They were all that remained.

At first Otto Frank had copies of the diary privately circulated as a memorial to his family. It was a Dutch university professor who urged formal publication of the book, and with only slight excisions by Mr. Frank *Het Achterhuis (The Secret Annexe)* was published in Amsterdam by Contact Publishers in June, 1947. The book soon went through several editions. In 1950 it was published in

Germany by the Heidelberg firm of Lambert Schneider. The first printing was only 4500 copies, and many booksellers were actually afraid to show it in their windows; but the book caught on rapidly, and sales of the pocket edition, published by S. Fischer Verlag, totaled 900,000. In 1950 the diary was published in France; in 1952, in England and the United States under the title *Anne Frank: The Diary of a Young Girl*. The book has been translated into thirty-one languages, including Bengali, Slovene, and Esperanto and has been published in thirty countries. In the United States the diary and *The Works of Anne Frank* were published by Doubleday & Company. The diary was also distributed by the Teen Age Book Club and the Book Find Club and was reprinted in the Modern Library. It was serialized by an American newspaper syndicate with an estimated audience of ten million readers, and millions more read it when it was condensed in *Omnibook* and *Compact* magazines. A German translation of the book has been used in the United States as a school reader, and a large-type edition has been published by Franklin Watts, Inc.

In 1955 a play by Frances Goodrich and Albert Hackett based on the diary and called simply *The Diary of Anne Frank* opened at the Cort Theatre in New York. A great success, it received the Pulitzer Prize, the Critics Circle Prize, and the Antoinette Perry Award for 1956. On October 1, 1956, *The Diary of Anne Frank* opened simultaneously in seven German cities. Audiences there greeted it in stunned silence. The play released a wave of emotion that finally broke through the silence with which Germans had treated the Nazi period. For the first time there were widespread expressions of guilt and shame for what Germans had done to the Jews only a few years before.

In Amsterdam, Queen Juliana attended the play's opening on November 27. This was the city where the events of the play had actually occurred, and many Netherlanders who had lost families and friends in the extermination of the Dutch Jews were in the audience. "There were audible sobs," *The New York Times* correspondent reported, "and one strangled cry as the drama struck its climax and conclusion—the sound of the Germans hammering at the door of the hideout. The audience sat in silence for several minutes after the curtain went down and then rose as the royal party left. There was no applause."

In the United States, *The Diary of Anne Frank* was made into a motion picture in 1959 and adapted for television in 1967.

But still the story was not finished. With the passing of the years, more and more details of Anne Frank's life became known. In 1958 Ernst Schnabel published his moving book, for which he interviewed forty-two people who had known Anne or whose lives had touched hers. In 1963 a Viennese police inspector, Karl Silberbauer, was identified as the Gestapo sergeant who had arrested the Franks in 1944. Silberbauer protested that he had merely followed orders. He was suspended from his post but was later acquitted of the charge of having concealed his past. In January, 1966, the Nazi police chief in the Netherlands during World War II, former S.S. lieutenant general Wilhelm Harster, together with two former aides, was arrested in Munich. The three were charged with having directed the deportation of nearly 100,000 Dutch Jews to Auschwitz. One of their victims had been Anne Frank. At their trial a year later, a former S.S. major, Wilhelm Zopf, testified that the Franks' betrayer—probably an employee in the warehouse—had received the usual reward of five gulden (about $1.40) for each of the persons taken from the "secret annexe." The German court sentenced Harster to fifteen years in prison, his accomplices to nine years and five years.

Anne Frank's wish—"I want to go on living even after my death"—has come true. Today the Anne Frank Foundation maintains the building on the Prinsengracht Canal where the Franks hid for twenty-five months as a memorial to Anne Frank. Each year the house is visited by thousands of people from all over the world. The Foundation is also working toward the future by helping to promote better understanding among young people from every part of the world. To this end it has established the International Youth Center, which serves as a meeting place for young people and which holds lectures, discussions, and conferences covering a wide range of international problems.

The Montessori School in Amsterdam is now the Anne Frank School. There are other memorials to her in Germany, Israel, and elsewhere to atone for the unmarked grave at Belsen. But above all, the diary remains. "Her voice was preserved," Ernst Schnabel wrote, "out of the millions that were silenced, this voice no louder than a child's whisper. . . . It has outlasted the shouts of the murderers and has soared above the voices of time."

Note: The page references on the following pages direct your attention to passages in the text (T for Top of page, M for Middle, and B for Bottom).

PICTORIAL BACKGROUND

My father was thirty-six when he married my mother, who was then twenty-five. My sister Margot was born in 1926 in Frankfort-on-Main. I followed on June 12, 1929, and, as we are Jewish, we emigrated to Holland in 1933, where my father was appointed Managing Director of Travies N.V. (p. 3M)

THE HOUSE WHERE ANNE WAS BORN *(Wide World Photos)*

In 1938 after the pogroms, my two uncles (my mother's brothers) escaped to the U.S.A. My old grandmother came to us, she was then seventy-three. After May 1940 good times rapidly fled: first the war, then the capitulation, followed by the arrival of the Germans, which is when the sufferings of us Jews really began. (p. 3M)

GERMAN TROOPS ARRIVING IN THE NETHERLANDS

The anti-Jewish movement in Germany began not long after Hitler came to power. By 1933, it had become a common sight in Berlin for Jews to be stopped in the streets, questioned in a hostile manner, and summarily removed. In most instances the victims were never seen again.

POLICE QUESTIONING AN OLD JEW IN BERLIN

Anti-Jewish decrees followed each other in quick succession. Jews must wear a yellow star, Jews must hand in their bicycles, Jews are banned from trains and are forbidden to drive. Jews are only allowed to do their shopping between three and five o'clock and then only in shops which bear the placard "Jewish shop." (p. 3B)

A JEWISH WOMAN WEARING A YELLOW STAR

Another form of persecution in the early years of the Nazi regime was the planned boycott of stores owned or operated by Jews. Hitler's bully boys, the storm troopers, would station themselves in front of stores, hold up placards warning Germans not to buy from Jews.

STORM TROOPERS WITH WARNING SIGN

I will describe the building: there is a large warehouse on the ground floor which is used as a store. The front door to the house is next to the warehouse door, and inside the front door is a second doorway which leads to a staircase. There is another door at the top of the stairs . . . (p. 15M)

THE ANNE FRANK HOUSE IN AMSTERDAM, NOW AN INTERNATIONAL YOUTH CENTER *(Wide World Photos)*

. . . *Miep took us quickly upstairs and into the "Secret Annexe." . . . Our living room and all the other rooms were chock-full of rubbish, indescribably so. . . . Mummy and Margot were not in a fit state to take part. . . . But the two "cleaners-up" of the family—Daddy and myself— wanted to start at once.* (p. 17M)

THE CLEANING-UP CHORE BEGINS.
(With permission of 20th Century-Fox)

At nine-thirty in the morning (we were still having break-fast) Peter arrived, the Van Daans' son, not sixteen yet, a rather soft, shy, gawky youth; can't expect much from his company. He brought his cat (Mouschi) with him. Mr. and Mrs. Van Daan arrived half an hour later, and to our great amusement she had a large pottie in her hat box. (p. 20T)

ANNE, PETER, AND MOUSCHI
(With permission of 20th Century-Fox)

I've only got dismal and depressing news for you today. Our many Jewish friends are being taken away by the dozen. These people are treated by the Gestapo without a shred of decency, being loaded into cattle trucks and sent to Westerbrook, the big Jewish camp in Drente. Westerbrook sounds terrible . . . (p. 34B)

A JEW BEING CARTED OFF TO A CONCENTRATION CAMP

It is impossible to escape; most of the people in the camp are branded as inmates by their shaven heads and many also by their Jewish appearance.

If it is as bad as this in Holland whatever will it be like in the distant and barbarous regions they are sent to? We assume that most of them are murdered. (p. 35T)

INMATES AT BUCHENWALD SMILE WEAKLY TO
WELCOME AMERICAN RESCUERS.
(Wide World Photos)

Prominent citizens—innocent people—are thrown into prisons to await their fate. If the saboteur can't be traced, the Gestapo simply put about five hostages against the wall. Announcements of their deaths appear in the papers frequently. These outrages are described as "fatal accidents." Nice people, the Germans! (p. 35B)

UNDERGROUND WORKERS LAY DUTCH FLAG
OVER DEAD HOSTAGES.

Mummy is frightfully irritable and that always seems to herald unpleasantness for me. Is it just a chance that Daddy and Mummy never rebuke Margot and that they always drop on me for everything? Yesterday evening, for instance: Margot was reading a book with lovely drawings in it . . . (p. 39M)

MUMMY SCOLDS ANNE.
(With permission of 20th Century-Fox)

In the evenings when it's dark, I often see rows of good, innocent people accompanied by crying children, walking on and on, in charge of a couple of these chaps, bullied and knocked about until they almost drop. No one is spared—old people, babies, expectant mothers, the sick— each and all join in the march of death. (p. 48M)

JEWS BEING HERDED ON TO A TRAIN BOUND
FOR A CONCENTRATION CAMP

Chanuka and St. Nicholas Day came almost together this year—just one day's difference. We didn't make much fuss about Chanuka: we just gave each other a few little presents and then we had the candles. Because of the shortage of candles we only had them alight for ten minutes . . . (p. 51M)

THE LIGHTING OF THE CANDLES AT CHANUKA
(With permission of 20th Century-Fox)

The Dutch people are anxious too, their sons are being sent to Germany. Everyone is afraid.

And every night hundreds of planes fly over Holland and go to German towns, where the earth is so plowed up by their bombs, and every hour hundreds and thousands of people are killed in Russia and Africa. (p. 57M)

DUTCH CITIZENS GATHER TO LEARN THE NEWS OF THE WAR.

This is exactly what the frightful puppet show on the radio was like. The wounded seemed to be proud of their wounds—the more the better. One of them felt so moved at being able to shake hands with the Führer (that is, if he still had a hand) that he could hardly get the words out of his mouth. (p. 65T)

HITLER AMIDST HIS FANATIC FOLLOWERS

The gentlemen who had been expected duly arrived; even before they came Daddy was trembling with anxiety as to how the talks would go. "If only I could be there, if only I was downstairs," he cried. "Why don't you go and lie with one ear pressed against the floor, then you'll be able to hear everything." Daddy's face cleared . . . (p. 68B)

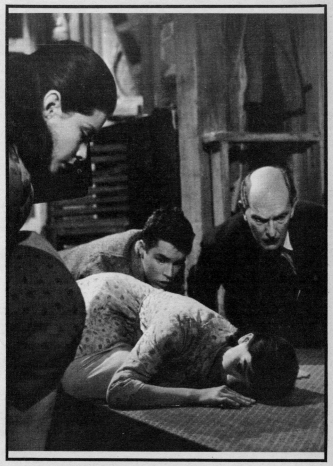

DESPERATE ATTEMPTS TO OVERHEAR A CONVERSATION
(With permission of 20th Century-Fox)

One good little piece of news is that the German department of the Labor Exchange has been set on fire by saboteurs. A few days after, the Registrar's Office went the same way. Men in German police uniforms gagged the guards and managed to destroy important papers. (p. 68T)

A DUTCH UNDERGROUND WORKER MAKING
INCENDIARY BOMBS

The Carlton Hotel is smashed to bits. Two British planes loaded with incendiary bombs fell right on top of the "Offiziersheim." The whole Vijzelstraat-Singel corner is burned down. The air raids on German towns are growing in strength every day. We don't have a single quiet night. (p. 70B)

THE COMING OF WAR TO AMSTERDAM

Today I have packed a suitcase with the most necessary things for an escape. But Mummy . . . says: "Where will you escape to?" The whole of Holland is being punished for the strikes which have been going on in many parts of the country. Therefore a state of siege has been declared and everyone gets one butter coupon less. (p. 72)

THE CENTRAL STATION IN AMSTERDAM DURING
THE RAILWAY STRIKE

The bustle of going to bed in the "Secret Annexe" begins and it is always really quite a business. Chairs are shoved about, beds are pulled down, blankets unfolded, nothing remains where it is during the day. . . . An eiderdown, sheets, pillows, blankets, are all fetched from Dussel's bed where they remain during the day. (p. 86M)

THE ORDEAL OF GOING TO BED
(With permission of 20th Century-Fox)

. . . *there is something wonderful going on. Last Wednesday evening, 8 September, we sat around listening to the seven o'clock news and the first thing we heard was: "Here follows the best news of the whole war. Italy has capitulated!" Italy's unconditional surrender! The Dutch program from England began at quarter past eight. (p. 97M)*

LISTENING IN ON SECRET RADIO EQUIPMENT
(With permission of 20th Century-Fox)

. . . Peter went on talking quite normally on what is otherwise such a painful subject, without meaning anything unpleasant, and finally put me sufficiently at my ease for me to be normal too. We played with Boche, amused ourselves, chattered together, and then sauntered through the large warehouse towards the door. (p. 128)

THE BUDDING ROMANCE BETWEEN ANNE AND PETER
(With permission of 20th Century-Fox)

EPILOGUE

Anne's diary ends here. On August 4, 1944, the Grüne Polizei made a raid on the "Secret Annexe." All the occupants, together with Kraler and Koophuis, were arrested and sent to German and Dutch concentration camps.

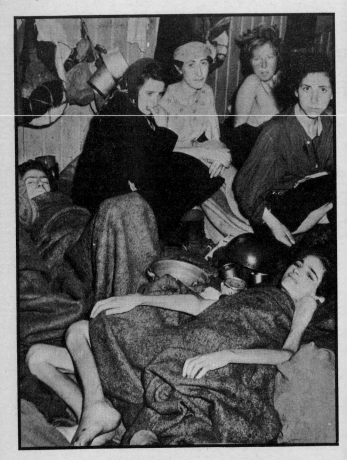

THE BERGEN-BELSEN CONCENTRATION CAMP, WHERE ANNE WAS SENT *(Wide World Photos)*

June 1, 1959, Wuppertal, Germany—Otto Frank, father of Anne, talks to former Belgian Foreign Minister Van Zeeland (left) and Nobel Peace Prize winner Father Dominique Pire, of Belgium, during cornerstone laying ceremonies for the new Anne Frank Village, not far from Wuppertal. The Anne Frank Village is the sixth European village to be built for refugees.

OTTO FRANK, THE SOLE SURVIVOR OF THE OCCUPANTS
OF THE "SECRET ANNEXE" (*Wide World Photos*)

LITERARY ALLUSIONS AND NOTES

Rin-Tin-Tin (p. 1B):
This famous dog actor starred in many films and was as eagerly adored by the young in his day as is *Lassie* of recent years.

pogroms (p. 3M):
Pogrom is a Russian word meaning "devastation" or "riot" that came into international usage after a number of anti-Semitic incidents in Russia between 1881 and 1917. Nazi anti-Semitism was based on race theories, which held that the Germanic peoples, or "Aryan" race, were destined by their inherent superiority to control all of Europe, at least, if not the world. In Hitler's book *Mein Kampf*, published in 1926, he laid out his plan to drive the Jews from Europe. Later, he decided that mass extermination was more expedient.

The pogroms of November, 1938, to which Anne is here referring were in reprisal for the assassination of a German embassy official in Paris by a 17-year-old Polish Jewish boy. In Germany, Jewish homes and shops were plundered. Jewish synagogues, orphanages, and hospitals were destroyed. More than 30,000 arrests were made and thousands were sent to concentration camps. A fine of 1,000,000,000 marks ($400,000,000) was also imposed on the Jews.

first the war, then the capitulation, followed by the arrival of the Germans (p. 3B):
The invasion of Poland by Germany on September 1, 1939, is generally said to mark the beginning of World War II. On September 3, France, England and Canada declared war on Germany. The Dutch government announced its intention to remain neutral. The German invasion of the Netherlands began on May 10, 1940. Queen Wilhelmina and her government escaped by ship to England. On May 14, Germany threatened destruction of all Dutch cities by aerial bombardment, and, while negotiations were in progress, the entire business section of Rotterdam was de-

stroyed in a show of power. After a war of just five days, the Dutch armies, which were not prepared for war on account of their declared neutrality, were forced to capitulate. Hitler's decree of May 18 established a German civil government in Holland. The persecution of Dutch Jewry, as Anne indicates, began almost immediately.

Jews must wear a yellow star (p. 3B):

Patterned after the "yellow patch" customary in some places and at some times during the Middle Ages, the black-bordered, six-pointed star of yellow cloth was about the size of the palm of a hand and bore the word "JOOD" (Jew) in black, Hebraized letters. They were obtainable for payment of a sum of money plus one stamp from the cloth ration card. The star was introduced into the occupied countries in 1942. Because the yellow star was humiliating as well as discriminatory, there were difficulties with the public about this decree and strong police action was frequently required to maintain it. In Denmark alone the ordinance had to be withdrawn after King Christian declared that he himself would be the first to wear the yellow star.

Montessori (p. 4M):

refers to the system of education originated by Maria Montessori (1870–1952). Dr. Montessori's methods emphasized freedom of movement in the classroom. The teacher provides learning materials and shows their use, but leaves the child to work by himself.

bicycle was stolen (p. 7B):

It is altogether likely that Anne's bicycle was also a victim of the Germans. In 1942, the S.S. was instructed to carry out bicycle raids, with the intention that the bicycles be sent to Germany for use by the police.

Zionist Movement (p. 9M):

Zionism is a Jewish national movement that has had as its goal the creation and support of a Jewish homeland in Palestine, where one of the hills of ancient Jerusalem was called Zion. The early 20th century Russian pogroms gave impetus to Zionism in eastern Europe, and Hitlerism brought many more to its ranks. The state of Israel was proclaimed after the war on May 14, 1948. During the Nazi occupation of the Netherlands, members of the movement also helped Jews that were in danger of arrest and deportation to escape to unoccupied territory or go underground like the members of the Secret Annexe.

S.S. (p. 12M) ... Gestapo (p. 34B):

The letters S.S. stand for "Schutzstaffel" or "Security Squad." The S.S. was the security organization of the German Nazi party which became the heart of the totalitarian state under Heinrich Himmler. The Dutch S.S. copied the initials of the German organization although the letters "S.S." had no meaning in Dutch.

The Gestapo was the secret state police. A plainclothes member of the Gestapo accompanied the uniformed Grune Polizei who arrested the members of the Secret Annexe. Originated in 1933 as the Prussian political police, after 1936 the Gestapo was expanded and effectively absorbed into the S.S. and merged with the S.D. (Security Service).

The powers of the Gestapo, S.S. and S.D. were vast; virtually anyone could be summarily arrested, executed, or imprisoned in a concentration camp. The S.S., which actually formed a separate army, was responsible only to Himmler, and thus wielded absolute power. The S.S. and Gestapo controlled the concentration and extermination camps and were therefore largely responsible for the crimes and atrocities of the World War II Nazi regime.

Westerbork (p. 35T):

The members of the Secret Annexe were all sent to Westerbork after their capture. Westerbork was a work camp, as opposed to an extermination camp, where the prisoners worked at such tasks as salvaging radio parts that were still usable from damaged equipment. But it also served as a sorting station where the fate of the Dutch Jews was decided, depending upon age, sex, and fitness for labor. From Westerbork, Anne was sent to Auschwitz. It was the last shipment out of the Netherlands.

fascist (p. 37B):

Fascism refers to a political party or an attitude which puts the nation-state or the race above individuals and their rights and above humanity in the exclusive interest of the nation. It combines an appeal to nationalistic expansion with a revolutionary call to the masses. Fascism is not so much an ideology as a technique which emphasizes violence, the absolute authority of the leader, military discipline, ruthless and direct action and the rejection of all ethical motives as weakening the resolve of the will to power. In sum, fascism holds that might is right.

The name fascism was first used by the movement started by Benito Mussolini in 1919, but later on became a general term for similar movements, such as German National Socialism.

Stalingrad (p. 42M):

The Battle of Stalingrad proved to be one of the most decisive battles in world history, and certainly the key battle in World War II. Against the advice of his generals, Hitler had decided upon a two-pronged offensive in Russia, thus dividing and weakening his eastern armies. Pathologically committed to the siege of Stalingrad in his hopeless strategy, he refused to allow retreat or surrender. In November of 1942, Anne reports that the fighting had been going on for three months.

Gandhi (p. 60M):

Mohandas Karamchand Gandhi, also known as Mahatma ("great soul"), was a pacifist revolutionary who devoted his life to freeing India of British rule. Gandhi called his non-violence *satyagraha* or "force which is born of truth and love." The fast to which Anne is referring here began on February 10 and lasted for 21 days in protest of British repression of the Indian nationalist movement for independence. This reference to the British empire in Asia is an interesting political sidelight on the Allied struggle to contain German expansion in Europe.

Rauter (p. 68T):

Hanns Albin Rauter, Higher S.S. and Police Leader, was one of the most influential German officials in the Netherlands. He was entrusted with the task of the annihilation of the Jews in Holland because he was a close confidant of Himmler, organizer and commander of the S.S. and the

Gestapo. In a speech to the Netherlands S.S., Rauter said: "It is my endeavor to dispose of the Jews as quickly as possible. This is not a pretty assignment, but it is a great work. The Germanic S.S. will show no pity if the whole Germanic race stands behind it. Whoever does not understand this and speaks of pity and humanism cannot be a leader in these times."

Benjamin (p. 74B):

According to the Book of Genesis, he was a son of Jacob by Rachel and the ancestor of one of the twelve tribes of Israel. As the youngest of Jacob's twelve sons, he was especially favored by his father after Joseph was sold into Egypt, and also favored by Joseph, his only full brother.

Benjamin stayed with his father when his brothers went down to Egypt to buy food during the famine. They were received by Joseph, who insisted the youngest brother come with them on their second visit, at which time he showed special favors to Benjamin. Joseph then put his brothers to a severe test by charging Benjamin with the theft of his silver cup. He threatened to keep Benjamin as a slave to see if his brothers would be as cruel and jealous of Benjamin as they had been of him. When they proved themselves to be dutiful sons and faithful brothers by defending Benjamin, Joseph revealed his true identity to his brothers.

Thus young Benjamin was the victim of Joseph's trick as well as the favorite brother and son. Since Anne often feels put upon by the adults, the comparison is apt in both respects.

the British have landed in Sicily (p. 76):

The capture of Sicily was of great strategic importance not only because the Mediterranean was thereby again opened as an Allied sea route but also because the path was opened for the invasion of Italy.

Danaidean (p. 90B):

This refers to the Danaïdes, the fifty daughters of Danaüs, a Greek mythological king. Danaüs was forced by his twin brother Aegyptus to agree to his daughters' marriage with Aegyptus' fifty sons. On the wedding night, Danaüs secretly gave his daughters swords and commanded them to kill their husbands. Only one had the courage to disobey. As punishment in the Underworld after their death, the others were required ceaselessly to draw water in leaky or bottomless jars which never filled.

Anne's comparison of this terrible punishment for the murders to Peter's appetite is amusing because of the criminality of the one and the healthy innocence of the other.

Lies (p. 107T and p. 113M):

In view of their eventual fates, this passage about Anne's girlhood friend Lies Goosens is ironic and doubly tragic, for it was Lies who was fated to help Anne, and Lies, not Anne, who survived the concentration camps.

Anne and Lies met again in Bergen-Belsen where they were in adjacent compounds. Because conditions were better for Lies, she managed to scrounge a pair of stockings and some bits of food for Anne. Shortly after, Anne was removed to another compound across the road. Several months later Lies encountered Mr. Frank in liberated Holland and learned from him that Anne and Margot had both died in Bergen-Belsen from typhus.

Goebbels (p. 135T):

Paul Joseph Goebbels (1897–1945) was made propaganda minister in 1933 by Hitler. He had complete control over radio, press, cinema and theater. As a hypnotic orator, he was second only to Hitler, and was unsurpassed in his staging of mass rallies and parades. His evil insight into mass psychology helped Hitler to power and spread Nazism abroad. In April of 1945, he committed suicide while Berlin was falling to the Russians.

N.S.B. (p. 182B):

The letters N.S.B. stand for Nationaal-Socialistische Beweging der Nederlanden. The party was founded in 1931. National Socialism proclaimed that the main goal of nature and therefore of human activity lay in the procreation and perfection of biologically higher forms of life. The main function of the National Socialist state was therefore the maintenance of Aryan racial purity and the acquisition of "living space" or *Lebensraum* in Europe for the Aryan

master race. In *Mein Kampf* Hitler declared his intention
to destroy France, to expand into Russian territory and
remove the Jews from Europe, but because of the supposed
racial purity of the Dutch, it was hoped that they would
be absorbed into Nazi Germany peacefully.

"Eldorado" (p. 195M):

In Spanish, El Dorado means "the gilded one." It denotes
a mythical South American country filled with gold and
wealth. Among early explorers in search of Eldorado were
Pizarro, Raleigh, and Coronado. Figuratively, Eldorado
means any place of fabulous wealth, a utopian dream, or
the land of desire. Peter's use of the word to describe a
person (Anne) rather than a place, while not wholly in-
correct, is awkward and amusing.

Theseus, Oedipus, Peleus, Orpheus, Jason, and Hercules (p. 209M):

Here is further evidence of Anne's great interest in mythology. Theseus slew the monster Minotaur, with the head of
a bull and the body of a man, who was confined in a
labyrinth (maze) and was annually fed seven youths and
seven maidens. Oedipus, in the great Greek tragedy, un-
knowingly killed his father and married his mother. Peleus
was a king of the Myrmidons who fought in the Trojan
War under the leadership of Achilles, son of Peleus. Orpheus was granted the right to release his wife Eurydice
from Hades on condition that he did not look back at her
until they had reached the upper world, but he couldn't
resist the temptation and, at the last moment, lost her again.
Jason, leader of the Argonauts, captured the Golden Fleece
despite the fire-breathing bulls and a dragon that guarded
it. Hercules proved he was the strongest man on earth by
successfully completing twelve labors that required extraordinary power and skill.

Myron, Phidias (p. 209B):

Myron was a Greek sculptor of the fifth century B.C., as was
Phidias.

Sodom, Gomorrah (p. 210T):

According to the Bible, both cities were destroyed by fire
because of the sinfulness of the people.

Atlantic Wall (p. 211T):

Hitler's "Atlantic Wall" stretched from the North Sea coast to Brittany and then southward to the Spanish border. This network of permanent fortifications protected by mine fields and underwater obstacles was devised in anticipation of a major Allied landing on the coast of occupied Europe.

Happy Whitsun (p. 217B):

Whitsun Day, literally "White Sunday," was named after the white garments worn by candidates for baptism, the seventh Sunday after Easter. This day is observed in some churches to commemorate the descent of the Holy Spirit upon the apostles.

Maria Theresa (p. 223T):

She was the queen of Hungary and Bohemia (1740–1780), archduchess of Austria, wife of Francis I of the Holy Roman Empire, and mother of Marie Antoinette.

CRITICAL EXCERPTS

1. *The Government Institute for War Documentation is in possession of about 200 similar diaries, but it would amaze me if there was one among them as pure, as intelligent, and yet as human as this one . . . For me this apparently insignificant diary, this* de profundis *in the stammering voice of a child, embodies the real hideousness of fascism more than all the trials of Nuremberg . . . If all signs do not deceive us, this girl, had she lived, would have become a talented writer . . . and she exhibited an insight into human nature—including her own—so faultless that it would be surprising in an adult, let alone a child. She also displayed, equally faultlessly, the limitless possibilities for humor, compassion, and love in human nature. These we should admire perhaps even more than her insight, and we might even shy away from them as we sometimes do from something very special, if her rejection and acceptance had not at the same time remained so profoundly childlike. That it was possible for this child to have been taken away and killed is proof for me that we have lost the battle against the beast in man.*

> "A Child's Voice," Jan Romein, first published in *Het Parool*, April 3, 1946; reprinted in *A Tribute to Anne Frank*, Anna G. Steenmeijer, Ed., Doubleday, New York, 1971.

2. *It is a war document, a document of the cruelty and heartbreaking misery of the persecution of the Jews, of human helpfulness and treason, of human adjustment and non-adjustment, of the small joys and the great and small miseries of life in hiding, written in a direct, non-literary, and therefore often excellent style, by this child who in any case possessed the one important characteristic of a great writer: an open mind, untouched by complacency and prejudice.*

But for me the most important thing about this diary is not the documentation, which so often is and will be recorded else-

where. When people in the tropics take a young plant from the temperate mountain zone and plant it in a very hot area, it will bloom once, richly and superabundantly, only to die soon after. That feeling is what touches me the most in this diary.

> Preface by Ammie Romein-Verschoor to the Dutch edition, *Het Achterhuis*, Amsterdam, 1947, reprinted in *A Tribute to Anne Frank.*

3. *It is a dialogue between one "I" and another, between a highly sensitive, thin-skinned being and another that seems to be armed with thorns. And it is a dialogue between the one "I" and the surrounding world, a discussion carried on with painstaking exactitude. No one could possibly miss the aggressive note that dominates the dialogue, and no one could miss the second tone that is not dominant and yet is the true keynote of the whole: the note of a genuine ability to love.*

> Preface by Albrecht Goes to the German edition, *Das Tagebuch der Anne Frank*, Germany, 1950, reprinted in Steenmeijer.

4. *It is sad, and idle, to speculate on what this brilliant young girl might have achieved had she lived. It is certain that her journal will strike many of our readers as the most moving personal record to come out of the years of the Nazi terror . . . it becomes one of the great documents of adolescence—true, of one gifted with a self-perception and power of expression beyond the ordinary, and yet who was nevertheless undergoing the familiar, turbulent unfolding of the personality that is the crisis of adolescence . . . Out of this experience of Anne's unnatural confinement for two years with seven other people, she re-creates for us the comedy drama of the compulsive banality of everyday life, even in a grim unbanal situation. In these descriptions, Anne's wit, one of her greatest gifts of spirit and style, flashes continually. It remains to be said that whatever childishness is naturally mingled with the star-*

tlingly mature reflections, there is not one false note of affectation.

> "The Secret Heart Within the Secret Annex," *Commentary*, May, 1952.

5. *So extraordinary a personality, and so authentic a talent, speak from every page, that the reader's first emotion after coming to the close of the unfinished diary is one of an overwhelming sadness at the destruction of this one mind, this one spirit, this one girl—an emotion which perhaps larger and more remote statistics have sometimes failed to arouse.*

> "The Secret Heart Within the Secret Annex," *Commentary*, June, 1952.

6. *Anne's diary shows a startling insight and a remarkable talent and wit. Her accounts of the daily life, the quarrels, the jealousies, the boredom, her criticism of her mother, the constant fear of discovery or sudden death, however, are expressions of amazing maturity . . . With her vivid and appealing diary she will be remembered as a talented and sensitive adolescent whose spirit could not be imprisoned or thwarted, and who preserved with genius her precocious observations of a life of almost unbearable strain.*

> *Newsweek*, June 16, 1952.

7. *It is extraordinary for its writer's candor and sensitivity, both to her environment and to her interior development . . . The picture thus assembled shows Anne's thoughts and emotions to have been typical of her age; their articulation is astonishingly mature . . . Against the grim background of the Jewish pogrom, these commonplaces are much more than usually touching . . . The Diary achieves several ends other than the recording of experience. In its way, it is one more impressive testimonial to the Dutch people's generosity toward Jewish refugees during World War II. And it constitutes also a tribute to youth; through its young writer, it restores to teen-*

agers some of the luster of honor and bravery which ought rightfully to be theirs.

> *Commonweal*, Jean Holzhauer, June 27, 1952.

8. *The . . . diary is one of the most moving stories that anyone, anywhere has managed to tell about World War II.*

> *Time*, June 16, 1952.

9. *The diary would not have such a deep hold on the affections of the world if it were merely a record of events and techniques. Fundamentally it is a portrait of adolescence. The privations and the emotional strains of the secret household are hardly more than background. In the foreground is the figure of an enchanting girl. Her vitality rushes at the reader. Anne's inner life flourishes. She had every reason to look forward to the career of a writer. For her diary is an extraordinary mirror of a human being on the threshold of life—temperamental, impulsive, brash, but also intelligent, thoughtful, affectionate and aspiring . . . None of the documents or statistics related to the abominations of the Nazis is so accusing as this diary.*

> From the Foreword by Brooks Atkinson to "The Diary of Anne Frank," by Frances Goodrich and Albert Hackett, New York, 1955.

"The Diary of Anne Frank" as a play first opened in New York in October of 1955. Most of the reviewers concern themselves more with the play as a drama of adolescence than as a political document, as evidenced by this sampling of reviews:

10. *If the diary of Anne Frank is remarkable for any one thing, it is the way in which she is able to command our deepest seriousness about everything she is going through—the way she makes us forget that she is an adolescent and makes us wish that this way of experiencing life were not so soon lost by some of us, and much sooner found by most of*

*us . . . It is impossible to consider why and how this myth of
adolescence has taken hold in America . . . Anne Frank was
not an "American" adolescent . . . She was an unaffected
young girl, exceedingly alive, deep and honest—experiencing
more, and in a better way perhaps, than many of us do in
the course of a lifetime.*

> "Anne Frank on Broadway," Al-
> gene Ballif, *Commentary*, Novem-
> ber, 1955.

11. *"The Diary of Anne Frank" consists of a series of episodes
which take place in an Amsterdam garret during the last
war . . . the flickering candle of hideaway life burns most
brightly in the person of a fifteen-year-old girl who spends
most of the play being a precocious brat. The close quarters
in which she and seven other Dutch Jews must hide out from
the Nazi army of occupation stretch her ingeniuty and resources. The presents she manages to scrape together for her
fellow inmates at Chanukah, her love-affair with the only
young boy available—romantic despite the difficult conditions
—and her gradual maturing towards a consideration of others,
these are the action of the play.*

> "Broadway   Postscript,"   Henry
> Hewes, *Saturday Review*, October
> 22, 1955.

12. *Contrary to most people's expectation, including mine,
the* Diary *proves to be a touching, charming, and not at all
harrowing piece of theatre, though it ends weakly with Anne
reflecting on the goodness of human nature—a principle which
the story is so far from confirming.*

> "Theatre," Eric Bentley, *New Re-
> public*, January 2, 1956.

"The Diary of Anne Frank" was translated into German,
and was performed in almost all West German cities, running
in some theaters for several months. In an article about the
guilt of the Germans for the Nazis' persecution and the
response to the German play, Alfred Werner concluded that

"the play became a symbol of murder protracted, not only of Anne and her relatives and friends, but of six million Jewish civilians and, indeed, of additional millions of Russians, Poles, French, Dutch and others." Werner went on to describe pilgrimages of thousands of young Germans to the gravesite of Anne Frank at Bergen-Belsen, and quoted this letter written by a sixteen-year-old participant in the pilgrimage, a letter published in newspapers in all parts of the Bonn Republic:

13. *I have sworn that we must do better! All must be made to realize that the highest and the most beautiful being is man —regardless of whether he is a Jew, a Dane, a Russian, an Englishman, a Frenchman, or a German. It does not matter, for they are all men.*

Ann [sic], you did not die in vain, We, today's youth, want to believe in what is good in man—like you did . . . we shall never forget you and all those innocent people who had to die like you. We do not want to forget, and we must never forget.

> Quoted in "Germany's New Flagellants," Alfred Werner, *The American Scholar,* Spring, 1958.

The New York Times reported that the phenomenal success of the German play had sparked a new interest in Jewish culture and history among German intellectuals, and added:

14. *A measure of Anne Frank's stature as an artist is that the play is appreciated in Germany as other than a slice of recent history. It is a particular favorite of students because of its perceptive comments on the relationships of adolescents to their elders . . . [But] the fact that many thousands [of adults] are ready to undertake with full knowledge the obviously shattering experience of witnessing "Das Tagebuch von Anne Frank" is sufficient evidence that the subject remains as alive today as in the autumn of 1945.*

> "Anne Frank Speaks to the Germans," Arthur J. Olsen, *The New York Times Magazine,* February 7, 1957.

Dr. Louis de Jong, a Dutch writer and editor who escaped from the Netherlands the day its army surrendered, a long-time friend of Otto Frank, and adviser to the authors of the play, quotes the Düsseldorf producer of the play:

15. Anne Frank *has succeeded because it enables the audience to come to grips with history, personally and without denunciation. We watch it as an indictment, in the most humble, pitiful terms, of inhumanity to fellow men. No one accuses us as Germans. We accuse ourselves.*

> "The Girl Who Was Anne Frank,"
> Louis de Jong, *Reader's Digest,*
> October, 1957.

Dr. de Jong also quotes a seventeen-year-old German schoolgirl who had made the pilgrimage to Bergen-Belsen:

16. *Anne Frank was younger than we are when her life was so horribly ended. She had to die because others had decided to destroy her race. Never again among our people must such a diseased and inhuman hatred arise.*

In 1958, a biography of Anne Frank was published in the United States. Ernst Schnabel, the author, followed up 76 persons who had known Anne. He found and interviewed 42 of them, and pieced together a portrait of the growing child before the time she went into hiding, and also learned the details of her imprisonment and death of typhus at Bergen-Belsen. Schnabel summed Anne up:

17. *She was gracious, capricious at times, and full of ideas. She had a tender, but also a critical spirit; a special gift for feeling deeply and for fear, but also her own special kind of courage. She had intelligence, but also many blind spots; a great deal of precocity alongside extraordinary childishness; and a sound and infrangible moral sense even in the most hopeless misery. All in all, she seems to have been what the Greeks would have called a good and beautiful person . . .*

Her voice was preserved out of the millions that were silenced, this voice no louder than a child's whisper. It tells how these millions lived, spoke, ate, and slept, and it has outlasted the shouts of the murderers and has soared above the voices of time.

> *Anne Frank: A Portrait in Courage,*
> Ernst Schnabel, New York, 1958.

The authors of the introduction to *The Works of Anne Frank*—a collection of the stories Anne mentions writing in the course of her diary—agreed that

18. *By now, in fact, Anne Frank has become a universal legend. Out of the millions that were gassed, burned, shot, hanged, starved, tortured, buried alive, the young girl who died so "peacefully" in Bergen-Belsen . . . has become a prime symbol of the innocence of all those who died in the middle of the twentieth century at the hands of the most powerful state in Western Europe . . . has become the personal example of the heartlessness, the bestiality, the still unbelievable cruelty of Germans in World War II. Upon her, at least, all agree; in her all peoples . . . can find a moment's occasion for compassion and awareness.*

> From the Introduction by Ann Birstein and Alfred Kazin to *The Works of Anne Frank*, New York, 1959.

In 1960, Dr. Henry F. Pommer published a review of the criticism of Anne Frank's *Diary*, pointing out that the critics were divided into two camps, those who held that the book was primarily a historical document and those who held that the book was primarily an intimate account of adolescence. Dr. Pommer is somewhat unique in considering the *Diary* also as a piece of literature:

19. *The chief literary merit of the diary is that it permits us to know intimately Anne's young, eager, difficult, lovable self.*

*We follow the quick alternations of her great depression, and
we benefit from the introspection generated by her sharply
contrasting moods. Some pages read as though they had been
written in the security of a Long Island suburb; on the next
page we are plunged into Nazi terror; and both passages use
vivid details . . . She sensed the need for variety in reporting,
and used effective techniques for achieving it. Life in the
Secret Annex was terribly repetitious, but there is little repeti-
tion in the diary itself.*

*Even if the last entry told of Jews liberated by the arrival
of Allied armies in Amsterdam, the book would still have
real interest and value. And it would still have its chief moral
significance.*

> "Anne Frank," Henry F. Pommer,
> *Judaism, a Quarterly Journal of
> Jewish Life and Thought,* winter,
> 1960, reprinted in Steenmeijer.

The author of the introduction to the British edition of
Anne's collected stories also agrees that besides being a legend
and a symbol, she is also an interesting writer:

20. *One thing is certain, that Anne was a writer in embryo.
Her title for the book she was planning to write after the war
was* Het Achterhuis . . . *referring of course to the house in
Amsterdam where they all lived cooped up and in hiding for
over two years, but it could also have stood for an unconsciously symbolic title to indicate that behind her pas-
sionate zest for life, we should find wisdom and a deeply
religious set of values.*

> From the Introduction by G. B.
> Stern to *Tales from the House
> Behind,* by Anne Frank, Kings-
> wood, 1962.

21. *Any analysis of the style used in the* Diary *must take two
things into account. First, we must note that the book, as we
read it, is a translation from the Dutch, and some of the*

original flavor of Anne Frank's native language may not have come through in English. A translator cannot always substitute word for word or phrase for phrase, since no two languages have exactly the same idioms or constructions.

Secondly, we must remember that a girl in her early teens is the author. A writer's technique rarely reaches full maturity in adolescence. But, in many ways, this is what makes Anne's diary so straightforward, so intensely human and personal, so sensitive to the changes that take place both about her and within herself. Her lack of sophistication and experience in writing removed any possibility that her style would contain the artificial flourishes and studied touches that so frequently mask the true character of older authors. The Diary is Anne Frank; it is her personality on paper; it reveals the complete human being behind the pen.

Anne tells us how self-conscious she feels about writing and then reveals her true motive in starting a diary: "paper is more patient than man." She wants to unburden herself, but she seems to sense that her words and sentences still retain the painful correctness, almost stiffness, of classroom "composition" writing.

However, the childish preciseness mixed with carelessness is far less pronounced than is the extraordinary maturity displayed in those passages that show keen insight, intelligent introspection, and self-analysis. Anne, like an accomplished novelist, rapidly sketches the character traits of the other inmates of the Secret Annexe and gives us hints of things to come with Peter. The emotions of a young girl who feels neglected by an elder sister and her mother are remarkably presented. A delightful talent for wry humor is evident when Anne talks of "using up" her brains keeping out of trouble. She recognizes and comments wisely on "growing pains" and keeps returning to her favorite problem, "Mumsie."

In all these journeys into herself, Anne drops her adolescent veneer and writes with the wisdom of an analyst. Her words express doubt, conviction, wonder, perplexity, understanding—and at these times we are not reading halting prose but are listening to a tape recording of a heart and brain. That Anne was aware of her strengths and shortcomings as a writer is touchingly noted when she calls herself the "best and sharpest critic of my own work."

Besides looking inwardly, Anne shows superior skill in observing the scene about her and commenting philosophically on the oddities and realities present. Witness her detached analysis of "grownups," her remarks on nature and God, her bitter charge against the "little man" (p. 201M), and her praise of work and religion (p. 230M). In examining the last two examples, you might want to compare the style of Anne when she is fifteen to what it was two years earlier. You can sense the assurance that is improving the shape of her language: the longer, more involved sentence structure; the more colorful detail; the greater depth of understanding. The Diary *offers the student of writing a fine opportunity to watch a style emerge from awkward uncertainty into grace and maturity. One grows heartsick at the thought of what this writer might have accomplished had she been granted the years to reach her full flowering as an artist.*

> Features of the Author's Style, Reader's Enrichment edition of *Anne Frank: The Diary of a Young Girl,* 1963.

Finally, from the guest book of the Anne Frank House, the museum now located at 263 Prinsengracht Canal, comes this sentiment about the life and death of Anne Frank:

22. *We cannot and we must not forget what has happened. We cannot bring back to life those who have died for the sanctification of the Name of God. (Ed. note: this refers to the belief that every Jewish deed which increases the prestige of Judaism in the eyes of non-Jews increases the honor of God at the same time.)*

We are here to do everything in our power to maintain the existence and the honor of the Jewish people.

> Golda Meir
> (Prime Minister of Israel)

February 27, 1964

Daddy. Funnily enough, Margot, who is much more shy than I am, isn't at all embarrassed.

I think what is happening to me is so wonderful, and not only what can be seen on my body, but all that is taking place inside. I never discuss myself or any of these things with anybody; that is why I have to talk to myself about them.

Each time I have a period—and that has only been three times—I have the feeling that in spite of all the pain, unpleasantness, and nastiness, I have a sweet secret, and that is why, although it is nothing but a nuisance to me in a way, I always long for the time that I shall feel that secret within me again.

Sis Heyster also writes that girls of this age don't feel quite certain of themselves, and discover that they themselves are individuals with ideas, thoughts, and habits. After I came here, when I was just fourteen, I began to think about myself sooner than most girls, and to know that I am a "person." Sometimes, when I lie in bed at night, I have a terrible desire to feel my breasts and to listen to the quiet rhythmic beat of my heart.

I already had these kinds of feelings subconsciously before I came here, because I remember that once when I slept with a girl friend I had a strong desire to kiss her, and that I did do so. I could not help being terribly inquisitive over her body, for she had always kept it hidden from me. I asked her whether, as proof of our friendship, we should feel one another's breasts, but she refused. I go into ecstasies every time I see the naked figure of a woman, such as Venus, for example. It strikes me as so wonderful and exquisite that I have difficulty in stopping the tears rolling down my cheeks.

If only I had a girl friend!

Yours, Anne

Dear Kitty,

My longing to talk to someone became so intense that somehow or other I took it into my head to choose Peter.

Sometimes if I've been upstairs into Peter's room during the day, it always struck me as very snug, but because Peter is so retiring and would never turn anyone out who became a nuisance, I never dared stay long, because I was afraid he might think me a bore. I tried to think of an excuse to stay in his room and get him talking, without it being too noticeable, and my chance came yesterday. Peter has a mania for crossword puzzles at the moment and hardly does anything else. I helped him with them and we soon sat opposite each other at his little table, he on the chair and me on the divan.

It gave me a queer feeling each time I looked into his deep blue eyes, and he sat there with that mysterious laugh playing round his lips. I was able to read his inward thoughts. I could see on his face that look of helplessness and uncertainty as to how to behave, and, at the same time, a trace of his sense of manhood. I noticed his shy manner and it made me feel very gentle; I couldn't refrain from meeting those dark eyes again and again, and with my whole heart I almost beseeched him: oh, tell me, what is going on inside you, oh, can't you look beyond this ridiculous chatter?

But the evening passed and nothing happened, except that I told him about blushing—naturally not what I have written, but just so that he would become more sure of himself as he grew older.

When I lay in bed and thought over the whole situation, I found it far from encouraging, and the idea that I should beg for Peter's patronage was simply repellent. One can do a lot to satisfy one's longings, which certainly sticks out in my case, for I have made up my mind to go and sit with Peter more often and to get him talking somehow or other.

Whatever you do, don't think I'm in love with Peter—not a bit of it! If the Van Daans had had a daughter instead of a son, I should have tried to make friends with her too.

I woke at about five to seven this morning and knew at once, quite positively, what I had dreamed. I sat on a chair and opposite me sat Peter . . . Wessel. We were looking together at a book of drawings by Mary Bos. The dream was so vivid that I can still partly remember the drawings. But that was not all—the dream went on. Suddenly Peter's eyes met mine and I looked into those fine, velvet brown eyes for a long time. Then Peter said very softly, "If I had only known, I would have come to you long before!" I turned around brusquely because the emotion was too much for me. And after that I felt a soft, and oh, such a cool kind cheek against mine and it felt so good, so good. . . .

I awoke at this point, while I could still feel his cheek against mine and felt his brown eyes looking deep into my heart, so deep, that there he read how much I had loved him and how much I still love him. Tears sprang into my eyes once more, and I was very sad that I had lost him again, but at the same time glad because it made me feel quite certain that Peter was still the chosen one.

It is strange that I should often see such vivid images in my dreams here. First I saw Grandma[1] so clearly one night that I could even distinguish her thick, soft, wrinkled velvety skin. Then Granny appeared as a guardian angel; then followed Lies, who seems to be a symbol to me of the sufferings of all my girl friends and all Jews. When I pray for her, I pray for all Jews and all those in need. And now Peter, my darling Peter—never before have I had such a clear picture of him in my mind. I don't need a photo of him, I can see him before my eyes, and oh, so well!

Yours, Anne

[1] Grandma is grandmother on Father's side, Granny on Mother's side.

Dear Kitty,

What a silly ass I am! I am quite forgetting that I have never told you the history of myself and all my boy friends.

When I was quite small—I was even still at a kindergarten—I became attached to Karel Samson. He had lost his father, and he and his mother lived with an aunt. One of Karel's cousins, Robby, was a slender, good-looking dark boy, who aroused more admiration than the litttle, humorous fellow, Karel. But looks did not count with me and I was very fond of Karel for years.

We used to be together a lot for quite a long time, but for the rest, my love was unreturned.

Then Peter crossed my path, and in my childish way I really fell in love. He liked me very much, too, and we were inseparable for one whole summer. I can still remember us walking hand in hand through the streets together, he in a white cotton suit and me in a short summer dress. At the end of the summer holidays he went into the first form of the high school and I into the sixth form of the lower school. He used to meet me from school and, vice versa, I would meet him. Peter was a very good-looking boy, tall, handsome, and slim, with an earnest, calm, intelligent face. He had dark hair, and wonderful brown eyes, ruddy cheeks, and a pointed nose. I was mad about his laugh, above all, when he looked so mischievous and naughty!

I went to the country for the holidays; when I returned, Peter had in the meantime moved, and a much older boy lived in the same house. He apparently drew Peter's attention to the fact that I was a childish little imp, and Peter gave me up. I adored him so that I didn't want to face the truth. I tried to hold on to him until it dawned on me that if I went on running after him I should soon get the name of being boy-mad. The years passed. Peter went around with girls of his own age and didn't even think of saying "Hello" to me any more; but I —couldn't forget him.

I went to the Jewish Secondary School. Lots of boys in our class were keen on me—I thought it was fun, felt honored, but was otherwise quite untouched. Then later on, Harry was mad about me, but, as I've already told you, I never fell in love again.

There is a saying "Time heals all wounds," and so it was with me. I imagined that I had forgotten Peter and that I didn't like him a bit any more. The memory of him, however, lived so strongly in my subconscious mind that I admitted to myself sometimes I was jealous of the other girls, and that was why I didn't like him any more. This morning I knew that nothing has changed; on the contrary, as I grew older and more mature my love grew with me. I can quite understand now that Peter thought me childish, and yet it still hurt that he had so completely forgotten me. His face was shown so clearly to me, and now I know that no one else could remain with me like he does.

I am completely upset by the dream. When Daddy kissed me this morning, I could have cried out: "Oh, if only you were Peter!" I think of him all the time and I keep repeating to myself the whole day, "Oh, Petel, darling, darling Petel . . . !"

Who can help me now? I must live on and pray to God that He will let Peter cross my path when I come out of here, and that when he reads the love in my eyes he will say, "Oh, Anne, if I had only known, I would have come to you long before!"

I saw my face in the mirror and it looks quite different. My eyes look so clear and deep, my cheeks are pink— which they haven't been for weeks—my mouth is much softer; I look as if I am happy, and yet there is something so sad in my expression and my smile slips away from my lips as soon as it has come. I'm not happy, because I might know that Peter's thoughts are not with me, and

121

yet I still feel his wonderful eyes upon me and his cool soft cheek against mine.

Oh, Petel, Petel, how will I ever free myself of your image? Wouldn't any other in your place be a miserable substitute? I love you, and with such a great love that it can't grow in my heart any more but has to leap out into the open and suddenly manifest itself in such a devastating way!

A week ago, even yesterday, if anyone had asked me, "Which of your friends do you consider would be the most suitable to marry?" I would have answered, "I don't know"; but now I would cry, "Petel, because I love him with all my heart and soul. I give myself completely!" But one thing, he may touch my face, but no more.

Once, when we spoke about sex, Daddy told me that I couldn't possibly understand the longing yet; I always knew that I did understand it and now I understand it fully. Nothing is so beloved to me now as he, my Petel.

Yours, Anne

Wednesday, 12 January, 1944

Dear Kitty,

Elli has been back a fortnight. Miep and Henk were away from their work for two days—they both had tummy upsets.

I have a craze for dancing and ballet at the moment, and practice dance steps every evening diligently: I have made a supermodern dance frock from a light blue petticoat edged with lace belonging to Mansa. A ribbon is threaded through round the top and ties in a bow in the center, and a pink corded ribbon completes the creation. I tried in vain to convert my gym shoes into real ballet shoes. My stiff limbs are well on the way to becoming supple again like they used to be. One terrific exercise is to sit on the floor, hold a heel in each hand, and then lift both legs up in the air. I have to have a cushion under me, otherwise my poor little behind has a rough time.

Everyone here is reading the book *Cloudless Morn*. Mummy thought it exceptionally good; there are a lot of youth problems in it. I thought to myself rather ironically: "Take a bit more trouble with your own young people first!"

I believe Mummy thinks there could be no better relationship between parents and their children, and that no one could take a greater interest in their children's lives than she. But quite definitely she only looks at Margot, who I don't think ever had such problems and thoughts as I do. Still, I wouldn't dream of pointing out to Mummy that, in the case of her daughters, it isn't at all as she imagines, because she would be utterly amazed and wouldn't know how to change anyway; I want to save her the unhappiness it would cause her, especially as I know that for me everything would remain the same anyway.

Mummy certainly feels that Margot loves her much more than I do, but she thinks that this just goes in phases! Margot has grown so sweet; she seems quite different from what she used to be, isn't nearly so catty these days and is becoming a real friend. Nor does she any longer regard me as a little kid who counts for nothing.

I have an odd way of sometimes, as it were, being able to see myself through someone else's eyes. Then I view the affairs of a certain "Anne" at my ease, and browse through the pages of her life as if she were a stranger. Before we came here, when I didn't think about things as much as I do now, I used at times to have the feeling that I didn't belong to Mansa, Pim, and Margot, and that I would always be a bit of an outsider. Sometimes I used to pretend I was an orphan, until I reproached and punished myself, telling myself it was all my own fault that I played this self-pitying role, when I was really so fortunate. Then came the time that I used to force myself to be friendly. Every morning, as soon as someone came downstairs I hoped that it would be Mummy who would say good morning to me; I greeted her warmly, because I really longed for her to look lovingly at me. Then she made some remark or other that seemed unfriendly, and I would go off to school again feeling thoroughly disheartened. On the way home I would make excuses for her because she had so many worries, arrive home very cheerful, chatter nineteen to the dozen, until I began repeating myself, and left the room wearing a pensive expression, my satchel under my arm. Sometimes I decided to remain cross, but when I came home from school I always had so much news that my resolutions were gone with the wind and Mummy, whatever she might be doing, had to lend an ear to all my adventures. Then the time came once more when I didn't listen for footsteps on the staircase any longer, and at night my pillow was wet with tears.

Everything grew much worse at that point; *enfin,* you know all about it.

Now God has sent me a helper—Peter . . . I just clasp my pendant, kiss it, and think to myself, "What do I care about the lot of them! Peter belongs to me and no one knows anything about it." This way I can get over all the snubs I receive. Who would ever think that so much can go on in the soul of a young girl?

Yours, Anne

Saturday, 15 January, 1944

Dear Kitty,

There is no point in telling you every time the exact details of our rows and arguments. Let it suffice to tell you that we have divided up a great many things, such as butter and meat, and that we fry our own potatoes. For some time now we've been eating whole-meal bread between meals as an extra, because by four o'clock in the afternoon we are longing for our supper so much that we hardly know how to control our rumbling tummies.

Mummy's birthday is rapidly approaching. She got some extra sugar from Kraler, which made the Van Daans jealous as Mrs. Van Daan had not been favored in this way for her birthday. But what's the use of annoying each other with yet more unkind words, tears, and angry outbursts. You can be sure of one thing, Kitty, that we are even more fed up with them than ever! Mummy has expressed the wish—one which cannot come true just now—not to see the Van Daan's for a fortnight.

I keep asking myself, whether one would have trouble in the long run, whoever one shared a house with. Or did we strike it extra unlucky? Are most people so selfish and stingy then? I think it's all to the good to have learned a bit about human beings, but now I think I've learned enough. The war goes on just the same, whether or not we choose to quarrel, or long for freedom and fresh air, and so we should try to make the best of our stay here. Now I'm preaching, but I also believe that if I stay here for very long I shall grow into a dried-up old beanstalk. And I did so want to grow into a real young woman!

Yours, Anne

Saturday, 22 January, 1944

Dear Kitty,

I wonder whether you can tell me why it is that people always try so hard to hide their real feelings? How is it that I always behave quite differently from what I should in other people's company?

Why do we trust one another so little? I know there must be a reason, but still I sometimes think it's horrible that you find you can never really confide in people, even in those who are nearest to you.

It seems as if I've grown up a lot since my dream the other night. I'm much more of an "independent being." You'll certainly be amazed when I tell you that even my attitude towards the Van Daans has changed. I suddenly see all the arguments and the rest of it in a different light, and am not as prejudiced as I was.

How can I have changed so much? Yes, you see it suddenly struck me that if Mummy had been different, a real Mumsie, the relationship might have been quite different. It's true that Mrs. Van Daan is by no means a nice person, but still I do think that half the quarrels

125

could be avoided if it weren't for the fact that when the conversation gets tricky Mummy is a bit difficult too.

Mrs. Van Daan has one good side, and that is that you can talk to her. Despite all her selfishness, stinginess, and underhandedness, you can make her give in easily, as long as you don't irritate her and get on the wrong side of her. This way doesn't work every time, but if you have patience you can try again and see how far you get.

All the problems of our "upbringing," of our being spoiled, the food—it could have been quite different if we'd remain perfectly open and friendly, and not always only on the lookout for something to seize on.

I know exactly what you'll say, Kitty: "But, Anne, do these words really come from *your* lips? From you, who have had to listen to so many harsh words from the people upstairs, from you, the girl who has suffered so many injustices?" And yet they come from me.

I want to start afresh and try to get to the bottom of it all, not be like the saying "the young always follow a bad example." I want to examine the whole matter carefully myself and find out what is true and what is exaggerated. Then if I myself am disappointed in them, I can adopt the same lines as Mummy and Daddy; if not, I shall try first of all to make them alter their ideas and if I don't succeed I shall stick to my own opinions and judgment. I shall seize every opportunity to discuss openly all our points of argument with Mrs. Van Daan and not be afraid of declaring myself neutral, even at the cost of being called a "know-all." It is not that I shall be going against my own family, but from today there will be no more unkind gossip on my part.

Until now I was immovable! I always thought the Van Daans were in the wrong, but we too are partly to blame. We have certainly been right over the subject matter; but handling of others from intelligent people (which we consider ourselves to be!) one expects more insight. I hope that I have acquired a bit of insight and will use it well when the occasion arises.

Yours, Anne

Dear Kitty,

Something has happened to me; or rather, I can hardly describe it as an event, except that I think it is pretty crazy. Whenever anyone used to speak of sexual problems at home or at school, it was something either mysterious or revolting. Words which had any bearing on the subject were whispered, and often if someone didn't understand he was laughed at. It struck me as very odd and I thought, "Why are people so secretive and tiresome when they talk about these things?" But as I didn't think that I could change things, I kept my mouth shut as much as possible, or sometimes asked girl friends for information. When I had learned quite a lot and had also spoken about it with my parents, Mummy said one day, "Anne, let me give you some good advice; never speak about this subject to boys and don't reply if they begin about it." I remember exactly what my answer was: I said, "No, of course not! The very idea!" And there it remained.

When we first came here, Daddy often told me about things that I would really have preferred to hear from Mummy, and I found out the rest from books and things I picked up from conversations. Peter Van Daan was never as tiresome over this as the boys at school—once or twice at first perhaps—but he never tried to get me talking.

Mrs. Van Daan told us that she had never talked about these things to Peter, and for all she knew neither had her husband. Apparently she didn't even know how much he knew.

Yesterday, when Margot, Peter, and I were peeling potatoes, somehow the conversation turned to Boche. "We still don't know what sex Boche is, do we?" I asked.

"Yes, certainly," Peter answered. "He's a tom."

I began to laugh. "A tomcat that's expecting, that's marvelous!"

Peter and Margot laughed too over this silly mistake.

127

You see, two months ago, Peter had stated that Boche would soon be having a family, her tummy was growing visibly. However, the fatness appeared to come from the many stolen bones, because the children didn't seem to grow fast, let alone make their appearance!

Peter just had to defend himself. "No," he said, "you can go with me yourself to look at him. Once when I was playing around with him, I noticed quite clearly that he's a tom."

I couldn't control my curiosity, and went with him to the warehouse. Boche, however, was not receiving visitors, and was nowhere to be seen. We waited for a while, began to get cold, and went upstairs again. Later in the afternoon I heard Peter go downstairs for the second time. I mustered up all my courage to walk through the silent house alone, and reached the warehouse. Boche stood on the packing table playing with Peter, who had just put him on the scales to weigh him.

"Hello, do you want to see him?" He didn't make any lengthy preparations, but picked up the animal, turned him over on to his back, deftly held his head and paws together, and the lesson began. "Those are the male organs, these are just a few stray hairs, and that is his bottom." The cat did another half turn and was standing on his white socks once more.

If any other boy had shown me "the male organs," I would never have looked at him again. But Peter went on talking quite normally on what is otherwise such a painful subject, without meaning anything unpleasant, and finally put me sufficiently at my ease for me to be normal too. We played with Boche, amused ourselves, chattered together, and then sauntered through the large warehouse towards the door.

"Usually, when I want to know something, I find it in some book or other, don't you?" I asked.

"Why on earth? I just ask upstairs. My father knows more than me and has had more experience in such things."

We were already on the stair, so I kept my mouth shut after that.

"Things may alter," as Brer Rabbit said. Yes. Really I shouldn't have discussed these things in such a normal way with a girl. I know too definitely that Mummy didn't mean it that way when she warned me not to discuss the subject with boys. I wasn't quite my usual self for the rest of the day though, in spite of everything. When I thought over our talk, it still seemed rather odd. But at least I'm wiser about one thing, that there really are young people —and of the opposite sex too—who can discuss these things naturally without making fun of them.

I wonder if Peter really does ask his parents much. Would he honestly behave with them as he did with me yesterday? Ah, what would I know about it!

Yours, Anne

Thursday, 27 January, 1944

Dear Kitty,

Lately I have developed a great love for family trees and genealogical tables of the royal families, and have come to the conclusion that, once you begin, you want to delve still deeper into the past, and can keep on making fresh and interesting discoveries. Although I am extraordinarily industrious over my lessons, and can already follow the English Home Service quite well on the wireless, I still devote many Sundays to sorting and looking over my large collection of film stars, which is quite a respectable size by now.

I am awfully pleased whenever Mr. Kraler brings the *Cinema and Theater* with him on Mondays. Although this little gift is often called a waste of money by the less worldly members of the household, they are amazed each time at how accurately I can state who is in a certain film, even after a year. Elli, who, on her days off, often goes to the movies with her boy friend, tells me the titles of the new films each week; and in one breath I rattle off the names of the stars who appear in them, together with what the reviews say. Not so long ago, Mum said that I wouldn't need to go to a cinema later on because I knew the plots, the names of the stars, and the opinions of the reviews all by heart.

If ever I come sailing in with a new hair style, they all look disapprovingly at me, and I can be quite sure that someone will ask which glamorous star I'm supposed to be imitating. They only half believe me if I reply that it's my own invention.

But to continue about the hair style—it doesn't stay put for more than half an hour; then I'm so tired of the remarks people pass that I quickly hasten to the bathroom and restore my ordinary house-garden-kitchen hair style.

Yours, Anne

Friday, 28 January, 1944

Dear Kitty,

I asked myself this morning whether you don't sometimes feel rather like a cow who has had to chew over all the old pieces of news again and again, and who finally yawns loudly and silently wishes that Anne would occasionally dig up something new.

Alas, I know it's dull for you, but try to put yourself in my place, and imagine how sick I am of the old cows who keep having to be pulled out of the ditch again. If the conversation at mealtimes isn't over politics or a delicious meal, then Mummy or Mrs. Van Daan trot out one of the old stories of their youth, which we've heard so many times before; or Dussel twaddles on about his wife's extensive wardrobe, beautiful race horses, leaking rowboats, boys who can swim at the age of four, muscular pains and nervous patients. What it all boils down to is this—that if one of the eight of us opens his mouth, the other seven can finish the story for him! We all know the point of every joke from the start, and the storyteller is alone in laughing at his witticisms. The various milkmen, grocers, and butchers of the two ex-housewives have already grown beards in our minds, so often have they been praised to the skies or pulled to pieces; it is impossible for anything in the conversation here to be fresh or new.

Still, all this would be bearable if the grownups didn't have their little way of telling the stories, with which Koophuis, Henk, or Miep oblige the company, ten times over and adding their own little frills and furbelows, so that I often have to pinch my arm under the table to prevent myself from putting them right. Little children such as Anne must never, under any circumstances, know better than the grownups, however many blunders they make, and to whatever extent they allow their imaginations to run away with them.

One favorite subject of Koophuis's and Henk's is that of people in hiding and in the underground movement. They know very well that anything to do with other people in hiding interests us tremendously, and how deeply we can sympathize with the sufferings of people who get taken away, and rejoice with the liberated prisoner.

We are quite as used to the idea of going into hiding, or "underground," as in bygone days one was used to Daddy's bedroom slippers warming in front of the fire.

There are a great number of organizations, such as "The Free Netherlands," which forge identity cards, supply money to people "underground," find hiding places for people, and work for young men in hiding, and it is amazing how much noble, unselfish work these people are doing, risking their own lives to help and save others. Our helpers are a very good example. They have pulled us through up till now and we hope they will bring us safely to dry land. Otherwise, they will have to share the same fate as the many others who are being searched for. Never have we heard *one* word of the burden which we certainly must be to them, never has one of them complained of all the trouble we give.

They all come upstairs every day, talk to the men about business and politics, to the women about food and wartime difficulties, and about newspapers and books with the children. They put on the brightest possible faces, bring flowers and presents for birthdays and bank holi-

131

days, are always ready to help and do all they can. That is
something we must never forget; although others may
show heroism in the war or against the Germans, our
helpers display heroism in their cheerfulness and affection.

The wildest tales are going around, but still they are
usually founded on fact. For instance, Koophuis told us
this week that in Gelderland two football elevens met,
and one side consisted solely of members of the "underground" and the other was made up of members of the
police. New ration books are being handed out in
Hilversum. In order that the many people in hiding may
also draw rations, the officials have given instructions to
those of them in the district to come at a certain time, so
that they can collect their documents from a separate
little table. Still, they'll have to be careful that such
impudent tricks do not reach the ears of the Germans.

Yours, Anne

Thursday, 3 February, 1944

Dear Kitty,

Invasion fever in the country is mounting daily. If you
were here, on the one hand, you would probably feel the
effect of all these preparations just as I do and, on the
other, you would laugh at us for making such a fuss—who
knows—perhaps for nothing.

All the newspapers are full of the invasion and are
driving people mad by saying that "In the event of the
English landing in Holland, the Germans will do all they
can to defend the country; if necessary they will resort to
flooding." With this, maps have been published, on which
the parts of Holland that will be under water are marked.
As this applies to large parts of Amsterdam, the first
question was, what shall we do if the water in the streets
rises to one meter? The answers given by different people
vary considerably.

"As walking or cycling is out of the question, we shall
have to wade through the stagnant water."

"Of course not, one will have to try and swim. We shall

all put on our bathing suits and caps and swim under water as much as possible, then no one will see that we are Jews."

"Oh, what nonsense! I'd like to see the ladies swimming, if the rats started biting their legs!" (That was naturally a man: just see who screams the loudest!)

"We shan't be able to get out of the house anyway; the warehouse will definitely collapse if there is a flood, it is so wobbly already."

"Listen, folks, all joking apart, we shall try and get a boat."

"Why bother? I know something much better. We each get hold of a wooden packing case from the attic and row with a soup ladle!"

"I shall walk on stilts: I used to be an expert at it in my youth."

"Henk Van Santen won't need to, he's sure to take his wife on his back, then she'll be on stilts."

This gives you a rough idea, doesn't it, Kit?

This chatter is all very amusing, but the truth may be otherwise. A second question about the invasion was bound to arise: what do we do if the Germans evacuate Amsterdam?

"Leave the city too, and disguise ourselves as best we can."

"Don't go, whatever happens, stay put! The only thing to do is to remain here! The Germans are quite capable of driving the whole population right into Germany, where they will all die."

"Yes, naturally, we shall stay here, since this is the safest place. We'll try and fetch Koophuis and his family over here to come and live with us. We'll try and get hold of a sack of wood wool, then we can sleep on the floor. Let's ask Miep and Koophuis to start bringing blankets here."

"We'll order some extra corn in addition to our sixty pounds. Let's get Henk to try and obtain more peas and beans; we have about sixty pounds of beans and ten pounds of peas in the house at present. Don't forget that we've got fifty tins of vegetables."

133

"Mummy, just count up how much we've got of other food, will you?"

"Ten tins of fish, forty tins of milk, ten kilos of milk powder, three bottles of salad oil, four preserving jars of butter, four ditto of meat, two wicker-covered bottles of strawberries, two bottles of raspberries, twenty bottles of tomatoes, ten pounds of rolled oats, eight pounds of rice; and that's all.

"Our stock's not too bad, but if you think that we may be having visitors as well and drawing from reserves each week, then it seems more than it actually is. We have sufficient coal and firewood in the house, also candles. Let's all make little moneybags, which could easily be hidden in our clothing, in case we want to take money with us.

"We'll make lists of the most important things to take, should we have to run for it, and pack rucksacks now in readiness. If it gets that far, we'll put two people on watch, one in the front and one in the back loft. I say, what's the use of collecting such stocks of food, if we haven't any water, gas, or electricity?"

"Then we must cook on the stove. Filter and boil our water. We'll clean out some large wicker bottles and store water in them."

I hear nothing but this sort of talk the whole day long, invasion and nothing but invasion, arguments about suffering from hunger, dying, bombs, fire extinguishers, sleeping bags, Jewish vouchers, poisonous gases, etc., etc. None of it is exactly cheering. The gentlemen in the "Secret Annexe" give pretty straightforward warnings; an example is the following conversation with Henk:

"Secret Annexe": "We are afraid that if the Germans withdraw, they will take the whole population with them."

Henk: "That is impossible, they haven't the trains at their disposal."

"S.A.": "Trains? Do you really think they'd put civilians in carriages? Out of the question. They could use 'shank's mare.'" (Per pedes apostolorum, Dussel always says.)

H.: "I don't believe a word of it, you look on the black

side of everything. What would be their object in driving all the civilians along with them?"

"S.A.": "Didn't you know that Goebbels said, 'If we have to withdraw, we shall slam the doors of all the occupied countries behind us'?"

H.: "They have said so much already."

"S.A.": "Do you think the Germans are above doing such a thing or too humane? What they think is this: 'If we have got to go down, then everybody in our clutches will go down with us.'"

H.: "Tell that to the Marines; I just don't believe it!"

"S.A.": "It's always the same song; no one will see danger approaching until it is actually on top of him."

H.: "But you know nothing definite; you just simply suppose."

"S.A.": "We have all been through it ourselves, first in Germany, and then here. And what is going on in Russia?"

H.: "You mustn't include the Jews. I don't think anyone knows what is going on in Russia. The English and the Russians are sure to exaggerate things for propaganda purposes, just like the Germans."

"S.A.": "Out of the question, the English have always told the truth over the wireless. And suppose they do exaggerate the news, the facts are bad enough anyway, because you can't deny that many millions of peace-loving people were just simply murdered or gassed in Poland and Russia."

I will spare you further examples of these conversations; I myself keep very quiet and don't take any notice of all the fuss and excitement. I have now reached the stage that I don't care much whether I live or die. The world will still keep on turning without me; what is going to happen, will happen, and anyway it's no good to resist.

I trust to luck and do nothing but work, hoping that all will end well.

Yours, Anne

Dear Kitty,

The sun is shining, the sky is a deep blue, there is a lovely breeze and I'm longing—so longing—for everything. To talk, for freedom, for friends, to be alone. And I do so long . . . to cry! I feel as if I'm going to burst, and I know that it would get better with crying; but I can't, I'm restless, I go from one room to the other, breathe through the crack of a closed window, feel my heart beating, as if it is saying, "Can't you satisfy my longings at last?"

I believe that it's spring within me, I feel that spring is awakening, I feel it in my whole body and soul. It is an effort to behave normally, I feel utterly confused, don't know what to read, what to write, what to do, I only know that I am longing . . . !

Yours, Anne

Sunday, 13 February, 1944

Dear Kitty,

Since Saturday a lot has changed for me. It came about like this. I longed—and am still longing—but . . . now something has happened, which has made it a little, just a little, less.

To my great joy—I will be quite honest about it— already this morning I noticed that Peter kept looking at me all the time. Not in the ordinary way, I don't know how, I just can't explain.

I used to think that Peter was in love with Margot, but yesterday I suddenly had the feeling that it is not so. I made a special effort not to look at him too much, because whenever I did, he kept on looking too and then—yes, then—it gave me a lovely feeling inside, but which I mustn't feel too often.

I desperately want to be alone. Daddy has noticed that

I'm not quite my usual self, but I really can't tell him everything. "Leave me in peace, leave me alone," that's what I'd like to keep crying out all the time. Who knows, the day may come when I'm left alone more than I would wish!

Yours, Anne

Monday, 14 February, 1944

Dear Kitty,

On Sunday evening everyone except Pim and me was sitting beside the wireless in order to listen to the "Immortal Music of the German Masters." Dussel fiddled with the knobs continually. This annoyed Peter, and the others too. After restraining himself for half an hour, Peter asked somewhat irritably if the twisting and turning might stop. Dussel answered in his most hoity-toity manner, "I'm getting it all right." Peter became angry, was rude, Mr. Van Daan took his side, and Dussel had to give in. That was all.

The reason in itself was very unimportant, but Peter seems to have taken it very much to heart. In any case, when I was rummaging about in the bookcase in the attic, he came up to me and began telling me the whole story. I didn't know anything about it, but Peter soon saw that he had found an attentive ear and got fairly into his stride.

"Yes, and you see," he said, "I don't easily say anything, because I know beforehand that I'll only become tongue-tied. I begin to stutter, blush, and twist around what I want to say, until I have to break off because I simply can't find the words. That's what happened yesterday, I wanted to say something quite different, but once I had started, I got in a hopeless muddle and that's frightful. I used to have a bad habit; I wish I still had it now. If I was angry with anyone, rather than argue it out I would get to work on him with my fists. I quite realize that this method doesn't get me anywhere; and that is why I admire you. You are never at a loss for a word, you say

137

exactly what you want to say to people and are never the least bit shy."

"I can tell you, you're making a big mistake," I answered. "I usually say things quite differently from the way I meant to say them, and then I talk too much and far too long, and that's just as bad."

I couldn't help laughing to myself over this last sentence. However, I wanted to let him go on talking about himself, so I kept my amusement to myself, went and sat on a cushion on the floor, put my arms around my bent knees, and looked at him attentively.

I am very glad that there is someone else in the house who can get into the same fits of rage as I get into. I could see it did Peter good to pull Dussel to pieces to his heart's content, without fear of my telling tales. And as for me, I was very pleased, because I sensed a real feeling of fellowship, such as I can only remember having had with my girl friends.

Yours, Anne

Wednesday, 16 February, 1944

Dear Kitty,

It's Margot's birthday. Peter came at half past twelve to look at the presents and stayed talking much longer than was strictly necessary—a thing he'd have never done otherwise. In the afternoon I went to get some coffee and, after that, potatoes, because I wanted to spoil Margot for just that one day in the year. I went through Peter's room; he took all his papers off the stairs at once and I asked whether I should close the trap door to the attic. "Yes," he replied, "knock when you come back, then I'll open it for you."

I thanked him, went upstairs, and searched at least ten minutes in the large barrel for the smallest potatoes. Then my back began to ache and I got cold. Naturally I didn't knock, but opened the trap door myself, but still he came to meet me most obligingly, and took the pan from me.

"I've looked for a long time, these are the smallest I could find," I said.

"Did you look in the big barrel?"

"Yes, I've been over them all."

By this time I was standing at the bottom of the stairs and he looked searchingly in the pan which he was still holding. "Oh, but these are first-rate," he said, and added when I took the pan from him, "I congratulate you!" At the same time he gave me such a gentle warm look which made a tender glow within me. I could really see that he wanted to please me, and because he couldn't make a long complimentary speech he spoke with his eyes. I understood him, oh, so well, and was very grateful. It gives me pleasure even now when I recall those words and that look he gave me.

When I went downstairs, Mummy said that I must get some more potatoes, this time for supper. I willingly offered to go upstairs again.

When I came into Peter's room, I apologized at having to disturb him again. When I was already on the stairs he got up, and went and stood between the door and the wall, firmly took hold of my arm, and wanted to hold me back by force.

"I'll go," he said. I replied that it really wasn't necessary and that I didn't have to get particularly small ones this time. Then he was convinced and let my arm go. On the way down, he came and opened the trap door and took the pan again. When I reached the door, I asked, "What are you doing?" "French," he replied. I asked if I might glance through the exercises, washed my hands, and went and sat on the divan opposite him.

We soon began talking, after I'd explained some of the French to him. He told me that he wanted to go to the Dutch East Indies and live on a plantation later on. He talked about his home life, about the black market, and then he said that he felt so useless. I told him that he certainly had a very strong inferiority complex. He talked about the Jews. He would have found it much easier if he'd been a Christian and if he could be one after the war. I asked if he wanted to be baptized, but that wasn't the case either. Who was to know whether he was a Jew when the war was over? he said.

This gave me rather a pang; it seems such a pity that there's always just a tinge of dishonesty about him. For the rest we chatted very pleasantly about Daddy, and about judging people's characters and all kinds of things, I can't remember exactly what now.

It was half past four by the time I left.

In the evening he said something else that I thought was nice. We were talking about a picture of a film star that I'd given him once, which has now been hanging in his room for at least a year and a half. He liked it very much and I offered to give him a few more sometime. "No," he replied, "I'd rather leave it like this. I look at these every day and they have grown to be my friends."

Now I understand more why he always hugs Mouschi. He needs some affection, too, of course.

I'd forgotten something else that he talked about. He said, "I don't know what fear is, except when I think of my own shortcomings. But I'm getting over that too."

Peter has a terrible inferiority complex. For instance, he always thinks that he is so stupid, and we are so clever. If I help him with his French, he thanks me a thousand times. One day I shall turn around and say: "Oh, shut up, you're much better at English and geography!"

Yours, Anne

Friday, 18 February, 1944

Dear Kitty,

Whenever I go upstairs now I keep on hoping that I shall see "him." Because my life now has an object, and I have something to look forward to, everything has become more pleasant.

At least the object of my feelings is always there, and I needn't be afraid of rivals, except Margot. Don't think I'm in love, because I'm not, but I do have the feeling all the time that something fine can grow up between us, something that gives confidence and friendship. If I get half a chance, I go up to him now. It's not like it used to be when he didn't know how to begin. It's just the opposite—he's still talking when I'm half out of the room.

Mummy doesn't like it much, and always says I'll be a nuisance and that I must leave him in peace. Honestly, doesn't she realize that I've got some intuition? She looks at me so queerly every time I go into Peter's little room. If I come downstairs from there, she asks me where I've been. I simply can't bear it, and think it's horrible.

Yours, Anne

Saturday, 19 February, 1944

Dear Kitty,

It is Saturday again and that really speaks for itself.

The morning was quiet. I helped a bit upstairs, but I didn't have more than a few fleeting words with "him." At half past two, when everyone had gone to their own rooms, either to sleep or to read, I went to the private office, with my blanket and everything, to sit at the desk and read or write. It was not long before it all became too much for me, my head drooped on to my arm, and I sobbed my heart out. The tears streamed down my cheeks and I felt desperately unhappy. Oh, if only "he" had come to comfort me. It was four o'clock by the time I went upstairs again. I went for some potatoes, with fresh hope in my heart of a meeting, but while I was still smartening up my hair in the bathroom he went down to see Boche in the warehouse.

Suddenly I felt the tears coming back and I hurried to the lavatory, quickly grabbing a pocket mirror as I passed. There I sat then, fully dressed, while the tears made dark spots on the red of my apron, and I felt very wretched.

This is what was going through my mind. Oh, I'll never reach Peter like this. Who knows, perhaps he doesn't like me at all and doesn't need anyone to confide in. Perhaps he only thinks about me in a casual sort of way. I shall have to go on alone once more, without friendship and without Peter. Perhaps soon I'll be without hope, without comfort, or anything to look forward to again. Oh, if I could nestle my head against his shoulder and not feel so hopelessly alone and deserted! Who knows, perhaps he doesn't care about me at all and looks at the others in just the same way. Perhaps I only imagined that it was especially for me? Oh, Peter, if only you could see or hear me. If the truth were to prove as bad as that, it would be more than I could bear.

However, a little later fresh hope and anticipation seemed to return, even though the tears were still streaming down my cheeks.

Yours, Anne

Wednesday, 23 February, 1944

Dear Kitty,

It's lovely weather outside and I've quite perked up since yesterday. Nearly every morning I go to the attic where Peter works to blow the stuffy air out of my lungs. From my favorite spot on the floor I look up at the blue sky and the bare chestnut tree, on whose branches little raindrops shine, appearing like silver, and at the seagulls and the other birds as they glide on the wind.

He stood with his head against a thick beam, and I sat down. We breathed the fresh air, looked outside, and both felt that the spell should not be broken by words. We remained like this for a long time, and when he had to go up to the loft to chop wood, I knew that he was a nice fellow. He climbed the ladder, and I followed, then he chopped wood for about a quarter of an hour, during which time we still remained silent. I watched him from where I stood, he was obviously doing his best to show off his strength. But I looked out of the open window too, over a large area of Amsterdam, over all the roofs and on to the horizon, which was such a pale blue that it was hard to see the dividing line. "As long as this exists," I thought,

142

"and I may live to see it, this sunshine, the cloudless skies, while this lasts, I cannot be unhappy."

The best remedy for those who are afraid, lonely, or unhappy is to go outside, somewhere where they can be quite alone with the heavens, nature, and God. Because only then does one feel that all is as it should be and that God wishes to see people happy, amidst the simple beauty of nature. As long as this exists, and it certainly always will, I know that then there will always be comfort for every sorrow, whatever the circumstances may be. And I firmly believe that nature brings solace in all troubles.

Oh, who knows, perhaps it won't be long before I can share this overwhelming feeling of bliss with someone who feels the way I do about it.

Yours, Anne

A thought:

We miss so much here, so very much and for so long now: I miss it too, just as you do. I'm not talking of outward things, for we are looked after in that way; no, I mean the inward things. Like you, I long for freedom and fresh air, but I believe now that we have ample compensation for our privations. I realized this quite suddenly when I sat in front of the window this morning. I mean inward compensation.

When I looked outside right into the depth of Nature and God, then I was happy, really happy. And Peter, so long as I have that happiness here, the joy in nature, health and a lot more besides, all the while one has that, one can always recapture happiness.

Riches can all be lost, but that happiness in your own heart can only be veiled, and it will still bring you happiness again, as long as you live. As long as you can look fearlessly up into the heavens, as long as you know that you are pure within and that you will still find happiness.

Sunday, 27 February, 1944

Dearest Kitty,

From early in the morning till late at night, I really do hardly anything else but think of Peter. I sleep with his image before my eyes, dream about him and he is still looking at me when I awake.

I have a strong feeling that Peter and I are really not so different as we would appear to be, and I will tell you why. We both lack a mother. His is too superficial, loves flirting and doesn't trouble much about what he thinks. Mine does bother about me, but lacks sensitiveness, real motherliness.

Peter and I both wrestle with our inner feelings, we are still uncertain and are really too sensitive to be roughly treated. If we are, then my reaction is to "get away from it all." But as that is impossible, I hide my feelings, throw my weight about the place, am noisy and boisterous, so that everyone wishes that I was out of the way.

He, on the contrary, shuts himself up, hardly talks at all, is quiet, day-dreams and in his way carefully conceals his true self.

But how and when will we finally reach each other? I don't know quite how long my common sense will keep this longing under control.

Yours, Anne

Monday, 28 February, 1944

Dearest Kitty,

It is becoming a bad dream—in daytime as well as at night. I see him nearly all the time and can't get at him, I mustn't show anything, must remain gay while I'm really in despair.

Peter Wessel and Peter Van Daan have grown into one

Peter, who is beloved and good, and for whom I long desperately.

Mummy is tiresome, Daddy sweet and therefore all the more tiresome, Margot the most tiresome because she expects me to wear a pleasant expression; and all I want is to be left in peace.

Peter didn't come to me in the attic. He went up to the loft instead and did some carpentry. At every creak and every knock some of my courage seemed to seep away and I grew more unhappy. In the distance a bell was playing "Pure in body, pure in soul." [1] I'm sentimental—I know. I'm desperate and silly—I know that too. Oh, help me!

Yours, Anne

Wednesday, 1 March, 1944

Dear Kitty,

My own affairs have been pushed into the background by—a burglary. I'm becoming boring with all my burglars, but what can I do, they seem to take such a delight in honoring Kolen & Co. with their visits. This burglary is much more complicated than the one in July 1943.

When Mr. Van Daan went to Kraler's office at half past seven, as usual, he saw that the communicating glass doors and the office door were open. Surprised at this, he walked through and was even more amazed to see that the doors of the little dark room were open too, and that there was a terrible mess in the main office. "There has been a burglar," he thought to himself at once, and to satisfy himself he went straight downstairs to look at the front door, felt the Yale lock, and found everything closed. "Oh, then both Peter and Elli must have been very slack this evening," he decided. He remained in Kraler's room for a while, then switched off the lamp, and went upstairs, without worrying much about either the open doors or the untidy office.

[1] The bells in old clock towers play tunes.

This morning Peter knocked at our door early and came with the not so pleasant news that the front door was wide open. He also told us that the projector and Kraler's new portfolio had both disappeared from the cupboard. Peter was told to close the door. Van Daan told us of his discoveries the previous evening and we were all awfully worried.

What must have happened is that the thief had a skeleton key, because the lock was quite undamaged. He must have crept into the house quite early and closed the door behind him, hidden himself when disturbed by Mr. Van Daan, and when he departed fled with his spoils, leaving the door open in his haste. Who can have our key? Why didn't the thief go to the warehouse? Might it be one of our own warehousemen, and would he perhaps betray us, since he certainly heard Van Daan and perhaps even saw him?

It is all very creepy, because we don't know whether this same burglar may not take it into his head to visit us again. Or perhaps it gave him a shock to find that there was someone walking about in the house?

Yours, Anne

Thursday, 2 March, 1944

Dear Kitty,

Margot and I were both up in the attic today; although we were not able to enjoy it together as I had imagined, still I do know that she shares my feelings over most things.

During dish washing Elli began telling Mummy and Mrs. Van Daan that she felt very discouraged at times. And what help do you think they gave her? Do you know what Mummy's advice was? She should try to think of all the other people who are in trouble! What is the good of thinking of misery when one is already miserable oneself? I said this too and was told, "You keep out of this sort of conversation."

Aren't the grownups idiotic and stupid? Just as if Peter,

Margot, Elli, and I don't all feel the same about things, and only a mother's love or that of a very, very good friend can help us. These mothers here just don't understand us at all. Perhaps Mrs. Van Daan does a little more than Mummy. Oh, I would have so liked to say something to poor Elli, something that I know from experience would have helped her. But Daddy came between us and pushed me aside.

Aren't they all stupid! We aren't allowed to have any opinions. People can tell you to keep your mouth shut, but it doesn't stop you having your own opinion. Even if people are still very young, they shouldn't be prevented from saying what they think.

Only great love and devotion can help Elli, Margot, Peter, and me, and none of us gets it. And no one, especially the stupid "know-alls" here, can understand us, because we are much more sensitive and much more advanced in our thoughts than anyone here would ever imagine in their wildest dreams.

Mummy is grumbling again at the moment—she is obviously jealous because I talk more to Mrs. Van Daan than to her nowadays.

I managed to get hold of Peter this afternoon and we talked for at least three quarters of an hour. Peter had the greatest difficulty in saying anything about himself; it took a long time to draw him out. He told me how often his parents quarrel over politics, cigarettes, and all kinds of things. He was very shy.

Then I talked to him about my parents. He defended Daddy: he thought him a "first-rate chap." Then we talked about "upstairs" and "downstairs" again; he was really rather amazed that we don't always like his parents. "Peter," I said, "you know I'm always honest, so why shouldn't I tell you that we can see their faults too." And among other things I also said, "I would so like to help you, Peter; can't I? You are in such an awkward position and, although you don't say anything, it doesn't mean that you don't care."

"Oh, I would always welcome your help."

"Perhaps you would do better to go to Daddy, he

wouldn't let anything go any further, take it from me; you can easily tell him!"

"Yes, he is a real pal."

"You're very fond of him, aren't you?" Peter nodded and I went on: "And he is of you too!"

He looked up quickly and blushed, it was really moving to see how these few words pleased him.

"Do you think so?" he asked.

"Yes," I said, "you can easily tell by little things that slip out now and then!"

Peter is a first-rate chap, too, just like Daddy!

Yours, Anne

Friday, 3 March, 1944

Dear Kitty,

When I looked into the candle this evening[1] I felt calm and happy. Oma seems to be in the candle and it is Oma too who shelters and protects me and who always makes me feel happy again.

But . . . there is someone else who governs all my moods and that is . . . Peter. When I went up to get potatoes today and was still standing on the stepladder with the pan, he at once asked, "What have you been doing since lunch?" I went and sat on the steps and we started talking. At a quarter past five (an hour later) the potatoes, which had been sitting on the floor in the meantime, finally reached their destinations.

Peter didn't say another word about his parents; we just talked about books and about the past. The boy has such warmth in his eyes; I believe I'm pretty near to being in love with him. He talked about that this evening. I went into his room, after peeling the potatoes, and said that I felt hot.

"You can tell what the temperature is by Margot and me; if it's cold we are white, and if it is hot we are red in the face," I said.

"In love?" he asked.

---

[1] In Jewish homes candles are lit on the Sabbath eve.

148

"Why should I be in love?" My answer was rather silly.

"Why not?" he said, and then we had to go for supper. Would he have meant anything by that question? I finally managed to ask him today whether he didn't find my chatter a nuisance; he only said: "It's okay, I like it!"

To what extent this answer was just shyness, I am not able to judge.

Kitty, I'm just like someone in love, who can only talk about her darling. And Peter really is a darling. When shall I be able to tell him so? Naturally, only if he thinks I'm a darling too. But I'm quite capable of looking after myself, and he knows that very well. And he likes his tranquillity, so I have no idea how much he likes me. In any case, we are getting to know each other a bit. I wish we dared to tell each other much more already. Who knows, the time may come sooner than I think! I get an understanding look from him about twice a day, I wink back, and we both feel happy.

I certainly seem quite mad to be talking about him being happy, and yet I feel pretty sure that he thinks just the same as I do.

Yours, Anne

Saturday, 4 March, 1944

Dear Kitty,

This is the first Saturday for months and months that hasn't been boring, dreary, and dull. And Peter is the cause.

This morning I went to the attic to hang up my apron, when Daddy asked whether I'd like to stay and talk some French. I agreed. First we talked French, and I explained something to Peter; then we did some English. Daddy read out loud to us from Dickens and I was in the seventh heaven, because I sat on Daddy's chair very close to Peter.

I went downstairs at eleven o'clock. When I came upstairs again at half past eleven, he was already waiting for me on the stairs. We talked until a quarter to one.

149

If, as I leave the room, he gets a chance after a meal, for instance, and if no one can hear, he says: "Good-by, Anne, see you soon."

Oh, I am so pleased! I wonder if he is going to fall in love with me after all? Anyway, he is a very nice fellow and no one knows what lovely talks I have with him!

Mrs. Van Daan quite approves when I go and talk to him, but she asked today teasingly, "Can I really trust you two up there together?"

"Of course," I protested, "really you quite insult me!"

From morn till night I look forward to seeing Peter.

Yours, Anne

Monday, 6 March, 1944

Dear Kitty,

I can tell by Peter's face that he thinks just as much as I do, and when Mrs. Van Daan yesterday evening said scoffingly: "The thinker!" I was irritated. Peter flushed and looked very embarrassed, and I was about to explode.

Why can't these people keep their mouths shut?

You can't imagine how horrible it is to stand by and see how lonely he is and yet not be able to do anything. I can so well imagine, just as if I were in his place, how desperate he must feel sometimes in quarrels and in love. Poor Peter, he needs love very much!

When he said he didn't need any friends how harsh the words sounded to my ears. Oh, how mistaken he is! I don't believe he meant it a bit.

He clings to his solitude, to his affected indifference and his grown-up ways, but it's just an act, so as never, never to show his real feelings. Poor Peter, how long will he be able to go on playing this role? Surely a terrible outburst must follow as the result of this superhuman effort?

Oh, Peter, if only I could help you, if only you would let me! Together we could drive away your loneliness and mine!

I think a lot, but I don't say much. I am happy if I

150

see him and if the sun shines when I'm with him. I was very excited yesterday; while I was washing my hair, I knew that he was sitting in the room next to ours. I couldn't do anything about; the more quiet and serious I feel inside, the more noisy I become outwardly.

Who will be the first to discover and break through this armor? I'm glad after all that the Van Daans have a son and not a daughter, my conquest could never have been so difficult, so beautiful, so good, if I had not happened to hit on someone of the opposite sex.

Yours, Anne

P.S. You know that I'm always honest with you, so I must tell you that I actually live from one meeting to the next. I keep hoping to discover that he too is waiting for me all the time and I'm thrilled if I notice a small shy advance from his side. I believe he'd like to say a lot just like I would; little does he know that it's just his clumsiness that attracts me.

Yours, Anne

Tuesday, 7 March, 1944

Dear Kitty,

If I think now of my life in 1942, it all seems so unreal. It was quite a different Anne who enjoyed that heavenly existence from the Anne who has grown wise within these walls. Yes, it was a heavenly life. Boy friends at every turn, about twenty friends and acquaintances of my own age, the darling of nearly all the teachers, spoiled from top to toe by Mummy and Daddy, lots of sweets, enough pocket money, what more could one want?

You will certainly wonder by what means I got around all these people. Peter's word "attractiveness" is not altogether true. All the teachers were entertained by my cute answers, my amusing remarks, my smiling face, and my questioning looks. That is all I was—a terrible flirt, coquettish and amusing. I had one or two advantages, which kept me rather in favor. I was industrious, honest, and frank. I would never have dreamed of cribbing from anyone else. I shared my sweets generously, and I wasn't conceited.

Wouldn't I have become rather forward with so much admiration? It was a good thing that in the midst of it, at the height of all this gaiety, I suddenly had to face reality, and it took me at least a year to get used to the fact that there was no more admiration forthcoming.

How did I appear at school? The one who thought of new jokes and pranks, always "king of the castle," never in a bad mood, never a crybaby. No wonder everyone liked to cycle with me, and I got other attentions.

Now I look back at that Anne as an amusing, but very superficial girl, who has nothing to do with the Anne of today. Peter said quite rightly about me: "If ever I saw you, you were always surrounded by two or more boys and a whole troupe of girls. You were always laughing and always the center of everything!"

What is left of this girl? Oh, don't worry, I haven't forgotten how to laugh or to answer back readily. I'm just as good, if not better, at criticizing people, and I can still flirt if . . . I wish. That's not it though, I'd like that sort of life again for an evening, a few days, or even a week; the life which seems so carefree and gay. But at the end of that week, I should be dead beat and would be only too thankful to listen to anyone who began to talk about something sensible. I don't want followers, but friends, admirers who fall not for a flattering smile but for what one does and for one's character.

I know quite well that the circle around me would be much smaller. But what does that matter, as long as one still keeps a few sincere friends?

Yet I wasn't entirely happy in 1942 in spite of everything; I often felt deserted, but because I was on the go the whole day long, I didn't think about it and enjoyed myself as much as I could. Consciously and unconsciously, I tried to drive away the emptiness I felt with jokes and pranks. Now I think seriously about life and what I have to do. One period of my life is over forever. The carefree schooldays are gone, never to return.

I don't even long for them any more; I have outgrown them, I can't just only enjoy myself as my serious side is always there.

I look upon my life up till the New Year, as it were, through a powerful magnifying glass. The sunny life at home, then coming here in 1942, the sudden change, the quarrels, the bickerings. I couldn't understand it, I was taken by surprise, and the only way I could keep up some bearing was by being impertinent.

The first half of 1943: my fits of crying, the loneliness, how I slowly began to see all my faults and shortcomings, which are so great and which seemed much greater then. During the day I deliberately talked about anything and everything that was farthest from my thoughts, tried to draw Pim to me; but couldn't. Alone I had to face the difficult task of changing myself, to stop the everlasting reproaches, which were so oppressive and which reduced me to such terrible despondency.

Things improved slightly in the second half of the year, I became a young woman and was treated more like a grownup. I started to think, and write stories, and came to the conclusion that the others no longer had the right to throw me about like an india-rubber ball. I wanted to change in accordance with my own desires. But *one* thing that struck me even more was when I realized that even Daddy would never become my confidant over everything. I didn't want to trust anyone but myself any more.

At the beginning of the New Year: the second great change, my dream. . . . And with it I discovered my longing, not for a girl friend, but for a boy friend. I also discovered my inward happiness and my defensive armor of superficiality and gaiety. In due time I quieted down and discovered my boundless desire for all that is beautiful and good.

And in the evening, when I lie in bed and end my prayers with the words, "I thank you, God, for all that is good and clear and beautiful," I am filled with joy. Then I think about "the good" of going into hiding, of my health and with my whole being of the "dearness" of Peter, of

153

that which is still embryonic and impressionable and which we neither of us dare to name or touch, of that which will come sometime; love, the future, happiness and of "the beauty" which exists in the world; the world, nature, beauty and all, all that is exquisite and fine.

I don't think then of all the misery, but of the beauty that still remains. This is one of the things that Mummy and I are so entirely different about. Her counsel when one feels melancholy is: "Think of all the misery in the world and be thankful you are not sharing in it!" My advice is: "Go outside, to the fields, enjoy nature and the sunshine, go out and try to recapture happiness in yourself and in God. Think of all the beauty that's still left in and around you and be happy!"

I don't see how Mummy's idea can be right, because then how are you supposed to behave if you go through the misery yourself? Then you are lost. On the contrary, I've found that there is always some beauty left—in nature, sunshine, freedom, in yourself; these can all help you. Look at these things, then you find yourself again, and God, and then you regain your balance.

And whoever is happy will make others happy too. He who has courage and faith will never perish in misery!

Yours, Anne

Sunday, 12 March, 1944

Dear Kitty,

I can't seem to sit still lately; I run upstairs and down and then back again. I love talking to Peter, but I'm always afraid of being a nuisance. He has told me a bit about the past, about his parents and about himself. It's not half enough though and I ask myself why it is that I always long for more. He used to think I was unbearable; and I returned the compliment; now I have changed my opinion, has he changed his too?

I think so; still it doesn't necessarily mean that we shall become great friends, although as far as I am concerned it would make the time here much more bearable. But

154

still, I won't get myself upset about it—I see quite a lot of him and there's no need to make you unhappy about it too, Kitty, just because I feel so miserable.

On Saturday afternoon I felt in such a whirl, after hearing a whole lot of sad news, that I went and lay on my divan for a sleep. I only wanted to sleep to stop myself thinking. I slept till four o'clock, then I had to go into the living room. I found it difficult to answer all Mummy's questions and think of some little excuse to tell Daddy, as an explanation for my long sleep. I resorted to a "headache," which wasn't a lie, as I had one . . . but inside!

Ordinary people, ordinary girls, teen-agers like myself, will think I'm a bit cracked with all my self-pity. Yes, that's what it is, but I pour out my heart to you, then for the rest of the day I'm as impudent, gay, and self-confident as I can be, in order to avoid questions and getting on my own nerves.

Margot is very sweet and would like me to trust her, but still, I can't tell her everything. She's darling, she's good and pretty, but she lacks the nonchalance for conducting deep discussion; she takes me so seriously, much too seriously, and then thinks about her queer little sister for a long time afterwards, looks searchingly at me, at every word I say, and keeps on thinking: "Is this just a joke or does she really mean it?" I think that's because we are together the whole day long, and that if I trusted someone completely, then I shouldn't want them hanging around me all the time.

When shall I finally untangle my thoughts, when shall I find peace and rest within myself again?

Yours, Anne

Tuesday, 14 March, 1944

Dear Kitty,

Perhaps it would be entertaining for you—though not in the least for me—to hear what we are going to eat today. As the charwoman is at work downstairs, I'm sitting on the Van Daans' table at the moment. I have a handkerchief soaked in some good scent (bought before we came here) over my mouth and held against my nose. You won't gather much from this, so let's "begin at the beginning."

The people from whom we obtained food coupons have been caught, so we just have our five ration cards and no extra coupons, and no fats. As both Miep and Koophuis are ill, Elli hasn't time to do any shopping, so the atmosphere is dreary and dejected, and so is the food. From tomorrow we shall not have a scrap of fat, butter, or margarine left. We can't have fried potatoes (to save bread) for breakfast any longer, so we have porridge instead, and as Mrs. Van Daan thinks we're starving, we have bought some full cream milk "under the counter." Our supper today consists of a hash made from kale which has been preserved in a barrel. Hence the precautionary measure with the handkerchief! It's incredible how kale can stink when it's a year old! The smell in the room is a mixture of bad plums, strong preservatives, and rotten eggs. Ugh! the mere thought of eating that muck makes me feel sick.

Added to this, our potatoes are suffering from such peculiar diseases that out of two buckets of *pommes de terre,* one whole one ends up on the stove. We amuse ourselves by searching for all the different kinds of diseases, and have come to the conclusion that they range from cancer and smallpox to measles! Oh, no, it's no joke to be in hiding during the fourth year of the war. If only the whole rotten business was over!

Quite honestly, I wouldn't care so much about the food, if only it were more pleasant here in other ways. There's the rub: this tedious existence is beginning to make us all touchy.

The following are the views of the five grownups on the present situation:

Mrs. Van Daan: "The job as queen of the kitchen lost its attraction a long time ago. It's dull to sit and do nothing, so I go back to my cooking again. Still, I have to complain that it's impossible to cook without any fats, and all these nasty smells make me feel sick. Nothing

156

but ingratitude and rude remarks do I get in return for my services. I am always the black sheep, always the guilty one. Moreover, according to me, very little progress is being made in the war; in the end the Germans will still win. I'm afraid we're going to starve, and if I'm in a bad mood I scold everyone."

Mr. Van Daan: "I must smoke and smoke and smoke, and then the food, the political situation, and Keril's moods don't seem so bad. Keril is a darling wife."

But if he hasn't anything to smoke, then nothing is right, and this is what one hears: "I'm getting ill, we don't live well enough, I must have meat. Frightfully stupid person, my Keril!" After this a terrific quarrel is sure to follow.

Mrs. Frank: "Food is not very important, but I would love a slice of rye bread now, I feel so terribly hungry. If I were Mrs. Van Daan I would have put a stop to Mr. Van Daan's everlasting smoking a long time ago. But now I must definitely have a cigarette, because my nerves are getting the better of me. The English make a lot of mistakes, but still the war is progressing. I must have a chat and be thankful I'm not in Poland."

Mr. Frank: "Everything's all right. I don't require anything. Take it easy, we've ample time. Give me my potatoes and then I will keep my mouth shut. Put some of my rations on one side for Elli. The political situation is very promising, I'm extremely optimistic!"

Mr. Dussel: "I must get my task for today, everything must be finished on time. Political situation 'outschtänding' and it is 'eempossible' that we'll be caught.

"I, I, I . . . !"

Yours, Anne

Wednesday, 15 March, 1944

Dear Kitty,

Phew! Oh dear, oh dear—released from the somber scenes for a moment! Today I hear nothing but "if this or that should happen, then we are going to be in difficulties . . . if he or she should become ill, then we'll be completely isolated, and then if . . ." *Enfin,* I expect you know the rest, at least I presume you know the "Secret Annexers" well enough by this time to be able to guess the trend of their conversations.

The reason for all this "if, if" is that Mr. Kraler has been called up to go digging. Elli has a streaming cold and will probably have to stay at home tomorrow. Miep hasn't fully recovered from her flu yet, and Koophuis has had such bad hemorrhage of the stomach that he lost consciousness. What a tale of woe!

The warehouse people are getting a free day tomorrow; Elli can stay at home, then the door will remain locked and we shall have to be as quiet as mice, so that the neighbors don't hear us. Henk is coming to visit the deserted ones at one o'clock—playing the role of zoo-keeper, as it were. For the first time in ages he told us something about the great wide world this afternoon. You should have seen the eight of us sitting around him; it looked exactly like a picture of grandmother telling a story. He talked nineteen to the dozen to his grateful audience about food, of course, and then Miep's doctor, and everything that we asked about. "Doctor," he said, "don't talk to me about the doctor! I rang him up this morning, had his assistant on the phone and asked for a prescription for flu. The reply was that I could come and get the prescription any time between eight and nine in the morning. If you have a very bad attack of flu, the doctor comes to the telephone himself and says 'Put out your tongue, say Aah, I can hear all right that your throat is inflamed. I'll write out a prescription for you to order from the chemist. Good-by.' And that's that." A fine practice that, run by telephone only.

But I don't want to criticize the doctors; after all, a person has but two hands, and in these days there's an abundance of patients and very few doctors to cope with them. Still, we couldn't help laughing when Henk repeated the telephone conversation to us.

I can just imagine what a doctor's waiting room must look like nowadays. One doesn't look down on panel patients any more, but on the people with minor ailments and thinks: "Hi, you, what are you doing here, end of the line, please; urgent cases have priority!"

Yours, Anne

Thursday, 16 March, 1944

Dear Kitty,

The weather is lovely, superb, I can't describe it; I'm going up to the attic in a minute.

Now I know why I'm so much more restless than Peter. He has his own room where he can work, dream, think, and sleep. I am shoved about from one corner to another. I hardly spend any time in my "double" room and yet it's something I long for so much. That is the reason too why I so frequently escape to the attic. There, and with you, I can be myself for a while just a little while. Still, I don't want to moan about myself, on the contrary, I want to be brave. Thank goodness the others can't tell what my inward feelings are, except that I'm growing cooler towards Mummy daily, I'm not so affectionate to Daddy and don't tell Margot a single thing. I'm completely closed up. Above all, I must maintain my outward reserve, no one must know that war still reigns incessantly within. War between desire and common sense. The latter has won up till now; yet will the former prove to be the stronger of the two? Sometimes I fear that it will and sometimes I long for it to be!

Oh, it is so terribly difficult never to say anything to Peter, but I know that the first to begin must be he; there's so much I want to say and do, I've lived it all in my dreams, it is so hard to find that yet another day has gone by, and none of it comes true! Yes, Kitty, Anne is a crazy child, but I do live in crazy times and under still crazier circumstances.

But, still, the brightest spot of all is that at least I can write down my thoughts and feelings, otherwise I would be absolutely stifled! I wonder what Peter thinks about all these things? I keep hoping that I can talk about it

159

to him one day. There must be something he has guessed about me, because he certainly can't love the outer Anne, which is the one he knows so far.

How can he, who loves peace and quiet, have any liking for all my bustle and din? Can he possibly be the first and only one to have looked through my concrete armor? And will it take him long to get there? Isn't there an old saying that love often springs from pity, or that the two go hand in hand? Is that the case with me too? Because I'm often just as sorry for him as I am for myself.

I really don't honestly know how to begin and however would he be able to, when he finds talking so much more difficult than I do? If only I could write to him, then at least I would know that he would grasp what I want to say, because it's so terribly difficult to put it into words!

Yours, Anne

Friday, 17 March, 1944

Dear Kitty,

A sigh of relief has gone through the "Secret Annexe." Kraler has been exempted from digging by the Court. Elli has given her nose a talking to and strictly forbidden it to be a nuisance to her today. So everything is all right again, except that Margot and I are getting a bit tired of our parents. Don't misunderstand me, I can't get on well with Mummy at the moment, as you know. I still love Daddy just as much, and Margot loves Daddy and Mummy, but when you are as old as we are, you do want to decide just a few things for yourself, you want to be independent sometimes.

If I go upstairs, then I'm asked what I'm going to do, I'm not allowed salt with my food, every evening regularly at a quarter past eight Mummy asks whether I ought not to start undressing, every book I read must be inspected. I must admit that they are not at all strict, and I'm allowed to read nearly everything, and yet we are both sick of all the remarks plus all the questioning that go on the whole day long.

Something else, especially about me, that doesn't please them: I don't feel like giving lots of kisses any more and I think fancy nicknames are terribly affected. In short, I'd really like to be rid of them for a while. Margot said last evening, "I think it's awfully annoying, the way they ask if you've got a headache, or whether you don't feel well, if you happen to give a sigh and put your hand to your head!"

It is a great blow to us both, suddenly to realize how little remains of the confidence and harmony that we used to have at home. And it's largely due to the fact that we're all "skew-wiff" here. By this I mean that we are treated as children over outward things, and we are much older than most girls of our age inwardly.

Although I'm only fourteen, I know quite well what I want, I know who is right and who is wrong, I have my opinions, my own ideas and principles, and although it may sound pretty mad from an adolescent, I feel more of a person than a child, I feel quite independent of anyone.

I know that I can discuss things and argue better than Mummy, I know I'm not so prejudiced, I don't exaggerate so much, I am more precise and adroit and because of this—you may laugh—I feel superior to her over a great many things. If I love anyone, above all I must have admiration for them, admiration and respect. Everything would be all right if only I had Peter, for I do admire him in many ways. He is such a nice, good-looking boy!

Yours, Anne

Sunday, 19 March, 1944

Dear Kitty,

Yesterday was a great day for me. I had decided to talk things out with Peter. Just as we were going to sit down to supper I whispered to him, "Are you going to do shorthand this evening, Peter?" "No," was his reply. "Then I'd just like to talk to you later!" He agreed. After the dishes were done, I stood by the window in his parents' room awhile for the look of things, but it wasn't

161

long before I went to Peter. He was standing on the left side of the open window, I went and stood on the right side, and we talked. It was much easier to talk beside the open window in the semidarkness than in bright light, and I believe Peter felt the same.

We told each other so much, so very very much, that I can't repeat it all, but it was lovely; the most wonderful evening I have ever had in the "Secret Annexe." I will just tell you briefly the various things we talked about. First we talked about the quarrels and how I regard them quite differently now, and then about the estrangement between us and our parents.

I told Peter about Mummy and Daddy, and Margot, and about myself.

At one moment he asked, "I suppose you always give each other a good night kiss, don't you?"

"*One*, dozens, why, don't you?"

"No, I have hardly ever kissed anyone."

"Not even on your birthday?"

"Yes, I have then."

We talked about how we neither of us confide in our parents, and how his parents would have loved to have his confidence, but that he didn't wish it. How I cry my heart out in bed, and he goes up into the loft and swears. How Margot and I really only know each other well for a little while, but that, even so, we don't tell each other everything, because we are always together. Over every imaginable thing—oh, he was just as I thought! Then we talked about 1942, how different we were then. We just don't recognize ourselves as the same people any more. How we simply couldn't bear each other in the beginning. He thought I was much too talkative and unruly, and I soon came to the conclusion that I'd no time for him. I couldn't understand why he didn't flirt with me, but now I'm glad. He also mentioned how much he isolated himself from us all. I said that there was not much difference between my noise and his silence. That I love peace and quiet too, and have nothing for myself alone, except my diary. How glad he is that my parents have children here, and that I'm glad he is here. That I

162

understand his reserve now and his relationship with his parents, and how I would love to be able to help him. "You always do help me," he said. "How?" I asked, very surprised. "By your cheerfulness." That was certainly the loveliest thing he said. It was wonderful, he must have grown to love me as a friend, and that is enough for the time being. I am so grateful and happy, I just can't find the words. I must apologize, Kitty, that my style is not up to standard today.

I have just written down what came into my head. I have the feeling now that Peter and I share a secret. If he looks at me with those eyes that laugh and wink, then it's just as if a little light goes on inside me. I hope it will remain like this and that we may have many, many more glorious times together!

Your grateful, happy Anne

Monday, 20 March, 1944

Dear Kitty,

This morning Peter asked me if I would come again one evening, and said that I really didn't disturb him, and if there's room for one there's room for two. I said that I couldn't come every evening, because they wouldn't like it downstairs, but he thought that I needn't let that bother me. Then I said that I would love to come one Saturday evening and especially asked him to warn me when there was a moon. "Then we'll go downstairs," he answered, "and look at the moon from there."

In the meantime a little shadow had fallen on my happiness. I've thought for a long time that Margot liked Peter quite a lot too. How much she loves him I don't know, but I think it's wretched. I must cause her terrible pain each time I'm with Peter, and the funny part of it is that she hardly shows it.

I know quite well that I'd be desperately jealous, but Margot only says that I needn't pity her.

"I think it's so rotten that you should be the odd one

163

out," I added. "I'm so used to that," she answered, somewhat bitterly.

I don't dare tell Peter this yet, perhaps later on, but we've got to talk about so many other things first.

I had a little ticking off yesterday evening from Mummy, which I certainly deserved. I mustn't overdo my indifference towards her. So in spite of everything, I must try once again to be friendly and keep my observations to myself.

Even Pim is different lately. He is trying not to treat me as such a child, and it makes him much too cool. See what comes of it!

Enough for now, I'm full to the brim with Peter and can do nothing but look at him!

Evidence of Margot's goodness: I received this today,

March 20th, 1944
Anne, when I said yesterday that I was not jealous of you I was only fifty per cent honest. It is like this; I'm jealous of neither you nor Peter. I only feel a bit sorry that I haven't found anyone yet, and am not likely to for the time being, with whom I can discuss my thoughts and feelings. But I should not grudge it to you for that reason. One misses enough here anyway, things that other people just take for granted.

On the other hand, I know for certain that I would never have got so far with Peter, anyway, because I have the feeling that if I wished to discuss a lot with anyone, I should want to be on rather intimate terms with him. I would want to have the feeling that he understood me through and through without my having to say much. But for that reason it would have to be someone whom I felt was my superior intellectually, and that is not the case with Peter. But I can imagine it being so with you and Peter.

You are not doing me out of anything which is my due; do not reproach yourself in the least on my account. You and Peter can only gain by the friendship.

My reply:

Dear Margot,
I thought your letter was exceptionally sweet, but I still don't feel quite happy about it and nor do I think that I shall.

164

*At present there is no question of such confidence as you
have in mind between Peter and myself, but in the twilight
beside an open window you can say more to each other than
in brilliant sunshine. Also it's easier to whisper your feelings
than to trumpet them forth out loud. I believe that you are
beginning to feel a kind of sisterly affection for Peter, and that
you would love to help him, just as much as I. Perhaps you
will still be able to do that sometime, although that is not the
kind of confidence we have in mind. I think it must come
from both sides, and I believe that's the reason why Daddy and
I have never got so far.*

*Let's not talk about it any more; but if you still want any-
thing please write to me about it, because I can say what I
mean much better on paper.*

*You don't know how much I admire you, and I only hope
that I may yet acquire some of the goodness that you and
Daddy have, because now I don't see much difference between
you and Daddy in that sense.*

Yours, Anne

Wednesday, 22 March, 1944

Dear Kitty,
I received this from Margot last evening:

*Dear Anne,
After your letter yesterday I have the unpleasant feeling that
you will have prickings of conscience when you visit Peter; but
really there is no reason for this. In my heart of hearts I feel
that I have the right to share mutual confidence with someone,
but I could not bear Peter in that role yet.*

*However, I do feel just as you say, that Peter is a bit like a
brother, but—a younger brother; we have put out feelers
towards each other, the affection of a brother and sister might
grow if they touched, perhaps they will later—perhaps never;
however, it has certainly not reached that stage yet.*

*Therefore you really needn't pity me. Now that you've found
companionship, enjoy it as much as you can.*

In the meantime it is getting more and more wonderful
here. I believe, Kitty, that we may have a real great love
in the "Secret Annexe." Don't worry, I'm not thinking of

marrying him. I don't know what he will be like when he grows up, nor do I know whether we should ever love each other enough to marry. I know now that Peter loves me, but just how I myself don't know yet.

Whether he only wants a great friend, or whether I attract him as a girl or as a sister, I can't yet discover.

When he said that I always helped him over his parents' quarrels, I was awfully glad; it was one step towards making me believe in his friendship. I asked him yesterday what he would do if there were a dozen Annes here who always kept coming to him. His reply was, "If they were all like you, it certainly wouldn't be too bad!" He's tremendously hospitable towards me and I really believe he likes to see me. Meanwhile he is working diligently at his French, even when he's in bed, going on until a quarter past ten. Oh, when I think about Saturday evening and recall it all, word for word, then for the first time I don't feel discontented about myself; I mean that I would still say exactly the same and wouldn't wish to change anything, as is usually the case.

He is so handsome, both when he laughs and when he looks quietly in front of him; he is such a darling and so good. I believe what surprised him most about me was when he discovered that I'm not a bit the superficial worldly Anne that I appear, but just as dreamy a specimen, with just as many difficulties as he himself.

Yours, Anne

Reply:

Dear Margot,
I think the best thing we can do is simply to wait and see what happens. It can't be very long before Peter and I come to a definite decision, either to go on as before or be different. Just which way it will go I don't know myself, and I don't bother to look beyond my own nose. But I shall certainly do one thing, if Peter and I decide to be friends, I shall tell him that you are very fond of him too and would always be prepared to help him should the need arise. The latter may not be what you wish, but I don't care now; I don't know what Peter thinks about you, but I shall ask him then.

166

I'm sure it's not bad—the opposite! You are always welcome to join us in the attic, or wherever we are; you honestly won't disturb us because I feel we have a silent agreement to talk only in the evenings when it's dark.

Keep your courage up! Like I do. Although it's not always easy; your time may come sooner than you think.

Yours, Anne

Thursday, 23 March, 1944

Dear Kitty,

Things are running more or less normally again now. Our coupon men are out of prison again, thank goodness!

Miep returned yesterday, Elli is better, although she still has a cough; Koophuis will have to stay at home for a long time still.

A plane crashed near here yesterday; the occupants were able to jump out in time by parachute. The machine crashed onto a school, but there were no children there at the time. The result was a small fire and two people killed. The Germans shot at the airmen terribly as they were coming down. The Amsterdammers who saw it nearly exploded with rage and indignation at the cowardliness of such a deed. We—I'm speaking of the ladies—nearly jumped out of our skins, I loathe the blasted shooting.

I often go upstairs after supper nowadays and take a breath of fresh evening air. I like it up there, sitting on a chair beside him and looking outside.

Van Daan and Dussel make very feeble remarks when I disappear into his room; "Anne's second home," they call it, or "Is it suitable for young gentlemen to receive young girls in semidarkness?" Peter shows amazing wit in his replies to these so-called humorous sallies. For that matter, Mummy too is somewhat curious and would love to ask what we talk about, if she wasn't secretly afraid of being snubbed. Peter says it's nothing but envy on the part of the grownups, because we are young and we don't pay much attention to their spitefulness. Sometimes he comes and gets me from downstairs, but he turns simply scarlet in spite of all precautions, and can hardly get the words out of his mouth. How thankful I am that I don't blush, it must be a highly unpleasant sensation. Daddy always says I'm prudish and vain but that's not true, I'm just simply vain! I have not often had anyone tell me I was pretty. Except a boy at school, who said I looked so attractive when I laughed. Yesterday I received a genuine compliment from Peter, and just for fun I will tell you roughly how the conversation went:

Peter so often used to say, "Do laugh, Anne!" This struck me as odd, and I asked, "Why must I always laugh?"

"Because I like it; you get such dimples in your cheeks when you laugh; how do they come, actually?"

"I was born with them. I've got one in my chin too. That's my only beauty!"

"Of course not, that's not true."

"Yes, it is, I know quite well that I'm not a beauty; I never have been and never shall be."

"I don't agree at all, I think you're pretty."

"That's not true."

"If I say so, then you can take it from me it is!"

Then I naturally said the same of him.

I hear a lot from all sides about the sudden friendship. We don't take much notice of all this parental chatter, their remarks are so feeble. Have the two sets of parents forgotten their own youth? It seems like it, at least they seem to take us seriously, if we make a joke, and laugh at us when we are serious.

Yours, Anne

Monday, 27 March, 1944

Dear Kitty,

One very big chapter of our history in hiding should really be about politics, but as this subject doesn't interest me personally very much, I've rather let it go. So for once I will devote my whole letter to politics today.

It goes without saying that there are very many different opinions on this topic, and it's even more logical that it should be a favorite subject for discussion in such critical times, but—it's just simply stupid that there should be so many quarrels over it.

They may speculate, laugh, abuse, and grumble, let them do what they will, as long as they stew in their own juice and don't quarrel, because the consequences are usually unpleasant.

The people from outside bring with them a lot of news that is not true; however, up till now our radio set hasn't lied to us. Henk, Miep, Koophuis, Elli, and Kraler all show ups and downs in their political moods, Henk least of all.

Political feeling here in the "Secret Annexe" is always about the same. During the countless arguments over invasion, air raids, speeches, etc., etc., one also always hears the countless cries of "impossible," or *"Um Gottes Willen,* if they are going to start now however long is it going to last?" "It's going splendidly, first class, good!" Optimists and pessimists, and, above all, don't let's forget the realists who give their opinions with untiring energy and, just as with everything else, each one thinking he is right. It annoys a certain lady that her spouse has such unparalleled faith in the British, and a certain gentleman attacks his lady because of her teasing and disparaging remarks about his beloved nation.

They never seem to tire of it. I have discovered something—the effects are stupendous, just like pricking someone with a pin and waiting to see how they jump. This is what I do: begin on politics. One question, one word, one sentence, and at once they're off!

Just as if the German Wehrmacht news bulletins and the English B.B.C. were not enough, they have now introduced "Special Air-Raid Announcements." In one word, magnificent; but on the other hand often disappointing too. The British are making a non-stop business of their air attacks, with the same zest as the Germans make a business of lying. The radio therefore goes on early in the morning and is listened to at all hours of the day, until nine, ten, and often eleven o'clock in the evening.

This is certainly a sign that the grownups have infinite patience, but it also means the power of absorption of their brains is pretty limited, with exceptions, of course— I don't want to hurt anyone's feelings. One or two news bulletins would be ample per day! But the old geese, well —I've said my piece!

Arbeiter-Programm, Radio "Oranje," Frank Phillips or Her Majesty Queen Wilhelmina, they each get their turn, and an ever attentive ear. And if they are not eating or sleeping, then they're sitting around the radio and discussing food, sleep, and politics.

Ugh! It gets so boring, and it's quite a job not to become a dull old stick oneself. Politics can't do much more harm to the parents!

I must mention one shining exception—a speech by our beloved Winston Churchill is quite perfect.

Nine o'clock on Sunday evening. The teapot stands, with the cozy over it, on the table, and the guests come in. Dussel next to the radio on the left, Mr. Van Daan in front of it, with Peter beside him. Mummy next to Mr. Van Daan and Mrs. Van Daan behind him, and Pim at the table, Margot and I beside. I see I haven't described very clearly how we sit. The gentlemen puff away at their pipes, Peter's eyes are popping out of his head with the strain of listening, Mummy wearing a long dark negligée, and Mrs. Van Daan trembling because of the planes, which take no notice of the speech but fly blithely on towards Essen, Daddy sipping tea, Margot and I united in a sisterly fashion by the sleeping Mouschi, who is monopolizing both our knees. Margot's hair is in curlers, I am wearing a nightdress, which is much too small, too narrow, and too short.

It all looks so intimate, snug, peaceful, and this time it is too; yet I await the consequences with horror. They can hardly wait till the end of the speech, stamping their feet, so impatient are they to get down to discussing it.

Brr, brr, brr—they egg each other on until the arguments lead to discord and quarrels.

Yours, Anne

Tuesday, 28 March, 1944

Dearest Kitty,

I could write a lot more about politics, but I have heaps of other things to tell you today. First, Mummy has more or less forbidden me to go upstairs so often, because, according to her, Mrs. Van Daan is jealous. Secondly, Peter has invited Margot to join us upstairs; I don't know whether it's just out of politeness or whether he really means it. Thirdly, I went and asked Daddy if he thought I need pay any regard to Mrs. Van Daan's jealousy, and he didn't think so. What next? Mummy is cross, perhaps jealous too. Daddy doesn't grudge us these times together, and thinks it's nice that we get on so well. Margot is fond of Peter too, but feels that two's company and three's a crowd.

Mummy thinks that Peter is in love with me; quite frankly, I only wish he were, then we'd be quits and really be able to get to know each other. She also says that he keeps on looking at me. Now, I suppose that's true, but still I can't help it if he looks at my dimples and we wink at each other occasionally, can I?

I'm in a very difficult position. Mummy is against me and I'm against her, Daddy closes his eyes and tries not to see the silent battle between us. Mummy is sad, because she does really love me, while I'm not in the least bit sad, because I don't think she understands. And Peter—I don't want to give Peter up, he's such a darling. I admire him so; it can grow into something beautiful between us; why do the "old 'uns" have to poke their noses in all the time? Luckily I'm quite used to hiding my feelings and I manage extremely well not to let them see how mad I am about him. Will he ever say anything? Will I ever feel his cheek against mine, like I felt Petel's cheek in my dream? Oh, Peter and Petel, you are one and the same!

171

They don't understand us; won't they ever grasp that we are happy, just sitting together and not saying a word. They don't understand what has driven us together like this. Oh, when will all these difficulties be overcome? And yet it is good to overcome them, because then the end will be all the more wonderful. When he lies with his head on his arm with his eyes closed, then he is still a child; when he plays with Boche, he is loving; when he carries potatoes or anything heavy, then he is strong; when he goes and watches the shooting, or looks for burglars in the darkness, then he is brave; and when he is so awkward and clumsy, then he is just a pet.

I like it much better if he explains something to me than when I have to teach him; I would really adore him to be my superior in almost everything.

What do we care about the two mothers? Oh, but if only he would speak!

Yours, Anne

Wednesday, 29 March, 1944

Dear Kitty,

Bolkestein, an M.P., was speaking on the Dutch News from London, and he said that they ought to make a collection of diaries and letters after the war. Of course, they all made a rush at my diary immediately. Just imagine how interesting it would be if I were to publish a romance of the "Secret Annexe." The title [1] alone would be enough to make people think it was a detective story.

But, seriously, it would seem quite funny ten years after the war if we Jews were to tell how we lived and what we ate and talked about here. Although I tell you a lot, still, even so, you only know very little of our lives.

How scared the ladies are during the air raids. For instance, on Sunday, when 350 British planes dropped half a million kilos of bombs on Ijmuiden, how the houses trembled like a wisp of grass in the wind, and who

[1] The original title of this diary was *Het Achterhuis*. There is no exact translation into English, the nearest being *The Secret Annexe.*

knows how many epidemics now rage. You don't know anything about all these things, and I would need to keep on writing the whole day if I were to tell you everything in detail. People have to line up for vegetables and all kinds of other things; doctors are unable to visit the sick, because if they turn their backs on their cars for a moment, they are stolen; burglaries and thefts abound, so much so that you wonder what has taken hold of the Dutch for them suddenly to have become such thieves. Little children of eight and eleven years break the windows of people's homes and steal whatever they can lay their hands on. No one dares to leave his house unoccupied for five minutes, because if you go, your things go too. Every day there are announcements in the newspapers offering rewards for the return of lost property, typewriters, Persian rugs, electric clocks, cloth, etc., etc. Electric clocks in the streets are dismantled, public telephones are pulled to pieces—down to the last thread. Morale among the population can't be good, the weekly rations are not enough to last for two days except the coffee substitute. The invasion is a long time coming, and the men have to go to Germany. The children are ill or undernourished, everyone is wearing old clothes and old shoes. A new sole costs 7.50 florins in the black market; moreover, hardly any of the shoemakers will accept shoe repairs or, if they do, you have to wait months, during which time the shoes often disappear.

There's one good thing in the midst of it all, which is that as the food gets worse and the measures against the people more severe, so sabotage against the authorities steadily increases. The people in the food offices, the police, officials, they all either work with their fellow citizens and help them or they tell tales on them and have them sent to prison. Fortunately, only a small percentage of Dutch people are on the wrong side.

Yours, Anne

Dear Kitty,

Think of it, it's still pretty cold, but most people have been without coal for about a month—pleasant, eh! In general public feeling over the Russian front is optimistic again, because that is terrific! You know I don't write much about politics, but I must just tell you where they are now; they are right by the Polish border and have reached the Pruth near Rumania. They are close to Odessa. Every evening here they expect an extra communiqué from Stalin.

They fire off so many salvos in Moscow to celebrate their victories that the city must rumble and shake just about every day—whether they think it's fun to pretend that the war is close at hand again or that they know of no other way of expressing their joy, I don't know!

Hungary is occupied by German troops. There are still a million Jews there, so they too will have had it now.

The chatter about Peter and me has calmed down a bit now. We are very good friends, are together a lot and discuss every imaginable subject. It is awfully nice never to have to keep a check on myself as I would have to with other boys, whenever we get on to precarious ground. We were talking, for instance, about blood and via that subject we began talking about menstruation. He thinks we women are pretty tough. Why on earth? My life has improved, greatly improved. God has not left me alone and will not leave me alone.

Yours, Anne

Saturday, 1 April, 1944

Dear Kitty,

And yet everything is still so difficult; I expect you can guess what I mean, can't you? I am so longing for a kiss, the kiss that is so long in coming. I wonder if all the time he still regards me as a friend? Am I nothing more?

You know and I know that I am strong, that I can carry most of my burdens alone. I have never been used to sharing my troubles with anyone, I have never clung to my mother, but now I would so love to lay my head on "his" shoulder just once and remain still.

I can't, I simply can't ever forget that dream of Peter's cheek, when it was all, all so good! Wouldn't he long for it too? Is it that he is just too shy to acknowledge his love? Why does he want me with him so often? Oh, why doesn't he speak?

I'd better stop, I must be quiet, I shall remain strong and with a bit of patience the other will come too, but— and that is the worst of it—it looks just as if I'm running after him; *I* am always the one who goes upstairs, *he* doesn't come to me.

But that is just because of the rooms, and he is sure to understand the difficulty.

Oh, yes, and there's more he'll understand.

Yours, Anne

Monday, 3 April, 1944

Dear Kitty,

Contrary to my usual custom, I will for once write more fully about food because it has become a very difficult and important matter, not only here in the "Secret Annexe" but in the whole of Holland, all Europe, and even beyond.

In the twenty-one months that we've spent here we have been through a good many "food cycles"—you'll understand what that means in a minute. When I talk of "food cycles" I mean periods in which one has nothing else to eat but one particular dish or kind of vegetable. We had nothing but endive for a long time, day in, day out, endive with sand, endive without sand, stew with endive, boiled or *en casserole;* then it was spinach, and after that followed kohlrabi, salsify, cucumbers, tomatoes, sauerkraut, etc., etc.

For instance, it's really disagreeable to eat a lot of sauerkraut for lunch and supper every day, but you do it if you're hungry. However, we have the most delightful period of all now, because we don't get any fresh vegetables at all. Our weekly menu for supper consists of kidney beans, pea soup, potatoes with dumplings, potato-chalet and, by the grace of God, occasionally turnip tops or rotten carrots, and then the kidney beans once again. We eat potatoes at every meal, beginning with breakfast, because of the bread shortage. We make our soup from kidney or haricot beans, potatoes, Julienne soup in packets. French beans in packets, kidney beans in packets. Everything contains beans, not to mention the bread!

In the evening we always have potatoes with gravy substitute and—thank goodness we've still got it—beetroot salad. I must still tell you about the dumplings, which we make out of government flour, water, and yeast. They are so sticky and tough, they lie like stones in one's stomach—ah, well!

The great attraction each week is a slice of liver sausage, and jam on dry bread. But we're still alive, and quite often we even enjoy our poor meals.

Yours, Anne

Tuesday, 4 April, 1944

Dear Kitty,

For a long time I haven't had any idea of what I was working for any more; the end of the war is so terribly far away, so unreal, like a fairy tale. If the war isn't over by September I shan't go to school any more, because I don't want to be two years behind. Peter filled my days—nothing but Peter, dreams and thoughts until Saturday, when I felt so utterly miserable; oh, it was terrible. I was holding back my tears all the while I was with Peter, then laughed with Van Daan over lemon punch, was cheerful and excited, but the moment I was alone I knew that I would have to cry my heart out. So, clad in my nightdress, I let myself go and slipped down onto the floor. First I said my long prayer very earnestly, then I cried with my head on my arms, my knees bent up, on the bare floor, completely folded up. One large sob brought me back to earth again, and I quelled my tears because I didn't want them to hear anything in the next room. Then I began trying to talk some courage into myself. I could only say: "I must, I must, I must . . ." Completely stiff from the unnatural position, I fell against the side of the bed and fought on, until I climbed into bed again just before half past ten. It was over!

And now it's all over. I must work, so as not to be a fool, to get on, to become a journalist, because that's what I want! I know that I can write, a couple of my stories are good, my descriptions of the "Secret Annexe" are humorous, there's a lot in my diary that speaks, but—whether I have real talent remains to be seen.

"Eva's Dream" is my best fairy tale, and the queer thing about it is that I don't know where it comes from. Quite a lot of "Cady's Life" is good too, but, on the whole, it's nothing.

I am the best and sharpest critic of my own work. I know myself what is and what is not well written. Anyone who doesn't write doesn't know how wonderful it is; I used to bemoan the fact that I couldn't draw at all, but now I am more than happy that I can at least write. And if I haven't any talent for writing books or newspaper articles, well, then I can always write for myself.

I want to get on; I can't imagine that I would have to lead the same sort of life as Mummy and Mrs. Van Daan and all the women who do their work and are then forgotten. I must have something besides a husband and children, something that I can devote myself to!

I want to go on living even after my death! And therefore I am grateful to God for giving me this gift, this possibility of developing myself and of writing, of expressing all that is in me.

I can shake off everything if I write; my sorrows disappear, my courage is reborn. But, and that is the great question, will I ever be able to write anything great, will I ever become a journalist or a writer? I hope so, oh, I hope so very much, for I can recapture everything when I write, my thoughts, my ideals and my fantasies.

I haven't done anything more to "Cady's Life" for ages; in my mind I know exactly how to go on, but somehow it doesn't flow from my pen. Perhaps I never shall finish it, it may land up in the wastepaper basket, or the fire . . . that's a horrible idea, but then I think to myself, "At the age of fourteen and with so little experience, how can you write about philosophy?"

So I go on again with fresh courage; I think I shall succeed, because I want to write!

Yours, Anne

Thursday, 6 April, 1944

Dear Kitty,

You asked me what my hobbies and interests were, so I want to reply. I warn you, however, that there are heaps of them, so don't get a shock!

First of all: writing, but that hardly counts as a hobby.

Number two: family trees. I've been searching for family trees of the French, German, Spanish, English, Austrian, Russian, Norwegian, and Dutch royal families in all the newspapers, books, and pamphlets I can find. I've made great progress with a lot of them, as, for a long time already, I've been taking down notes from all the biographies and history books that I read; I even copy out many passages of history.

My third hobby then is history, on which Daddy has already bought me a lot of books. I can hardly wait for the day that I shall be able to comb through the books in a public library.

Number four is Greek and Roman mythology. I have various books about this too.

Other hobbies are film stars and family photos. Mad on books and reading. Have a great liking for history of art, poets and painters. I may go in for music later on. I have a great loathing for algebra, geometry, and figures.

178

I enjoy all the other school subjects, but history above all!

Yours, Anne

Tuesday, 11 April, 1944

Dear Kitty,

My head throbs, I honestly don't know where to begin. On Friday (Good Friday) we played Monopoly, Saturday afternoon too. These days passed quickly and uneventfully. On Sunday afternoon, on my invitation, Peter came to my room at half past four; at a quarter past five we went to the front attic, where we remained until six o'clock. There was a beautiful Mozart concert on the radio from six o'clock until a quarter past seven. I enjoyed it all very much, but especially the "Kleine Nachtmusik." I can hardly listen in the room because I'm always so inwardly stirred when I hear lovely music.

On Sunday evening Peter and I went to the front attic together and, in order to sit comfortably, we took with us a few divan cushions that we were able to lay our hands on. We seated ourselves on one packing case. Both the case and the cushions were very narrow, so we sat absolutely squashed together, leaning against other cases. Mouschi kept us company too, so we weren't unchaperoned.

Suddenly, at a quarter to nine, Mr. Van Daan whistled and asked if we had one of Dussel's cushions. We both jumped up and went downstairs with cushion, cat, and Van Daan.

A lot of trouble arose out of this cushion, because Dussel was annoyed that we had one of his cushions, one that he used as a pillow. He was afraid that there might be fleas in it and made a great commotion about his beloved cushion! Peter and I put two hard brushes in his bed as a revenge. We had a good laugh over this little interlude!

Our fun didn't last long. At half past nine Peter knocked softly on the door and asked Daddy if he would just help him upstairs over a difficult English sentence.

"That's a blind," I said to Margot, "anyone could see through that one!" I was right. They were in the act of breaking into the warehouse. Daddy, Van Daan, Dussel, and Peter were downstairs in a flash. Margot, Mummy, Mrs. Van Daan, and I stayed upstairs and waited.

Four frightened women just have to talk, so talk we did, until we heard a bang downstairs. After that all was quiet, the clock struck a quarter to ten. The color had vanished from our faces; we were still quiet, although we were afraid. Where could the men be? What was that bang? Would they be fighting the burglars? Ten o'clock, footsteps on the stairs: Daddy, white and nervous, entered, followed by Mr. Van Daan. "Lights out, creep upstairs, we expect the police in the house!"

There was no time to be frightened: the lights went out, I quickly grabbed a jacket, and we were upstairs. "What has happened? Tell us quickly!" There was no one to tell us, the men having disappeared downstairs again. Only at ten past ten did they reappear; two kept watch at Peter's open window, the door to the landing was closed, the swinging cupboard shut. We hung a jersey round the night light, and after that they told us:

Peter heard two loud bangs on the landing, ran downstairs, and saw there was a large plank out of the left half of the door. He dashed upstairs, warned the "Home Guard" of the family, and the four of them proceeded downstairs. When they entered the warehouse, the burglars were in the act of enlarging the hole. Without further thought Van Daan shouted: "Police!"

A few hurried steps outside, and the burglars had fled. In order to avoid the hole being noticed by the police, a plank was put against it, but a good hard kick from outside sent it flying to the ground. The men were perplexed at such impudence, and both Van Daan and Peter felt murder welling up within them; Van Daan beat on the ground with a chopper, and all was quiet again. Once more they wanted to put the plank in front of the hole. Disturbance! A married couple outside shone a torch through the opening, lighting up the whole warehouse. "Hell!" muttered one of the men, and now they switched over from their role of police to that of burglars. The four of them sneaked upstairs, Peter quickly opened the doors and windows of the kitchen and private office, flung the telephone onto the floor, and finally the four of them landed behind the swinging cupboard.

END OF PART ONE

The married couple with the torch would probably have warned the police: it was Sunday evening, Easter Sunday, no one at the office on Easter Monday, so none of us could budge until Tuesday morning. Think of it, waiting in such fear for two nights and a day! No one had anything to suggest, so we simply sat there in pitch-darkness, because Mrs. Van Daan in her fright had unintentionally turned the lamp right out; talked in whispers, and at every creak one heard "Sh! sh!"

It turned half past ten, eleven, but not a sound; Daddy and Van Daan joined us in turns. Then a quarter past eleven, a bustle and noise downstairs. Everyone's breath was audible, otherwise no one moved. Footsteps in the house, in the private office, kitchen, then . . . on our staircase. No one breathed audibly now, footsteps on our staircase, then a rattling of the swinging cupboard. This moment is indescribable. "Now we are lost!" I said, and could see us all being taken away by the Gestapo that very night. Twice they rattled at the cupboard, then there was nothing, the footsteps withdrew, we were saved so far. A shiver seemed to pass from one to another, I heard someone's teeth chattering, no one said a word.

There was not another sound in the house, but a light was burning on our landing, right in front of the cupboard. Could that be because it was a secret cupboard? Perhaps the police had forgotten the light? Would someone come back to put it out? Tongues loosened, there was no one in the house any longer, perhaps there was someone on guard outside.

Next we did three things: we went over again what we supposed had happened, we trembled with fear, and we

181

had to go to the lavatory. The buckets were in the attic, so all we had was Peter's tin wastepaper basket. Van Daan went first, then Daddy, but Mummy was too shy to face it. Daddy brought the wastepaper basket into the room, where Margot, Mrs. Van Daan, and I gladly made use of it. Finally Mummy decided to do so too. People kept on asking for paper—fortunately I had some in my pocket!

The tin smelled ghastly, everything went on in a whisper, we were tired, it was twelve o'clock. "Lie down on the floor then and sleep." Margot and I were each given a pillow and one blanket; Margot lying just near the store cupboard and I between the table legs. The smell wasn't quite so bad when one was on the floor, but still Mrs. Van Daan quietly brought some chlorine, a tea towel over the pot serving as a second expedient.

Talk, whispers, fear, stink, flatulation, and always someone on the pot; then try to go to sleep! However, by half past two I was so tired that I knew no more until half past three. I awoke when Mrs. Van Daan laid her head on my foot.

"For heaven's sake, give me something to put on!" I asked. I was given something, but don't ask what—a pair of woolen knickers over my pajamas, a red jumper, and a black skirt, white oversocks and a pair of sports stockings full of holes. Then Mrs. Van Daan sat in the chair and her husband came and lay on my feet. I lay thinking till half past three, shivering the whole time, which prevented Van Daan from sleeping. I prepared myself for the return of the police, then we'd have to say that we were in hiding; they would either be good Dutch people, then we'd be saved, or N.S.B.-ers,[1] then we'd have to bribe them!

"In that case, destroy the radio," sighed Mrs. Van Daan. "Yes, in the stove!" replied her husband. "If they find us, then let them find the radio as well!"

"Then they will find Anne's diary," added Daddy. "Burn it then," suggested the most terrified member of the

[1] The Dutch National Socialist Movement.

party. This, and when the police rattled the cupboard door, were my worst moments. "Not my diary; if my diary goes, I go with it!" But luckily Daddy didn't answer.

There is no object in recounting all the conversations that I can still remember; so much was said. I comforted Mrs. Van Daan, who was very scared. We talked about escaping and being questioned by the Gestapo, about ringing up, and being brave.

"We must behave like soldiers, Mrs. Van Daan. If all is up now, then let's go for Queen and Country, for freedom, truth, and the right, as they always say on the Dutch News from England. The only thing that is really rotten is that we get a lot of other people into trouble too."

Mr. Van Daan changed places with his wife after an hour, and Daddy came and sat beside me. The men smoked non-stop, now and then there was a deep sigh, then someone went on the pot and everything began all over again.

Four o'clock, five o'clock, half past five. Then I went and sat with Peter by his window and listened, so close together that we could feel each other's bodies quivering; we spoke a word or two now and then, and listened attentively. In the room next door they took down the blackout. They wanted to call up Koophuis at seven o'clock and get him to send someone around. Then they wrote down everything they wanted to tell Koophuis over the phone. The risk that the police on guard at the door, or in the warehouse, might hear the telephone was very great, but the danger of the police returning was even greater.

The points were these:

Burglars broken in: police have been in the house, as far as the swinging cupboard, but no further.

Burglars apparently disturbed, forced open the door in the warehouse and escaped through the garden.

Main entrance bolted, Kraler must have used the second door when he left. The typewriters and adding machine are safe in the black case in the private office.

Try to warn Henk and fetch the key from Elli, then go

and look around the office—on the pretext of feeding the cat.

Everything went according to plan. Koophuis was phoned, the typewriters which we had upstairs were put in the case. Then we sat around the table again and waited for Henk or the police.

Peter had fallen asleep and Van Daan and I were lying on the floor, when we heard loud footsteps downstairs. I got up quietly: "That's Henk."

"No, no, it's the police," some of the others said.

Someone knocked at the door, Miep whistled. This was too much for Mrs. Van Daan, she turned as white as a sheet and sank limply into a chair; had the tension lasted one minute longer she would have fainted.

Our room was a perfect picture when Miep and Henk entered, the table alone would have been worth photographing! A copy of *Cinema and Theater*, covered with jam and a remedy for diarrhea, opened at a page of dancing girls, two jam pots, two started loaves of bread, a mirror, comb, matches, ash, cigarettes, tobacco, ash tray, books, a pair of pants, a torch, toilet paper, etc., etc., lay jumbled together in variegated splendor.

Of course Henk and Miep were greeted with shouts and tears. Henk mended the hole in the door with some planks, and soon went off again to inform the police of the burglary. Miep had also found a letter under the warehouse door from the night watchman Slagter, who had noticed the hole and warned the police, whom he would also visit.

So we had half an hour to tidy ourselves. I've never seen such a change take place in half an hour. Margot and I took the bedclothes downstairs, went to the W.C., washed, and did our teeth and hair. After that I tidied the room a bit and went upstairs again. The table there was already cleared, so we ran off some water and made coffee and tea, boiled the milk, and laid the table for lunch. Daddy and Peter emptied the potties and cleaned them with warm water and chlorine.

At eleven o'clock we sat round the table with Henk,

who was back by that time, and slowly things began to be more normal and cozy again. Henk's story was as follows:

Mr. Slagter was asleep, but his wife told Henk that her husband had found the hole in our door when he was doing his tour round the canals, and that he had called a policeman, who had gone through the building with him. He would be coming to see Kraler on Tuesday and would tell him more then. At the police station they knew nothing of the burglary yet, but the policeman had made a note of it at once and would come and look round on Tuesday. On the way back Henk happened to meet our greengrocer at the corner, and told him that the house had been broken into. "I know that," he said quite coolly. "I was passing last evening with my wife and saw the hole in the door. My wife wanted to walk on, but I just had a look in with my torch; then the thieves cleared at once. To be on the safe side, I didn't ring up the police, as with you I didn't think it was the thing to do. I don't know anything, but I guess a lot."

Henk thanked him and went on. The man obviously guesses that we're here, because he always brings the potatoes during the lunch hour. Such a nice man!

It was one by the time Henk had gone and we'd finished doing the dishes. We all went for a sleep. I awoke at a quarter to three and saw that Mr. Dussel had already disappeared. Quite by chance, and with my sleepy eyes, I ran into Peter in the bathroom; he had just come down. We arranged to meet downstairs.

I tidied myself and went down. "Do you still dare to go to the front attic?" he asked. I nodded, fetched my pillow, and we went up to the attic. It was glorious weather, and soon the sirens were wailing; we stayed where we were. Peter put his arm around my shoulder, and I put mine around his and so we remained, our arms around each other, quietly waiting until Margot came to fetch us for coffee at four o'clock.

We finished our bread, drank lemonade and joked (we were able to again), otherwise everything went normally. In the evening I thanked Peter because he was the bravest of us all.

185

None of us has ever been in such danger as that night. God truly protected us; just think of it—the police at our secret cupboard, the light on right in front of it, and still we remained undiscovered.

If the invasion comes, and bombs with it, then it is each man for himself, but in this case the fear was also for our good, innocent protectors. "We are saved, go on saving us!" That is all we can say.

This affair has brought quite a number of changes with it. Mr. Dussel no longer sits downstairs in Kraler's office in the evenings, but in the bathroom instead. Peter goes round the house for a checkup at half past eight and half past nine. Peter isn't allowed to have his window open at nights any more. No one is allowed to pull the plug after half past nine. This evening there's a carpenter coming to make the warehouse doors even stronger.

Now there are debates going on all the time in the "Secret Annexe." Kraler reproached us for our carelessness. Henk, too, said that in a case like that we must never go downstairs. We have been pointedly reminded that we are in hiding, that we are Jews in chains, chained to one spot, without any rights, but with a thousand duties. We Jews mustn't show our feelings, must be brave and strong, must accept all inconveniences and not grumble, must do what is within our power and trust in God. Sometime this terrible war will be over. Surely the time will come when we are people again, and not just Jews.

Who has inflicted this upon us? Who has made us Jews different from all other people? Who has allowed us to suffer so terribly up till now? It is God that has made us as we are, but it will be God, too, who will raise us up again. If we bear all this suffering and if there are still Jews left, when it is over, then Jews, instead of being doomed, will be held up as an example. Who knows, it might even be our religion from which the world and all peoples learn good, and for that reason and that reason only do we have to suffer now. We can never become just Netherlanders, or just English, or representatives of any country for that matter, we will always remain Jews, but we want to, too.

Be brave! Let us remain aware of our task and not grumble, a solution will come, God has never deserted our people. Right through the ages there have been Jews, through all the ages they have had to suffer, but it has made them strong too; the weak fall, but the strong will remain and never go under!

During that night I really felt that I had to die, I waited for the police, I was prepared, as the soldier is on the battlefield. I was eager to lay down my life for the country, but now, now I've been saved again, now my first wish after the war is that I may become Dutch! I love the Dutch, I love this country, I love the language and want to work here. And even if I have to write to the Queen myself, I will not give up until I have reached my goal.

I am becoming still more independent of my parents, young as I am, I face life with more courage than Mummy; my feeling for justice is immovable, and truer than hers. I know what I want, I have a goal, an opinion, I have a religion and love. Let me be myself and then I am satisfied. I know that I'm a woman, a woman with inward strength and plenty of courage.

If God lets me live, I shall attain more than Mummy ever has done, I shall not remain insignificant, I shall work in the world and for mankind!

And now I know that first and foremost I shall require courage and cheerfulness!

Yours, Anne

Friday, 14 April, 1944

Dear Kitty,

The atmosphere here is still extremely strained. Pim has just about reached boiling point. Mrs. Van Daan is in bed with a cold and trumpeting away. Mr. Van Daan grows pale without his fags, Dussel, who is giving up a lot of his comfort, is full of observations, etc., etc.

187

There is no doubt that our luck's not in at the moment. The lavatory leaks and the washer of the tap has gone, but, thanks to our many connections, we shall soon be able to get these things put right.

I am sentimental sometimes, I know that, but there is occasion to be sentimental here at times, when Peter and I are sitting somewhere together on a hard, wooden crate in the midst of masses of rubbish and dust, our arms around each other's shoulders, and very close, he with one of my curls in his hand; when the birds sing outside and you see the trees changing to green, the sun invites one to be out in the open air, when the sky is so blue, then—oh, then, I wish for so much!

One sees nothing but dissatisfied, grumpy faces here, nothing but sighs and suppressed complaints; it really would seem as if suddenly we were very badly off here. If the truth is told, things are just as bad as you yourself care to make them. There's no one here that sets a good example; everyone should see that he gets the better of his own moods. Every day you hear, "If only it was all over."

My work, my hope, my love, my courage, all these things keep my head above water and keep me from complaining.

I really believe, Kits, that I'm slightly bats today, and yet I don't know why. Everything here is so mixed up, nothing's connected any more, and sometimes I very much doubt whether in the future anyone will be interested in all my tosh.

"The unbosomings of an ugly duckling" will be the title of all this nonsense. My diary really won't be much use to Messrs. Bolkestein or Gerbrandy.[1]

Yours, Anne

---

[1] Two members of the wartime Dutch Cabinet-in-Exile in London.

Saturday, 15 April, 1944

Dear Kitty,

"Shock upon shock. Will there ever be an end?" We honestly can ask ourselves that question now. Guess what's the latest. Peter forgot to unbolt the front door (which is bolted on the inside at night) and the lock of the other door doesn't work. The result was that Kraler and the men could not get into the house, so he went to the neighbors, forced open the kitchen window, and entered the building from the back. He is livid at us for being so stupid.

I can tell you, it's upset Peter frightfully. At one meal, when Mummy said she felt more sorry for Peter than anyone else, he almost started to cry. We're all just as much to blame as he is, because nearly every day the men ask whether the door's been unbolted and, just today, no one did.

Perhaps I shall be able to console him a bit later on; I would so love to help him.

Yours, Anne

Sunday morning, just before eleven o'clock,
16 April, 1944

Darlingest Kitty,

Remember yesterday's date, for it is a very important day in my life. Surely it is a great day for every girl when she receives her first kiss? Well, then, it is just as important for me too! Bram's kiss on my right cheek doesn't count any more, likewise the one from Mr. Walker on my right hand.

How did I suddenly come by this kiss? Well, I will tell you.

Yesterday evening at eight o'clock I was sitting with Peter on his divan, it wasn't long before his arm went

189

round me. "Let's move up a bit," I said, "then I don't bump my head against the cupboard." He moved up, almost into the corner, I laid my arm under his and across his back, and he just about buried me, because his arm was hanging on my shoulder.

Now we've sat like this on other occasions, but never so close together as yesterday. He held me firmly against him, my left shoulder against his chest; already my heart began to beat faster, but we had not finished yet. He didn't rest until my head was on his shoulder and his against it. When I sat upright again after about five minutes, he soon took my head in his hands and laid it against him once more. Oh, it was so lovely, I couldn't talk much, the joy was too great. He stroked my cheek and arm a bit awkwardly, played with my curls and our heads lay touching most of the time. I can't tell you, Kitty, the feeling that ran through me all the while. I was too happy for words, and I believe he was as well.

We got up at half past eight. Peter put on his gym shoes, so that when he toured the house he wouldn't make a noise, and I stood beside him. How it came about so suddenly, I don't know, but before we went downstairs he kissed me, through my hair, half on my left cheek, half on my ear; I tore downstairs without looking round, and am simply longing for today!

Yours, Anne

Monday, 17 April, 1944

Dear Kitty,

Do you think that Daddy and Mummy would approve of my sitting and kissing a boy on a divan—a boy of seventeen and a half and a girl of just under fifteen? I don't really think they would, but I must rely on myself over this. It is so quiet and peaceful to lie in his arms and to dream, it is so thrilling to feel his cheek against mine, it is so lovely to know that there is someone waiting for me. But there is indeed a big "but," because will Peter be content to leave it at this? I haven't forgotten his promise already, but . . . he *is* a boy!

I know myself that I'm starting very soon, not even fifteen, and so independent already! It's certainly hard for other people to understand, I know almost for certain that Margot would never kiss a boy unless there had been some talk of an engagement or marriage, but neither Peter nor I have anything like that in mind. I'm sure too that Mummy never touched a man before Daddy. What would my girl friends say about it if they knew that I lay in Peter's arms, my heart against his chest, my head on his shoulder and with his head against mine!

Oh, Anne, how scandalous! But honestly, I don't think it is; we are shut up here, shut away from the world, in fear and anxiety, especially just lately. Why, then, should we who love each other remain apart? Why should we wait until we've reached a suitable age? Why should we bother?

I have taken it upon myself to look after myself; he would never want to cause me sorrow or pain. Why shouldn't I follow the way my heart leads me, if it makes us both happy? All the same, Kitty, I believe you can sense that I'm in doubt, I think it must be my honesty which rebels against doing anything on the sly! Do you think it's my duty to tell Daddy what I'm doing? Do you think we should share our secret with a third person? A lot of the beauty would be lost, but would my conscience feel happier? I will discuss it with "him."

Oh, yes, there's still so much I want to talk to him about, for I don't see the use of only just cuddling each other. To exchange our thoughts, that shows confidence and faith in each other, we would both be sure to profit by it!

Yours, Anne

Dear Kitty,

Everything goes well here. Daddy's just said that he definitely expects large-scale operations to take place before the twentieth of May, both in Russia and Italy, and also in the West; I find it more and more difficult to imagine our liberation from here.

Yesterday Peter and I finally got down to our talk, which had already been put off for at least ten days. I explained everything about girls to him and didn't hesitate to discuss the most intimate things. The evening ended by each giving the other a kiss, just about beside my mouth, it's really a lovely feeling.

Perhaps I'll take my diary up there sometime, to go more deeply into things for once. I don't get any satisfaction out of lying in each other's arms day in, day out, and would so like to feel that he's the same.

We are having a superb spring after our long, lingering winter; April is really glorious, not too hot and not too cold, with little showers now and then. Our chestnut tree is already quite greenish and you can even see little blooms here and there.

Elli gave us a treat on Saturday, by bringing four bunches of flowers, three bunches of narcissus and one of grape hyacinths, the latter being for me.

I must do some algebra, Kitty—good-by.

Yours, Anne

Wednesday, 19 April, 1944

My darling,

Is there anything more beautiful in the world than to sit before an open window and enjoy nature, to listen to the birds singing, feel the sun on your cheeks and have a darling boy in your arms? It is so soothing and peaceful to feel his arms around me, to know that he is close by and yet to remain silent, it can't be bad, for this tranquillity is good. Oh, never to be disturbed again, not even by Mouschi.

Yours, Anne

Friday, 21 April, 1944

Dear Kitty,

Yesterday afternoon I was lying in bed with a sore throat, but since I was already bored on the first day and did not have a temperature, I got up again today. It's the eighteenth birthday of Her Royal Highness Princess Elizabeth of York. The B.B.C. has said that she will not be declared of age yet, though it's usually the case with royal children. We have been asking ourselves what prince this beauty is going to marry, but cannot think of anyone suitable. Perhaps her sister, Princess Margaret Rose, can have Prince Baudouin of Belgium one day.

Here we are having one misfortune after another, Scarcely had the outside doors been strengthened than the warehouse man appeared again. In all probability it was he who stole the potato meal and wants to put the blame on to Elli's shoulders. The whole "Secret Annexe" is understandably het up again. Elli is beside herself with anger.

I want to send in to some paper or other to see if they will take one of my stories, under a pseudonym, of course.

Till next time, darling!

Yours, Anne

Tuesday, 25 April, 1944

Dear Kitty,

Dussel has not been on speaking terms with Van Daan for ten days and just because, ever since the burglary, a whole lot of fresh security measures have been made that don't suit him. He maintains that Van Daan has been shouting at him.

"Everything here happens upside down," he told me. "I am going to speak to your father about it." He is not supposed to sit in the office downstairs on Saturday afternoons and Sundays any more, but he goes on doing it just the same. Van Daan was furious and Father went downstairs to talk to him. Naturally, he kept on inventing excuses, but this time he could not get around even Father. Father now talks to him as little as possible, as Dussel has insulted him. None of us know in what way, but it must have been very bad.

I have written a lovely story called "Blurr, the Explorer," which pleased the three to whom I read it very much.

Yours, Anne

Thursday, 27 April, 1944

Dear Kitty,

Mrs. Van Daan was in such a bad mood this morning, nothing but complaints! First, there's her cold, and she can't get any lozenges, and so much nose-blowing is unendurable. Next, it's that the sun's not shining, that the invasion doesn't come, that we can't look out of the windows, etc., etc. We all had to laugh at her; and she was sporting enough to join in. At the moment I'm reading *The Emperor Charles V*, written by a professor at Göttingen University; he worked at the book for forty years. I read fifty pages in five days; it's impossible to do more. The book has 598 pages, so now you can work out how long it will take me—and there is a second volume to follow. But very interesting.

What doesn't a schoolgirl get to know in a single day! Take me, for example. First, I translated a piece from Dutch into English, about Nelson's last battle. After that, I went through some more of Peter the Great's war against Norway (1700-1721), Charles XII, Augustus the Strong,

194

Stanislavs Leczinsky, Mazeppa, Von Görz, Brandenburg, Pomerania and Denmark, plus the usual dates.

After that I landed up in Brazil, read about Bahia tobacco, the abundance of coffee and the one and a half million inhabitants of Rio de Janeiro, of Pernambuco and Sao Paulo, not forgetting the river Amazon; about Negroes, Mulattos, Mestizos, Whites, more than fifty per cent of the population being illiterate, and the malaria. As there was still some time left, I quickly ran through a family tree. Jan the Elder, Willem Lodewijk, Ernst Casimir I, Hendrik Casimir I, right up to the little Margriet Franciskạ (born in 1943 in Ottawa).

Twelve o'clock: In the attic, I continued my program with the history of the Church—Phew! Till one o'clock.

Just after two, the poor child sat working ('hm, 'hm!) again, this time studying narrow- and broad-nosed monkeys. Kitty, tell me quickly how many toes a hippopotamus has! Then followed the Bible, Noah and the Ark, Shem, Ham, and Japheth. After that Charles V. Then with Peter: *The Colonel*, in English by Thackeray. Heard my French verbs and then compared the Mississippi with the Missouri.

I've still got a cold and have given it to Margot as well as to Mummy and Daddy. As long as Peter doesn't get it! He called me his "Eldorado" and wanted a kiss. Of course, I couldn't! Funny boy! But still, he's a darling.

Enough for today, good-by!

Yours, Anne

Friday, 28 April, 1944

Dear Kitty,

I have never forgotten my dream about Peter Wessel (see beginning of January). If I think of it, I can still feel his cheek against mine now, and recall that lovely feeling that made everything good.

Sometimes I have had the same feeling here with Peter, but never to such an extent, until yesterday, when we were, as usual, sitting on the divan, our arms around each

195

other's waists. Then suddenly the ordinary Anne slipped away and a second Anne took her place, a second Anne who is not reckless and jocular, but one who just wants to love and be gentle.

I sat pressed closely against him and felt a wave of emotion come over me, tears sprang into my eyes, the left one trickled onto his dungarees, the right one ran down my nose and also fell onto his dungarees. Did he notice? He made no move or sign to show that he did. I wonder if he feels the same as I do? He hardly said a word. Does he know that he has two Annes before him? These questions must remain unanswered.

At half past eight I stood up and went to the window, where we always say good-by. I was still trembling, I was still Anne number two. He came towards me, I flung my arms around his neck and gave him a kiss on his left cheek, and was about to kiss the other cheek, when my lips met his and we pressed them together. In a whirl we were clasped in each other's arms, again and again, never to leave off. Oh, Peter does so need tenderness. For the first time in his life he has discovered a girl, has seen for the first time that even the most irritating girls have another side to them, that they have hearts and can be different when you are alone with them. For the first time in his life he has given of himself and, having never had a boy or girl friend in his life before, shown his real self. Now we have found each other. For that matter, I didn't know him either, like him having never had a trusted friend, and this is what it has come to. . . .

Once more there is a question which gives me no peace: "Is it right? Is it right that I should have yielded so soon, that I am so ardent, just as ardent and eager as Peter himself? May I, a girl, let myself go to this extent?" There is but *one* answer: "I have longed so much and for so long —I am so lonely—and now I have found consolation."

In the mornings we just behave in an ordinary way, in the afternoons more or less so (except just occasionally); but in the evenings the suppressed longings of the whole day, the happiness and the blissful memories of all the previous occasions come to the surface and we only think of each other. Every evening, after the last kiss, I would like to dash away, not to look into his eyes any more—away, away, alone in the darkness.

And what do I have to face, when I reach the bottom of the staircase? Bright lights, questions, and laughter; I have to swallow it all and not show a thing. My heart still feels too much; I can't get over a shock such as I received yesterday all at once. The Anne who is gentle shows herself too little anyway, and, therefore, will not allow herself to be suddenly driven into the background. Peter has touched my emotions more deeply than anyone has ever done before—except in my dreams. Peter has taken possession of me and turned me inside out; surely it goes without saying that anyone would require a rest and a little while to recover from such an upheaval?

Oh Peter, what have you done to me? What do you want of me? Where will this lead us? Oh, now I understand Elli; now, now that I am going through this myself, now I understand her doubt; if I were older and he should ask me to marry him, what should I answer? Anne, be honest! You would not be able to marry him, but yet, it would be hard to let him go. Peter hasn't enough character yet, not enough will power, too little courage and strength. He is still a child in his heart of hearts, he is no older than I am; he is only searching for tranquillity and happiness.

Am I only fourteen? Am I really still a silly little schoolgirl? Am I really so inexperienced about everything? I have more experience than most; I have been through things that hardly anyone of my age has undergone. I am afraid of myself, I am afraid that in my longing I am giving myself too quickly. How, later on, can it ever go right with other boys? Oh, it is so difficult, always battling with one's heart and reason; in its own time, each will speak, but do I know for certain that I have chosen the right time?

Yours, Anne

Dear Kitty,

On Saturday evening I asked Peter whether he thought that I ought to tell Daddy a bit about us; when we'd discussed it a little, he came to the conclusion that I should. I was glad, for it shows that he's an honest boy. As soon as I got downstairs I went off with Daddy to get some water; and while we were on the stairs I said, "Daddy, I expect you've gathered that when we're together Peter and I don't sit miles apart. Do you think it's wrong?" Daddy didn't reply immediately, then said, "No, I don't think it's wrong, but you must be careful, Anne, you're in such a confined space here." When we went upstairs, he said something else on the same lines. On Sunday morning he called me to him and said, "Anne, I have thought more about what you said." I felt scared already. "It's not really very right—here in this house; I thought that you were just pals. Is Peter in love?"

"Oh, of course not," I replied.

"You know that I understand both of you, but you must be the one to hold back. Don't go upstairs so often, don't encourage him more than you can help. It is the man who is always the active one in these things; the woman can hold him back. It is quite different under normal circumstances, when you are free, you see other boys and girls, you can get away sometimes, play games and do all kinds of other things; but here, if you're together a lot, and you want to get away, you can't; you see each other every hour of the day—in fact, all the time. Be careful, Anne, and don't take it too seriously!"

"I don't, Daddy, but Peter is a decent boy, really a nice boy!"

"Yes, but he is not a strong character; he can be easily influenced, for good, but also for bad; I hope for his sake that his good side will remain uppermost, because, by nature, that is how he is."

198

We talked on for a bit and agreed that Daddy should talk to him too.

On Sunday morning in the attic he asked, "And have you talked to your father, Anne?"

"Yes," I replied, "I'll tell you about it. Daddy doesn't think it's bad, but he says that here, where we're so close together all the time, clashes may easily arise."

"But we agreed, didn't we, never to quarrel; and I'm determined to stick to it!"

"So will I, Peter, but Daddy didn't think that it was like this, he just thought we were pals; do you think that we still can be?"

"I can—what about you?"

"Me too, I told Daddy that I trusted you. I do trust you, Peter, just as much as I trust Daddy, and I believe you to be worthy of it. You are, aren't you, Peter?"

"I hope so." (He was very shy and rather red in the face.)

"I believe in you, Peter," I went on, "I believe that you have good qualities, and that you'll get on in the world."

After that, we talked about other things. Later I said, "If we come out of here, I know quite well that you won't bother about me any more!"

He flared right up. "That's not true, Anne, oh no, I won't let you think that of me!"

Then I was called away.

Daddy has talked to him; he told me about it today. "Your father thought that the friendship might develop into love sooner or later," he said. But I replied that we would keep a check on ourselves.

Daddy doesn't want me to go upstairs so much in the evenings now, but I don't want that. Not only because I like being with Peter; I have told him that I trust him. I do trust him and I want to show him that I do, which can't happen if I stay downstairs through lack of trust.

No, I'm going!

In the meantime the Dussel drama has righted itself again. At supper on Saturday evening he apologized in beautiful Dutch. Van Daan was nice about it straight away; it must have taken Dussel a whole day to learn that little lesson off by heart.

Sunday, his birthday, passed peacefully. We gave him a bottle of good 1919 wine, from the Van Daans (who could give their presents now after all), a bottle of piccalilli and a packet of razor blades, a jar of lemon jam from Kraler, a book, *Little Martin*, from Miep, and a plant from Elli. He treated each one of us to an egg.

Yours, Anne

Wednesday, 3 May, 1944

Dear Kitty,

First, just the news of the week. We're having a holiday from politics; there is nothing, absolutely nothing to announce. I too am gradually beginning to believe that the invasion will come. After all, they can't let the Russians clear up everything; for that matter, they're not doing anything either at the moment.

Mr. Koophuis comes to the office every morning again now. He's got a new spring for Peter's divan, so Peter will have to do some upholstering, about which, quite understandably, he doesn't feel a bit happy.

Have I told you that Boche has disappeared? Simply vanished—we haven't seen a sign of her since Thursday of last week. I expect she's already in the cats' heaven, while some animal lover is enjoying a succulent meal from her. Perhaps some little girl will be given a fur cap out of her skin. Peter is very sad about it.

Since Saturday we've changed over, and have lunch at half past eleven in the morning, so we have to last out with one cupful of porridge; this saves us a meal. Vegetables are still very difficult to obtain: we had rotten boiled lettuce this afternoon. Ordinary lettuce, spinach, and boiled lettuce, there's nothing else. With these we eat rotten potatoes, so it's a delicious combination!

As you can easily imagine we often ask ourselves here

despairingly: "What, oh, what is the use of the war? Why can't people live peacefully together? Why all this destruction?"

The question is very understandable, but no one has found a satisfactory answer to it so far. Yes, why do they make still more gigantic planes, still heavier bombs and, at the same time, prefabricated houses for reconstruction? Why should millions be spent daily on the war and yet there's not a penny available for medical services, artists, or for poor people?

Why do some people have to starve, while there are surpluses rotting in other parts of the world? Oh, why are people so crazy?

I don't believe that the big men, the politicians and the capitalists alone, are guilty of the war. Oh no, the little man is just as guilty, otherwise the peoples of the world would have risen in revolt long ago! There's in people simply an urge to destroy, an urge to kill, to murder and rage, and until all mankind, without exception, undergoes a great change, wars will be waged, everything that has been built up, cultivated, and grown will be destroyed and disfigured, after which mankind will have to begin all over again.

I have often been downcast, but never in despair; I regard our hiding as a dangerous adventure, romantic and interesting at the same time. In my diary I treat all the privations as amusing. I have made up my mind now to lead a different life from other girls and, later on, different from ordinary housewives. My start has been so very full of interest, and that is the sole reason why I have to laugh at the humorous side of the most dangerous moments.

I am young and I possess many buried qualities; I am young and strong and am living a great adventure; I am still in the midst of it and can't grumble the whole day long. I have been given a lot, a happy nature, a great deal of cheerfulness and strength. Every day I feel that I am developing inwardly, that the liberation is drawing nearer and how beautiful nature is, how good the people are about me, how interesting this adventure is! Why, then, should I be in despair?

Yours, Anne

Friday, 5 May, 1944

Dear Kitty,

Daddy is not pleased with me; he thought that after our talk on Sunday I automatically wouldn't go upstairs every evening. He doesn't want any "necking," a word I can't bear. It was bad enough talking about it, why must he make it so unpleasant now? I shall talk to him today. Margot has given me some good advice, so listen; this is roughly what I want to say:

"I believe, Daddy, that you expect a declaration from me, so I will give it you. You are disappointed in me, as you had expected more reserve from me, and I suppose you want me to be just as a fourteen-year-old should be. But that's where you're mistaken!

"Since we've been here, from July 1942 until a few weeks ago, I can assure you that I haven't had an easy time. If you only knew how I cried in the evening, how unhappy I was, how lonely I felt, then you would understand that I want to go upstairs!

"I have now reached the stage that I can live entirely on my own, without Mummy's support or anyone else's for that matter. But it hasn't just happened in a night; it's been a bitter, hard struggle and I've shed many a tear, before I became as independent as I am now. You can laugh at me and not believe me, but that can't harm me. I know that I'm a separate individual and I don't feel in the least bit responsible to any of you. I am only telling you this because I thought that otherwise you might think that I was underhand, but I don't have to give an account of my deeds to anyone but myself.

"When I was in difficulties you all closed your eyes and stopped up your ears and didn't help me; on the contrary, I received nothing but warnings not to be so boisterous. I was only boisterous so as not to be miserable all the time.

I was reckless so as not to hear that persistent voice within me continually. I played a comedy for a year and a half, day in, day out, I never grumbled, never lost my cue, nothing like that—and now, now the battle is over. I have won! I am independent both in mind and body. I don't need a mother any more, for all this conflict has made me strong.

"And now, now that I'm on top of it, now that I know that I've fought the battle, now I want to be able to go on in my own way too, the way that I think is right. You can't and mustn't regard me as fourteen, for all these troubles have made me older; I shall not be sorry for what I have done, but shall act as I think I can. You can't coax me into not going upstairs; *either* you forbid it, *or* you trust me through thick and thin, but then leave me in peace as well!"

Yours, Anne

Saturday, 6 May, 1944

Dear Kitty,

I put a letter, in which I wrote what I explained to you yesterday, in Daddy's pocket before supper yesterday. After reading it, he was, according to Margot, very upset for the rest of the evening. (I was upstairs doing the dishes.) Poor Pim, I might have known what the effect of such an epistle would be. He is so sensitive! I immediately told Peter not to ask or say anything more. Pim hasn't said any more about it to me. Is that yet in store, I wonder?

Here everything is going on more or less normally again. What they tell us about the prices and the people outside is almost unbelievable, half a pound of tea costs 350 florins,[1] a pound of coffee 80 florins, butter 35 florins per pound, an egg 1.45 florin. People pay 14 florins for an ounce of Bulgarian tobacco! Everyone deals in the black market, every errand boy has something to offer. Our baker's boy got hold of some sewing silk, 0.9 florin for a

[1] A florin is equal to approximately twenty-eight cents.

203

thin little skein, the milkman manages to get clandestine
ration cards, the undertaker delivers the cheese. Burglaries, murders, and theft go on daily. The police and
night watchmen join in just as strenuously as the profes-
sionals, everyone wants something in their empty stomachs and because wage increases are forbidden the people
simply have to swindle. The police are continually on the
go, tracing girls of fifteen, sixteen, seventeen and older,
who are reported missing every day.

Yours, Anne

Sunday morning, 7 May, 1944

Dear Kitty,
Daddy and I had a long talk yesterday afternoon, I
cried terribly and he joined in. Do you know what he said
to me, Kitty? "I have received many letters in my life, but
this is certainly the most unpleasant! You, Anne, who have
received such love from your parents, you, who have
parents who are always ready to help you, who have always defended you whatever it might be, can you talk of
feeling no responsibility towards us? You feel wronged
and deserted; no, Anne, you have done us a great injustice!

"Perhaps you didn't mean it like that, but it is what you
wrote; no, Anne, we haven't deserved such a reproach as
this!"

Oh, I have failed miserably; this is certainly the worst
thing I've ever done in my life. I was only trying to show
off with my crying and my tears, just trying to appear big,
so that he would respect me. Certainly, I have had a lot
of unhappiness, but to accuse the good Pim, who has done
and still does do everything for me—no, that was too low
for words.

It's right that for once I've been taken down from my
inaccessible pedestal, that my pride has been shaken a bit,
for I was becoming much too taken up with myself again.
What Miss Anne does is by no means always right! Anyone who can cause such unhappiness to someone else,

someone he professes to love, and on purpose, too, is low, very low!

And the way Daddy has forgiven me makes me feel more than ever ashamed of myself, he is going to throw the letter in the fire and is so sweet to me now, just as if he had done something wrong. No, Anne, you still have a tremendous lot to learn, begin by doing that first, instead of looking down on others and accusing them!

I have had a lot of sorrow, but who hasn't at my age? I have played the clown a lot too, but I was hardly conscious of it; I felt lonely, but hardly ever in despair! I ought to be deeply ashamed of myself, and indeed I am.

What is done cannot be undone, but one can prevent it happening again. I want to start from the beginning again and it can't be difficult, now that I have Peter. With him to support me, I can and will!

I'm not alone any more; he loves me. I love him, I have my books, my storybook and my diary, I'm not so frightfully ugly, not utterly stupid, have a cheerful temperament and want to have a good character!

Yes, Anne, you've felt deeply that your letter was too hard and that it was untrue. To think that you were even proud of it! I will take Daddy as my example, and I *will* improve.

Yours, Anne

Monday, 8 May, 1944

Dear Kitty,

Have I ever really told you anything about our family? I don't think I have, so I will begin now. My father's parents were very rich. His father had worked himself right up and his mother came from a prominent family, who were also rich. So in his youth Daddy had a real little rich boy's upbringing, parties every week, balls, festivities, beautiful girls, dinners, a large home, etc., etc.

After Grandpa's death all the money was lost during the World War and the inflation that followed. Daddy was therefore extremely well brought up and he laughed very much yesterday when, for the first time in his fifty-five years, he scraped out the frying pan at table.

Mummy's parents were rich too and we often listen openmouthed to stories of engagement parties of two hundred and fifty people, private balls and dinners. One certainly could not call us rich now, but all my hopes are pinned on after the war.

I can assure you I'm not at all keen on a narrow, cramped existence like Mummy and Margot. I'd adore to go to Paris for a year and London for a year to learn the languages and study the history of art. Compare that with Margot, who wants to be a midwife in Palestine! I always long to see beautiful dresses and interesting people.

I want to see something of the world and do all kinds of exciting things. I've already told you this before. And a little money as well won't do any harm.

Miep told us this morning about a party she went to, to celebrate an engagement. Both the future bride and bridegroom came from rich families and everything was very grand. Miep made our mouths water telling us about the food they had: vegetable soup with minced meat balls in it, cheese, rolls, hors d'oeuvre with eggs and roast beef, fancy cakes, wine and cigarettes, as much as you wanted of everything (black market). Miep had ten drinks—can that be the woman who calls herself a teetotaler? If Miep had all those, I wonder however many her spouse managed to knock back? Naturally, everyone at the party was a bit tipsy. There were two policemen from the fighting squad, who took photos of the engaged couple. It seems as if we are never far from Miep's thoughts, because she took down the addresses of these men at once, in case anything should happen at some time or other, and good Dutchmen might come in useful.

She made our mouths water. We, who get nothing but two spoonfuls of porridge for our breakfast and whose tummies were so empty that they were positively rattling, we, who get nothing but half-cooked spinach (to preserve the vitamins) and rotten potatoes day after day, we, who get nothing but lettuce, cooked or raw, spinach and yet again spinach in our hollow stomachs. Perhaps we may yet grow to be as strong as Popeye, although I don't see much sign of it at present!

If Miep had taken us to the party we shouldn't have left any rolls for the other guests. I can tell you, we positively drew the words from Miep's lips, we gathered round her, as if we'd never heard about delicious food or smart people in our lives before!

And these are the granddaughters of a millionaire. The world is a queer place!

Yours, Anne

Tuesday, 9 May, 1944

Dear Kitty,

I've finished my story of Ellen the fairy. I have copied it once on nice note paper. It certainly looks very attractive, but is it really enough for Daddy's birthday? I don't know. Margot and Mummy have both written poems for him.

Mr. Kraler came upstairs this afternoon with the news that Mrs. B., who used to act as demonstrator for the business, wants to eat her box lunch in the office here at two o'clock every afternoon. Think of it! No one can come upstairs any more, the potatoes cannot be delivered, Elli can't have any lunch, we can't go to the W.C., we mustn't move, etc., etc. We thought up the wildest and most varied suggestions to wheedle her away. Van Daan thought that a good laxative in her coffee would be sufficient. "No," replied Koophuis, "I beg of you not, then we'd never get her off the box!" Resounding laughter. "Off the box," asked Mrs. Van Daan, "what does that mean?" An explanation followed. "Can I always use it?" she then asked stupidly. "Imagine it," Elli giggled, "if one asked for the box in Bijenkorf's[1] they wouldn't even understand what you mean!"

Oh, Kit, it's such wonderful weather, if only I could go outdoors!

Yours, Anne

[1] "Bijenkorf" is a large store in Amsterdam.

Wednesday, 10 May, 1944

Dear Kitty,

We were sitting in the attic doing some French yesterday afternoon when I suddenly heard water pattering down behind me. I asked Peter what it could be, but he didn't even reply, simply tore up to the loft, where the source of the disaster was, and pushed Mouschi, who, because of the wet earth box, had sat down beside it, harshly back to the right place. A great din and disturbance followed, and Mouschi, who had finished by that time, dashed downstairs.

Mouschi, seeking the convenience of something similar to his box, had chosen some wood shavings. The pool had trickled down from the loft into the attic immediately and, unfortunately, landed just beside and in the barrel of potatoes. The ceiling was dripping, and as the attic floor is not free from holes either, several yellow drips came through the ceiling into the dining room between a pile of stockings and some books, which were lying on the table. I was doubled up with laughter; it really was a scream. There was Mouschi crouching under a chair, Peter with water, bleaching powder, and floor cloth, and Van Daan trying to soothe everyone. The calamity was soon over, but it's a well-known fact that cats' puddles positively stink. The potatoes proved this only too clearly and also the wood shavings that Daddy collected in a bucket to be burned. Poor Mouschi! How were you to know that peat is unobtainable?

Yours, Anne

P.S. Our beloved Queen spoke to us yesterday and this evening. She is taking a holiday in order to be strong for her return to Holland. She used words like "soon, when I am back, speedy liberation, heroism, and heavy burdens."

A speech by Gerbrandy followed. A clergyman concluded with a prayer to God to take care of the Jews, the people in concentration camps, in prisons, and in Germany.

Yours, Anne

Thursday, 11 May, 1944

Dear Kitty,

I'm frightfully busy at the moment, and although it sounds mad, I haven't time to get through my pile of work. Shall I tell you briefly what I have got to do? Well, then, by tomorrow I must finish reading the first part of *Galileo Galilei*, as it has to be returned to the library. I only started it yesterday, but I shall manage it.

Next week I have got to read *Palestine at the Crossroads* and the second part of *Galilei*. Next I finished reading the first part of the biography of *The Emperor Charles V* yesterday, and it's essential that I work out all the diagrams and family trees that I have collected from it. After that I have three pages of foreign words gathered from various books, which have all got to be recited, written down, and learned. Number four is that my film stars are all mixed up together and are simply gasping to be tidied up; however, as such a clearance would take several days, and since Professor Anne, as she's already said, is choked with work, the chaos will have to remain a chaos.

Next Theseus, Oedipus, Peleus, Orpheus, Jason, and Hercules are all awaiting their turn to be arranged, as their different deeds lie crisscross in my mind like fancy threads in a dress; it's also high time Myron and Phidias had some treatment, if they wish to remain at all coherent. Likewise it's the same with the seven and nine years' war; I'm mixing everything up together at this rate. Yes, but what can one do with such a memory! Think how forgetful I shall be when I'm eighty!

Oh, something else, the Bible, how long is it still going to take before I meet the bathing Suzanna? And what do they mean by the guilt of Sodom and Gomorrah? Oh, there is still such a terrible lot to find out and to learn. And in the meantime I've left Lisolette of the Pfalz completely in the lurch.

Kitty, can you see that I'm just about bursting?

Now, about something else: you've known for a long time that my greatest wish is to become a journalist some-day and later on a famous writer. Whether these leanings towards greatness (or insanity?) will ever materialize remains to be seen, but I certainly have the subjects in my mind. In any case, I want to publish a book entitled *Het Achterhuis* after the war. Whether I shall succeed or not, I cannot say, but my diary will be a great help. I have other ideas as well, besides *Het Achterhuis*. But I will write more fully about them some other time, when they have taken a clearer form in my mind.

Yours, Anne

Saturday, 13 May, 1944

Dearest Kitty,

It was Daddy's birthday yesterday. Mummy and Daddy have been married nineteen years. The charwoman wasn't below and the sun shone as it has never shone before in 1944. Our horse chestnut is in full bloom, thickly covered with leaves and much more beautiful than last year.

Daddy received a biography of the life of Linnaeus from Koophuis, a book on nature from Kraler, *Amsterdam by the Water* from Dussel, a gigantic box from Van Daan, beautifully done up and almost professionally decorated, containing three eggs, a bottle of beer, a bottle of yoghourt, and a green tie. It made our pot of syrup seem rather small. My roses smelled lovely compared with Miep's and Elli's carnations, which had no smell, but were very pretty too. He was certainly spoiled. Fifty fancy pastries have arrived, heavenly! Daddy himself treated us to spiced gingerbread, beer for the gentlemen, and yoghourt for the ladies. Enjoyment all around!

Yours, Anne

Tuesday, 16 May, 1944

Dearest Kitty,

Just for a change, as we haven't talked about them for so long, I want to tell you a little discussion that went on between Mr. and Mrs. Van Daan yesterday.

Mrs. Van Daan: "The Germans are sure to have made the Atlantic Wall very strong indeed, they will certainly do all in their power to hold back the English. It's amazing how strong the Germans are!"

Mr. Van Daan: "Oh, yes, incredibly."

Mrs. Van Daan: "Ye-es."

Mr. Van Daan: "The Germans are so strong they're sure to win the war in the end, in spite of everything!"

Mrs. Van Daan: "It's quite possible, I'm not convinced of the opposite yet."

Mr. Van Daan: "I won't bother to reply any more."

Mrs. Van Daan: "Still you always do answer me, you can't resist capping me every time."

Mr. Van Daan: "Of course not, but my replies are the bare minimum."

Mrs. Van Daan: "But still you do reply, and you always have to be in the right! Your prophecies don't always come true by a long shot."

Mr. Van Daan: "They have up till now."

Mrs. Van Daan: "That's not true. The invasion was to have come last year, and the Finns were to have been out of the war by now. Italy was finished in the winter, but the Russians would already have Lemberg; oh, no, I don't think much of your prophecies."

Mr. Van Daan (standing up): "It's about time you shut your mouth. One day I'll show you that I'm right; sooner or later you'll get enough of it. I can't bear any more of your grousing. You're so infuriating but you'll stew in your own juice one day."

211

End of Part I.

I really couldn't help laughing. Mummy too, while Peter sat biting his lip. Oh, those stupid grownups, they'd do better to start learning themselves, before they have so much to say to the younger generation!

Yours, Anne

Friday, 19 May, 1944

Dear Kitty,

I felt rotten yesterday, really out of sorts (unusual for Anne!), with tummy-ache and every other imaginable misery. I'm much better today, feel very hungry, but I'd better not touch the kidney beans we're having today.

All goes well with Peter and me. The poor boy seems to need a little love even more than I do. He blushes every evening when he gets his good-night kiss and simply begs for another. I wonder if I'm a good substitute for Boche? I don't mind, he is so happy now that he knows that someone loves him.

After my laborious conquest I've got the situation a bit more in hand now, but I don't think my love has cooled off. He's a darling, but I soon closed up my inner self from him. If he wants to force the lock again he'll have to work a good deal harder than before!

Yours, Anne

Saturday, 20 May, 1944

Dear Kitty,

Last evening I came downstairs from the attic and as I entered the room saw at once the lovely case of carnations lying on the floor, Mummy down on hands and knees mopping up and Margot fishing up some papers from the floor.

"What's happened here?" I asked, full of misgivings and, not even waiting for their answer, tried to sum up the damage from a distance. My whole portfolio of family

212

trees, writing books, textbooks, everything was soaked. I nearly wept and was so worked up that I can hardly remember what I said, but Margot said that I let fly something about "incalculable loss, frightful, terrible, can never be repaired," and still more. Daddy burst out laughing, Mummy and Margot joined in, but I could have cried over all the toil that was wasted, and the diagrams I'd so carefully worked out.

On closer inspection the "incalculable loss" didn't turn out to be as bad as I'd thought. I carefully sorted out all the papers that were stuck together and separated them in the attic. After that I hung them all up on the clothes lines to dry. It was a funny sight and I couldn't help laughing myself. Maria de Medici beside Charles V, William of Orange and Marie Antoinette; it's a "racial outrage," was Mr. Van Daan's joke on the subject. After I'd entrusted my papers into Peter's care I went downstairs again.

"Which books are spoiled?" I asked Margot, who was checking up on them. "Algebra," she said. I hurried to her side, but unfortunately not even the algebra book was spoiled. I wish it had fallen right in the vase; I've never loathed *any* other book so much as that one. There are the names of at least twenty girls in the front, all previous owners; it is old, yellow, full of scribbles and improvements. If I'm ever in a really very wicked mood, I'll tear the blasted thing to pieces!

Yours, Anne

Monday, 22 May, 1944

Dear Kitty,

On May 20th Daddy lost five bottles of yoghourt on a bet with Mrs. Van Daan. The invasion still hasn't come yet; it's no exaggeration to say that all Amsterdam, all Holland, yes, the whole west coast of Europe, right down to Spain, talks about the invasion day and night, debates about it, and makes bets on it and . . . hopes.

The suspense is rising to a climax. By no means everyone we had regarded as "good" Dutch have stuck to their faith in the English; by no means everyone thinks the English bluff a masterly piece of strategy, oh no, the people want to see deeds at last, great, heroic deeds. Nobody sees beyond his own nose, no one thinks that the English are fighting for their own land and their own people, everyone thinks that it's their duty to save Holland, as quickly and as well as they can.

What obligations have the English towards us? How have the Dutch earned the generous help that they seem so explicitly to expect? Oh no, the Dutch will have made a big mistake, the English, in spite of all their bluff, are certainly no more to blame than all the other countries, great and small, which are not under occupation. The English really won't offer us their apologies, for even if we do reproach them for being asleep during the years when Germany was rearming, we cannot deny that all the other countries, especially those bordering Germany, also slept. We shan't get anywhere by following an ostrich policy. England and the whole world have seen that only too well now, and that is why, one by one, England, no less than the rest, will have to make heavy sacrifices.

No country is going to sacrifice its men for nothing and certainly not in the interests of another. England is not going to do that either. The invasion, with liberation and freedom, will come sometime, but England and America will appoint the day, not all the occupied countries put together.

To our great horror and regret we hear that the attitude of a great many people towards us Jews has changed. We hear that there is anti-Semitism now in circles that never thought of it before. This news has affected us all very, very deeply. The cause of this hatred of the Jews is understandable, even human sometimes, but not good. The Christians blame the Jews for giving secrets away to the Germans, for betraying their helpers and for the fact that, through the Jews a great many Christians have gone the way of so many others before them, and suffered terrible punishments and a dreadful fate.

214

This is all true, but one must always look at these things from both sides. Would Christians behave differently in our place? The Germans have a means of making people talk. Can a person, entirely at their mercy, whether Jew or Christian, always remain silent? Everyone knows that is practically impossible. Why, then, should people demand the impossible of the Jews?

It's being murmured in underground circles that the German Jews who emigrated to Holland and who are now in Poland may not be allowed to return here; they once had the right of asylum in Holland, but when Hitler has gone they will have to go back to Germany again.

When one hears this one naturally wonders why we are carrying on with this long and difficult war. We always hear that we're all fighting together for freedom, truth, and right! Is discord going to show itself while we are still fighting, is the Jew once again worth less than another? Oh, it is sad, very sad, that once more, for the umpteenth time, the old truth is confirmed: "What *one* Christian does is his own responsibility, what *one* Jew does is thrown back at all Jews."

Quite honestly, I can't understand that the Dutch, who are such a good, honest, upright people, should judge us like this, we, the most oppressed, the unhappiest, perhaps the most pitiful of all peoples of the whole world.

I hope *one* thing only, and that is that this hatred of the Jews will be a passing thing, that the Dutch will show what they are after all, and that they will never totter and lose their sense of right. For anti-Semitism is unjust!

And if this terrible threat should actually come true, then the pitiful little collection of Jews that remain will have to leave Holland. We, too, shall have to move on again with our little bundles, and leave this beautiful country, which offered us such a warm welcome and which now turns it back on us.

I love Holland. I who, having no native country, had hoped that it might become my fatherland, and I still hope it will!

Yours, Anne

Dear Kitty,

There's something fresh every day. This morning our vegetable man was picked up for having two Jews in his house. It's a great blow to us, not only that those poor Jews are balancing on the edge of an abyss, but it's terrible for the man himself.

The world has turned topsy-turvy, respectable people are being sent off to concentration camps, prisons, and lonely cells, and the dregs that remain govern young and old, rich and poor. One person walks into the trap through the black market, a second through helping the Jews or other people who've had to go "underground"; anyone who isn't a member of the N.S.B. doesn't know what may happen to him from one day to another.

This man is a great loss to us too. The girls can't and aren't allowed to haul along our share of potatoes, so the only thing to do is to eat less. I will tell you how we shall do that; it's certainly not going to make things any pleasanter. Mummy says we shall cut out breakfast altogether, have porridge and bread for lunch, and for supper fried potatoes and possibly once or twice per week vegetables or lettuce, nothing more. We're going to be hungry, but anything is better than being discovered.

Yours, Anne

Dear Kitty,

At last, at last I can sit quietly at my table in front of a crack of window and write you everything.

I feel so miserable, I haven't felt like this for months; even after the burglary I didn't feel so utterly broken. On the one hand, the vegetable man, the Jewish question, which is being discussed minutely over the whole house, the invasion delay, the bad food, the strain, the miserable atmosphere, my disappointment in Peter; and on the other hand, Elli's engagement, Whitsun reception, flowers, Kraler's birthday, fancy cakes, and stories about cabarets, films, and concerts. That difference, that huge difference, it's always there; one day we laugh and see the funny side of the situation, but the next we are afraid, fear, suspense, and despair staring from our faces. Miep and Kraler carry the heaviest burden of the eight in hiding, Miep in all she does, and Kraler through the enormous responsibility, which is sometimes so much for him that he can hardly talk from pent-up nerves and strain. Koophuis and Elli look after us well too, but they can forget us at times, even if it's only for a few hours, or a day, or even two days. They have their own worries, Koophuis over his health, Elli over her engagement, which is not altogether rosy, but they also have their little outings, visits to friends, and the whole life of ordinary people. For them the suspense is sometimes lifted, even if it is only for a short time, but for us it never lifts for a moment. We've been here for two years now; how long have we still to put up with this almost unbearable, ever increasing pressure?

The sewer is blocked, so we mustn't run water, or rather only a trickle; when we go to the W.C. we have to take a lavatory brush with us, and we keep dirty water in a large Cologne pot. We can manage for today, but what do we do if the plumber can't do the job alone? The municipal scavenging service doesn't come until Tuesday.

Miep sent us a currant cake, made up in the shape of a doll, with the words "Happy Whitsun" on the note attached to it. It's almost as if she's ridiculing us; our present frame of mind and our uneasiness could hardly be called "happy." The affair of the vegetable man has made us more nervous, you hear "shh, shh" from all sides again, and we're being quieter over everything. The police forced the door there, so they could do it to us too! If one day we too should . . . no, I mustn't write it, but I can't put the question out of my mind today. On the contrary, all the fear I've already been through seems to face me again in all its frightfulness.

This evening at eight o'clock I had to go to the downstairs lavatory all alone; there was no one down there, as everyone was listening to the radio; I wanted to be brave, but it was difficult. I always feel much safer here upstairs than alone downstairs in that large, silent house; alone with the mysterious muffled noises from upstairs and the tooting of motor horns in the street. I have to hurry for I start to quiver if I begin thinking about the situation.

Again and again I ask myself, would it not have been better for us all if we had not gone into hiding, and if we were dead now and not going through all this misery, especially as we shouldn't be running our protectors into danger any more. But we all recoil from these thoughts too, for we still love life; we haven't yet forgotten the voice of nature, we still hope, hope about everything. I hope something will happen soon now, shooting if need be—nothing can crush us *more* than this restlessness. Let the end come, even if it is hard; then at least we shall know whether we are finally going to win through or go under.

Yours, Anne

Wednesday, 31 May, 1944

Dear Kitty,

It was so frightfully hot on Saturday, Sunday, Monday, and Tuesday that I simply couldn't hold a fountain pen in my hand. That's why it was impossible to write to you. The drains went shut again on Friday, were mended again on Saturday; Mr. Koophuis came to see us in the afternoon and told us masses about Corry and her being in the same hockey club as Jopie.

On Sunday Elli came to make sure no one had broken in and stayed for breakfast, on Whit Monday Mr. Van Santen acted as the hide-out watchman, and, finally, on Tuesday the windows could be opened again at last.

There's seldom been such a beautiful, warm, one can even say hot, Whitsun. The heat here in the "Secret Annexe" is terrible; I will briefly describe these warm days by giving you a sample of the sort of complaints that arise:

Saturday: "Lovely, what perfect weather," we all said in the morning. "If only it wasn't quite so warm," in the afternoon when the windows had to be closed.

Sunday: "It's positively unbearable, this heat. The butter's melting, there's not a cool spot anywhere in the house, the bread's getting so dry, the milk's going sour, windows can't be opened, and we, wretched outcasts, sit here suffocating while other people enjoy their Whitsun holiday."

Monday: "My feet hurt me, I haven't got any thin clothes. I can't wash the dishes in this heat," all this from Mrs. Van Daan. It was extremely unpleasant.

I still can't put up with heat and am glad that there's a stiff breeze today, and yet the sun still shines.

Yours, Anne

Monday, 5 June, 1944

Dear Kitty,

Fresh "Secret Annexe" troubles, a quarrel between Dussel and the Franks over something very trivial: the sharing out of the butter. Dussel's capitulation. Mrs. Van Daan and the latter very thick, flirtations, kisses and friendly little laughs. Dussel is beginning to get longings for women. The Fifth Army has taken Rome. The city has been spared devastation by both armies and air forces, and is undamaged. Very few vegetables and potatoes. Bad weather. Heavy bombardments against the French coast and Pas de Calais continue.

Yours, Anne

Tuesday, 6 June, 1944

Dear Kitty,

"This is D-day," came the announcement over the English news and quite rightly, "this is *the* day." [1] The invasion has begun!

[1] Original English.

219

The English gave the news at eight o'clock this morning: Calais, Boulogne, Le Havre, and Cherbourg, also the Pas de Calais (as usual), were heavily bombarded. Moreover, as a safety measure for all occupied territories, all people who live within a radius of thirty-five kilometers from the coast are warned to be prepared for bombardments. If possible, the English will drop pamphlets one hour beforehand.

According to German news, English parachute troops have landed on the French coast, English landing craft are in battle with the German Navy, says the B.B.C.

We discussed it over the "Annexe" breakfast at nine o'clock: Is this just a trial landing like Dieppe two years ago?

English broadcast in German, Dutch, French, and other languages at ten o'clock: "The invasion has begun!" that means the "real" invasion. English broadcast in German at eleven o'clock, speech by the Supreme Commander, General Dwight Eisenhower.

The English news at twelve o'clock in English: "This is D-day." General Eisenhower said to the French people: "Stiff fighting will come now, but after this the victory. The year 1944 is the year of complete victory; good luck." [1]

English news in English at one o'clock (translated): 11,000 planes stand ready, and are flying to and fro nonstop, landing troops and attacking behind the lines; 4000 landing boats, plus small craft, are landing troops and matériel between Cherbourg and Le Havre incessantly. English and American troops are already engaged in hard fighting. Speeches by Gerbrandy, by the Prime Minister of Belgium, King Haakon of Norway, De Gaulle of France, the King of England, and last, but not least, Churchill.

Great commotion in the "Secret Annexe"! Would the long-awaited liberation that has been talked of so much, but which still seems *too* wonderful, *too* much like a fairy tale, ever come true? Could we be granted victory this year, 1944? We don't know yet, but hope is revived within us; it gives us fresh courage, and makes us strong

[1] Original English.

again. Since we must put up bravely with all the fears, privations, and sufferings, the great thing now is to remain calm and steadfast. Now more than ever we must clench our teeth and not cry out. France, Russia, Italy, and Germany, too, can all cry out and give vent to their misery, but we haven't the right to do that yet!

Oh, Kitty, the best part of the invasion is that I have the feeling that friends are approaching. We have been oppressed by those terrible Germans for so long, they have had their knives so at our throats, that the thoughts of friends and delivery fills us with confidence!

Now it doesn't concern the Jews any more; it concerns Holland and all occupied Europe. Perhaps, Margot says, I may yet be able to go back to school in September or October.

Yours, Anne

P.S. I'll keep you up to date with all the latest news!

Friday, 9 June, 1944

Dear Kitty,

Super news of the invasion. The Allies have taken Bayeux, a small village on the French coast, and are now fighting for Caen. It's obvious that they intend to cut off the peninsula where Cherbourg lies. Every evening war correspondents give news from the battle front, telling us of the difficulties, courage, and enthusiasm of the army; they manage to get hold of the most incredible stories. Also some of the wounded who are already back in England again came to the microphone. The air force is up all the time in spite of the miserable weather. We heard over the B.B.C. that Churchill wanted to land with the troops on D-Day, however, Eisenhower and the other generals managed to get him out of the idea. Just think of it, what pluck he has for such an old man—he must be seventy at least.

The excitement here has worn off a bit; still, we're hoping that the war will be over at the end of this year.

It'll be about time too! Mrs. Van Daan's grizzling is absolutely unbearable; now she can't any longer drive us crazy over the invasion, she nags us the whole day long about the bad weather. It really would be nice to dump her in a bucket of cold water and put her up in the loft.

The whole of the "Secret Annexe" except Van Daan and Peter have read the trilogy *Hungarian Rhapsody*. This book deals with the life history of the composer, virtuoso, and child prodigy, Franz Liszt. It is a very interesting book, but in my opinion there is a bit too much about women in it. In his time Liszt was not only the greatest and most famous pianist, but also the greatest ladies' man —right up to the age of seventy. He lived with the Duchess Marie d'Agould, Princess Caroline Sayn-Wittgenstein, the dancer Lola Montez, the pianist Agnes Kingworth, the pianist Sophie Menter, Princess Olga Janina, Baroness Olga Meyendorff, the actress Lilla what's-her-name, etc., etc.; it is just endless. The parts of the book that deal with music and art are much more interesting. Among those mentioned are Schumann, Clara Wieck, Hector Berlioz, Johannes Brahms, Beethoven, Joachim, Richard Wagner, Hans von Bülow, Anton Rubinstein, Frédéric Chopin, Victor Hugo, Honoré de Balzac, Hiller, Hummel, Czerny, Rossini, Cherubini, Paganini, Mendelssohn, etc., etc.

Liszt was personally a fine man, very generous, and modest about himself though exceptionally vain. He helped everyone, his art was everything to him, he was mad about cognac and about women, could not bear to see tears, was a gentleman, would never refuse to do anyone a favor, didn't care about money, loved religious liberty and world freedom.

Yours, Anne

Tuesday, 13 June, 1944

Dear Kitty,

Another birthday has gone by, so now I'm fifteen. I received quite a lot of presents.

All five parts of Sprenger's *History of Art,* a set of underwear, a handkerchief, two bottles of yoghourt, a pot of jam, a spiced gingerbread cake, and a book on botany from Mummy and Daddy, a double bracelet from Margot, a book from the Van Daans, sweet peas from Dussel, sweets and exercise books from Miep and Elli and, the high spot of all, the book *Maria Theresa* and three slices of full-cream cheese from Kraler. A lovely bunch of peonies from Peter; the poor boy took a lot of trouble to try and find something, but didn't have any luck.

There's still excellent news of the invasion, in spite of the wretched weather, countless gales, heavy rains, and high seas.

Yesterday Churchill, Smuts, Eisenhower, and Arnold visited French villages which have been conquered and liberated. The torpedo boat that Churchill was in shelled the coast. He appears, like so many men, not to know what fear is—makes me envious!

It's difficult for us to judge from our secret redoubt how people outside have reacted to the news. Undoubtedly people are pleased that the idle (?) English have rolled up their sleeves and are doing something at last. Any Dutch people who still look down on the English, scoff at England and her government of old gentlemen, call the English cowards, and yet hate the Germans deserve a good shaking. Perhaps it would put some sense into their woolly brains.

I hadn't had a period for over two months, but it finally started again on Saturday. Still, in spite of all the unpleasantness and bother, I'm glad it hasn't failed me any longer.

Yours, Anne

Wednesday, 14 June, 1944

Dear Kitty,

My head is haunted by so many wishes and thoughts, accusations and reproaches. I'm really not as conceited as so many people seem to think, I know my own faults and shortcomings better than anyone, but the difference is that I also know that I want to improve, shall improve, and have already improved a great deal.

Why is it then, I so often ask myself, that everyone still thinks I'm so terribly knowing and forward? Am I so knowing? Is it that I really am, or that maybe the others aren't? That sounds queer, I realize now, but I shan't cross out the last sentence, because it really isn't so crazy. Everyone knows that Mrs. Van Daan, one of my chief accusers, is unintelligent. I might as well put it plainly and say "stupid." Stupid people usually can't take it if others do better than they do.

Mrs. Van Daan thinks I'm stupid because I'm not quite so lacking in intelligence as she is; she thinks I'm forward because she's even more so; she thinks my dresses are too short, because hers are even shorter. And that's also the reason that she thinks I'm knowing, because she's twice as bad about joining in over subjects she knows absolutely nothing about. But one of my favorite sayings is "There's no smoke without fire," and I readily admit that I'm knowing.

Now the trying part about me is that I criticize and scold myself far more than anyone else does. Then if Mummy adds her bit of advice the pile of sermons becomes so insurmountable that in my despair I become rude and start contradicting and then, of course, the old well-known Anne watchword comes back: "No one understands me!" This phrase sticks in my mind; I know it sounds silly, yet there is some truth in it. I often accuse myself to such an extent that I simply long for a word of comfort, for someone who could give me sound advice and also draw out some of my real self; but, alas, I keep on looking, but I haven't found anyone yet.

I know that you'll immediately think of Peter, won't you, Kit? It's like this: Peter loves me not as a lover but as a friend and grows more affectionate every day. But what is the mysterious something that holds us both back? I don't understand it myself. Sometimes I think that my terrible longing for him was exaggerated, yet that's really not it, because if I don't go up to see him for two days, then I long for him more desperately than ever before. Peter is good and he's a darling, but still there's no denying that there's a lot about him that disappoints me. Especially his dislike of religion and all his talk about food and various other things don't appeal to me. Yet I feel quite convinced that we shall never quarrel now that we've made that straightforward agreement together. Pete is a peace-loving person; he's tolerant and gives in very easily. He lets me say a lot of things to him that he would never accept from his mother, he tries most persistently to keep his things in order. And yet why should he keep his innermost self to himself and why am I never allowed there? By nature he is more closed-up than I am, I agree, but I know—and from my own experience—that at some time or other even the most uncommunicative people long just as much, if not more, to find someone in whom they can confide.

Both Peter and I have spent our most meditative years in the "Secret Annexe." We often discuss the future, the past, and the present, but, as I've already said, I still seem to miss the real thing and yet I know that it's there.

Yours, Anne

Thursday, 15 June, 1944

Dear Kitty,

I wonder if it's because I haven't been able to poke my nose outdoors for so long that I've grown so crazy about everything to do with nature? I can perfectly well remember that there was a time when a deep blue sky, the song of the birds, moonlight and flowers could never have kept me spellbound. That's changed since I've been here.

At Whitsun, for instance, when it was so warm, I stayed awake on purpose until half past eleven one evening in order to have a good look at the moon for once by myself. Alas, the sacrifice was all in vain, as the moon gave far too much light and I didn't dare risk opening a window. Another time, some months ago now, I happened to be upstairs one evening when the window was open. I didn't go downstairs until the window had to be shut. The dark, rainy evening, the gale, the scudding clouds held me entirely in their power; it was the first time in a year and a half that I'd seen the night face to face. After that evening my longing to see it again was greater than my fear of burglars, rats, and raids on the house. I went downstairs all by myself and looked outside through the windows in the kitchen and the private office. A lot of people are fond of nature, many sleep outdoors occasionally, and people in prisons and hospitals long for the day when they will be free to enjoy the beauties of nature, but few are so shut away and isolated from that which can be shared alike by rich and poor. It's not imagination on my part when I say that to look up at the sky, the clouds, the moon, and the stars makes me calm and patient. It's a better medicine than either Valerian or bromine; Mother Nature makes me humble and prepared to face every blow courageously.

Alas, it has had to be that I am only able—except on a few rare occasions—to look at nature through dirty net curtains hanging before very dusty windows. And it's no pleasure looking through these any longer, because nature is just the one thing that really must be unadulterated.

Yours, Anne

Friday, 16 June, 1944

Dear Kitty,

New problems: Mrs. Van Daan is desperate, talks about a bullet through her head, prison, hanging, and suicide. She's jealous that Peter confides in me and not her. She's offended that Dussel doesn't enter into her flirtations with him, as she'd hoped, afraid that her husband is smoking all the fur-coat money away, she quarrels, uses abusive language, cries, pities herself, laughs, and then starts a fresh quarrel again. What on earth can one do with such a foolish, blubbering specimen? No one takes her seriously, she hasn't any character, and she grumbles to everyone. The worst of it is that it makes Peter rude, Mr. Van Daan irritable, and Mummy cynical. Yes, it's a frightful situation! There's *one* golden rule to keep before you: laugh about everything and don't bother yourself about the others! It sounds selfish, but it's honestly the only cure for anyone who has to seek consolation in himself.

Kraler has received another call-up to go digging for four weeks. He's trying to get out of it with a doctor's certificate and a letter from the business. Koophuis wants to have an operation on his stomach. All private telephones were cut off at eleven o'clock yesterday.

Yours, Anne

Friday, 23 June, 1944

Dear Kitty,

Nothing special going on here. The English have begun their big attack on Cherbourg; according to Pim and Van Daan, we're sure to be free by October 10. The Russians are taking part in the campaign, and yesterday began their offensive near Vitebsk; it's exactly three years to a day since the Germans attacked. We've hardly got any potatoes; from now on we're going to count them out for each person, then everyone knows what he's getting.

Yours, Anne

Tuesday, 27 June, 1944

Dearest Kitty,

The mood has changed, everything's going wonderfully. Cherbourg, Vitebsk, and Sloben fell today. Lots of prisoners and booty. Now the English can land what they want now they've got a harbor, the whole Cotentin Peninsula three weeks after the English invasion! A tremendous achievement! In the three weeks since D-day not a day has gone by without rain and gales, both here and in France, but a bit of bad luck didn't prevent the English and Americans from showing their enormous strength, and how! Certainly the "wonder weapon" is in full swing,

227

but of what consequence are a few squibs apart from a bit of damage in England and pages full of it in the Boche newspapers! For that matter, when they really realize in "Bocheland" that the Bolshevists really are on the way, they'll get even more jittery.

All German women not in military service are being evacuated to Groningen, Friesland, and Gelderland with their children. Mussert [1] has announced that if they get as far as here with the invasion he'll put on a uniform. Does the old fatty want to do some fighting? He could have done so in Russia before now. Some time ago Finland turned down a peace offer, now the negotiations have just been broken off again, they'll be sorry for it later, the silly fools!

How far do you think we'll be on July 27?

Yours, Anne

Friday, 30 June, 1944

Dear Kitty,

Bad weather, or *bad weather at a stretch to the thirtieth of June*.[2] Isn't that well said! Oh yes, I have a smattering of English already; just to show that I can, I'm reading *An Ideal Husband* with the aid of a dictionary. War going wonderfully! Bobroisk, Mogilef, and Orsa have fallen, lots of prisoners.

Everything's all right here and tempers are improving. The superoptimists are triumphing. Elli has changed her hair style, Miep has the week off. That's the latest news.

Yours, Anne

---

[1] Mussert was the Dutch National Socialist leader.
[2] In English in the original.

Dear Kitty,

It strikes fear to my heart when Peter talks of later being a criminal, or of gambling; although it's meant as a joke, of course, it gives me the feeling that he's afraid of his own weakness. Again and again I hear from both Margot and Peter: "Yes, if I was as strong and plucky as you are, if I always stuck to what I wanted, if I had such persistent energy, yes then . . . !"

I wonder if it's really a good quality not to let myself be influenced. Is it really good to follow almost entirely my own conscience?

Quite honestly, I can't imagine how anyone can say: "I'm weak," and then remain so. After all, if you know it, why not fight against it, why not try to train your character? The answer was: "Because it's so much easier not to!" This reply rather discouraged me. Easy? Does that mean that a lazy, deceitful life is an easy life? Oh, no, that can't be true, it mustn't be true, people can so easily be tempted by slackness . . . and by money.

I thought for a long time about the best answer to give Peter, how to get him to believe in himself and, above all to try and improve himself; I don't know whether my line of thought is right though, or not.

I've so often thought how lovely it would be to have someone's complete confidence, but now, now that I'm that far, I realize how difficult it is to think what the other person is thinking and then to find the *right* answer. More especially because the very ideas of "easy" and "money" are something entirely foreign and new to me. Peter's beginning to lean on me a bit and that mustn't happen under any circumstances. A type like Peter finds it difficult to stand on his own feet, but it's even harder to stand on your own feet as a conscious, living being. Because if you do, then it's twice as difficult to steer a right path through the sea of problems and still remain constant through it all. I'm just drifting around, have been searching for days, searching for a good argument against that terrible word "easy," something to settle it once and for all.

How can I make it clear to him that what appears easy and attractive will drag him down into the depths, depths where there is no comfort to be found, no friends and no beauty, depths from which it is almost impossible to raise oneself?

We all live, but we don't know the why or the wherefore. We all live with the object of being happy; our lives are all different and yet the same. We three have been brought up in good circles, we have the chance to learn, the possibility of attaining something, we have all reason to hope for much happiness, but . . . we must earn it for ourselves. And that is never easy. You must work and do good, not be lazy and gamble, if you wish to earn happiness. Laziness may *appear* attractive, but work *gives* satisfaction.

I can't understand people who don't like work, yet that isn't the case with Peter; he just hasn't got a fixed goal to aim at, and he thinks he's too stupid and too inferior to achieve anything. Poor boy, he's never known what it feels like to make other people happy, and I can't teach him that either. He has no religion, scoffs at Jesus Christ, and swears, using the name of God; although I'm not orthodox either, it hurts me every time I see how deserted, how scornful, and how poor he really is.

People who have a religion should be glad, for not everyone has the gift of believing in heavenly things. You don't necessarily even have to be afraid of punishment after death; purgatory, hell, and heaven are things that a lot of people can't accept, but still a religion, it doesn't matter which, keeps a person on the right path. It isn't the fear of God but the upholding of one's honor and conscience. How noble and good everyone could be if, every evening before falling asleep, they were to recall to their minds the events of the whole day and consider exactly what has been good and bad. Then, without realizing it, you try to improve yourself at the start of each new day; of course, you achieve quite a lot in the course of time. Anyone can do this, it costs nothing and is certainly very helpful. Whoever doesn't know it must learn and find by experience that: "A quiet conscience makes one strong!"

Yours, Anne

Saturday, 8 July, 1944

Dear Kitty,

The chief representative of the business, Mr. B., has been in Beverwijk and managed, just like that, to get strawberries at the auction sale.[1] They arrived here dusty, covered with sand, but in large quantities. No less then twenty-four trays for the office people and us. That very same evening we bottled six jars and made eight pots of jam. The next morning Miep wanted to make jam for the office people.

At half past twelve, no strangers in the house, front door bolted, trays fetched, Peter, Daddy, Van Daan clattering on the stairs: Anne, get hot water; Margot, bring a bucket; all hands on deck! I went into the kitchen, which was chock-full, with a queer feeling in my tummy, Miep, Elli, Koophuis, Henk, Daddy, Peter: the families in hiding and their supply column, all mingling together, and in the middle of the day too!

People can't see in from outside because of the net curtains, but, even so, the loud voices and banging doors positively gave me the jitters. Are we really supposed to be in hiding? That's what flashed through my mind, and it gives me a very queer feeling to be able to appear in the world again. The pan was full, and I dashed upstairs again. The rest of the family was seated round our table in the kitchen busy stalk-picking—at least that's what they were supposed to be doing; more went into mouths than into buckets. Another bucket would soon be required. Peter went to the downstairs kitchen again—the

[1] It is compulsory in Holland for all growers to sell their produce at public auction.

231

bell rang twice; the bucket stayed where it was, Peter tore upstairs, locked the cupboard door. We were kicking our heels impatiently, couldn't turn on a tap, even though the strawberries were only half washed; the rule: "If anyone in the house, use no water, because of the noise," was strictly maintained.

At one o'clock Henk came and told us that it was the postman. Peter hurried downstairs again. Ting-a-ling . . . the bell, right about turn. I go and listen to see if I can hear anyone coming, first at our cupboard door and then creep to the top of the stairs. Finally Peter and I both lean over the banisters like a couple of thieves, listening to the din downstairs. No strange voices, Peter sneaks down, stops halfway, and calls out: "Elli!" No answer, one more: "Elli!" Peter's voice is drowned by the din in the kitchen. He goes right down and into the kitchen. I stand looking down tensely. "Get upstairs at once, Peter, the accountant is here, clear out!" It was Koophuis speaking. Peter comes upstairs sighing, the cupboard door closes. Finally Kraler arrives at half past one. "Oh, dearie me, I see nothing but strawberries, strawberries at breakfast, strawberries stewed by Miep, I smell strawberries, must have a rest from them and go upstairs—what is being washed up here . . . strawberries."

The remainder are being bottled. In the evening: two jars unsealed. Daddy quickly makes them into jam. The next morning: two more unsealed and four in the afternoon. Van Daan hadn't brought them to the right temperature for sterilizing. Now Daddy makes jam every evening.

We eat strawberries with our porridge, skimmed milk with strawberries, bread and butter with strawberries, strawberries for dessert, strawberries with sugar, strawberries with sand. For two whole days strawberries and nothing but strawberries, then the supply was finished or in bottles and under lock and key.

"I say, Anne," Margot calls out, "the greengrocer on the corner has let us have some green peas, nineteen pounds." "That's nice of him," I replied. And it certainly is, but oh, the work . . . ugh!

"You've all got to help shelling peas on Saturday morning," Mummy announced when we were at table. And, sure enough, the big enamel pan duly appeared this morning, filled to the brim. Shelling peas is a boring job, but you ought to try "skinning" the pods. I don't think many people realize how soft and tasty the pod is when the skin on the inside has been removed. However, an even greater advantage is that the quantity which can be eaten is about triple the amount of when one only eats the peas. It's an exceptionally precise, finicky job, pulling out this skin; perhaps it's all right for pedantic dentists or precise office workers, but for an impatient teen-ager like me, it's frightful. We began at half past nine, I got up at half past ten, at half past eleven I sat down again. This refrain hummed in my ears: bend the top, pull the skin, remove the string, throw out the pod, etc., etc., they dance before my eyes, green, green, green maggots, strings, rotten pods, green, green, green. Just for the sake of doing something, I chatter the whole morning, any nonsense that comes into my head, make everyone laugh, and bore them stiff. But every string that I pull makes me feel more certain that I never, never want to be just a housewife only!

We finally have breakfast at twelve o'clock, but from half past twelve until quarter past one we've got to go skinning pods again. I'm just about seasick when I stop, the others a bit too. I go and sleep till four o'clock, but I'm still upset by those wretched peas.

Yours, Anne

Saturday, 15 July, 1944

Dear Kitty,
We have had a book from the library with the challenging title of: *What Do You Think of the Modern Young Girl?* I want to talk about this subject today.

The author of this book criticizes "the youth of today" from top to toe, without, however, condemning the whole of the young brigade as "incapable of anything good." On the contrary, she is rather of the opinion that if young people wished, they have it in their hands to make a bigger, more beautiful and better world, but that they occupy themselves with superficial things, without giving a thought to real beauty.

In some passages, the writer gave me very much the feeling she was directing her criticism at me, and that's why I want to lay myself completely bare to you for once and defend myself against this attack.

I have one outstanding trait in my character, which must strike anyone who knows me for any length of time, and that is my knowledge of myself. I can watch myself and my actions, just like an outsider. The Anne of every day I can face entirely without prejudice, without making excuses for her and watch what's good and what's bad about her. This "self-consciousness" haunts me, and every time I open my mouth I know as soon as I've spoken whether "that ought to have been different" or "that was right as it was." There are so many things about myself that I condemn; I couldn't begin to name them all. I understand more and more how true Daddy's words were when he said: "All children must look after their own upbringing." Parents can only give good advice or put them on the right paths, but the final forming of a person's character lies in their own hands.

In addition to this, I have lots of courage, I always feel so strong and as if I can bear a great deal, I feel so free and so young! I was glad when I first realized it, because I don't think I shall easily bow down before the blows that inevitably come to everyone.

But I've talked about these things so often before. Now I want to come to the chapter of "Daddy and Mummy don't understand me." Daddy and Mummy have always thoroughly spoiled me, were sweet to me, defended me, and have done all that parents could do. And yet I've felt so terribly lonely for a long time, so left out, neglected, and misunderstood. Daddy tried all he could to check my rebellious spirit, but it was no use, I have cured myself, by seeing for myself what was wrong in my behavior and keeping it before my eyes.

How is it that Daddy was never any support to me in

my struggle, why did he completely miss the mark when he wanted to offer me a helping hand? Daddy tried the wrong methods, he always talked to me as a child who was going through difficult phases. It sounds crazy, because Daddy's the only one who has always taken me into his confidence, and no one but Daddy has given me the feeling that I'm sensible. But there's one thing he's omitted: you see, he hasn't realized that for me the fight to get on top was more important than all else. I didn't want to hear about "symptoms of your age," or "other girls," or "it wears off by itself"; I didn't want to be treated as a girl-like-all-others, but as Anne-on-her-own-merits. Pim didn't understand that. For that matter, I can't confide in anyone, unless they tell me a lot about themselves, and as I know very little about Pim, I don't feel that I can tread upon more intimate ground with him. Pim always takes up the older, fatherly attitude, tells me that he too has had similar passing tendencies. But still he's not able to feel with me like a friend, however hard he tries. These things have made me never mention my views on life nor my well-considered theories to anyone but my diary and, occasionally, to Margot. I concealed from Daddy everything that perturbed me; I never shared my ideals with him. I was aware of the fact that I was pushing him away from me.

I couldn't do anything else. I have acted entirely according to my feelings, but I have acted in the way that was best for my peace of mind. Because I should completely lose my repose and self-confidence, which I have built up so shakily, if, at this stage, I were to accept criticisms of my half-completed task. And I can't do that even from Pim, although it sounds very hard, for not only have I not shared my secret thoughts with Pim but I have often pushed him even further from me, by my irritability.

This is a point that I think a lot about: why is it that Pim annoys me? So much so that I can hardly bear him teaching me, that his affectionate ways strike me as being put on, that I want to be left in peace and would really prefer it if he dropped me a bit, until I felt more certain in my attitude towards him. Because I still have a gnawing feeling of guilt over that horrible letter that I dared to write him when I was so wound up. Oh, how hard it is to be really strong and brave in every way!

Yet this was not my greatest disappointment; no, I ponder far more over Peter than Daddy. I know very well that I conquered him instead of he conquering me. I created an image of him in my mind, pictured him as a quiet, sensitive, lovable boy, who needed affection and friendship. I needed a living person to whom I could pour out my heart; I wanted a friend who'd help to put me on the right road. I achieved what I wanted, and slowly but surely, I drew him towards me. Finally, when I had made him feel friendly, it automatically developed into an intimacy which, on second thought, I don't think I ought to have allowed.

We talked about the most private things, and yet up till now we have never touched on those things that filled, and still fill, my heart and soul. I still don't know quite what to make of Peter, is he superficial, or does he still feel shy, even of me? But dropping that, I committed one error in my desire to make a real friendship: I switched over and tried to get at him by developing it into a more intimate relation, whereas I should have explored all other possibilities. He longs to be loved and I can see that he's beginning to be more and more in love with me. He gets satisfaction out of our meetings, whereas they just have the effect of making me want to try it out with him again. And yet I don't seem able to touch on the subjects that I'm so longing to bring out into the daylight. I drew Peter towards me, far more than he realizes. Now he clings to me, and for the time being, I don't see any way of shaking him off and putting him on his own feet. When I realized that he could not be a friend for my understanding, I thought I would at least try to lift him up out of his narrow-mindedness and make him do something with his youth.

"For in its innermost depths youth is lonelier than old age." I read this saying in some book and I've always remembered it, and found it to be true. Is it true then that

236

grownups have a more difficult time here than we do? No. I know it isn't. Older people have formed their opinions about everything, and don't waver before they act. It's twice as hard for us young ones to hold our ground, and maintain our opinions, in a time when all ideals are being shattered and destroyed, when people are showing their worst side, and do not know whether to believe in truth and right and God.

Anyone who claims that the older ones have a more difficult time here certainly doesn't realize to what extent our problems weigh down on us, problems for which we are probably much too young, but which thrust themselves upon us continually, until, after a long time, we think we've found a solution, but the solution doesn't seem able to resist the facts which reduce it to nothing again. That's the difficulty in these times: ideals, dreams, and cherished hopes rise within us, only to meet the horrible truth and be shattered.

It's really a wonder that I haven't dropped all my ideals, because they seem so absurd and impossible to carry out. Yet I keep them, because in spite of everything I still believe that people are really good at heart. I simply can't build up my hopes on a foundation consisting of confusion, misery, and death. I see the world gradually being turned into a wilderness, I hear the ever approaching thunder, which will destroy us too, I can feel the sufferings of millions and yet, if I look up into the heavens, I think that it will all come right, that this cruelty too will end, and that peace and tranquillity will return again.

In the meantime, I must uphold my ideals, for perhaps the time will come when I shall be able to carry them out.

Yours, Anne

Friday, 21 July, 1944

Dear Kitty,

Now I am getting really hopeful, now things are going well at last. Yes, really, they're going well! Super news! An attempt has been made on Hitler's life and not even by Jewish communists or English capitalists this time, but by a proud German general, and what's more, he's a count, and still quite young. The Führer's life was saved by Divine Providence and, unfortunately, he managed to get off with just a few scratches and burns. A few officers and generals who were with him have been killed and wounded. The chief culprit was shot.

Anyway, it certainly shows that there are lots of officers and generals who are sick of the war and would like to see Hitler descend into a bottomless pit. When they've disposed of Hitler, their aim is to establish a military dictator, who will make peace with the Allies, then they intend to rearm and start another war in about twenty years' time. Perhaps the Divine Power tarried on purpose in getting him out of the way, because it would be much easier and more advantageous to the Allies if the impeccable Germans kill each other off; it'll make less work for the Russians and the English and they'll be able to begin rebuilding their own towns all the sooner.

But still, we're not that far yet, and I don't want to anticipate the glorious events too soon. Still, you must have noticed, this is all sober reality and that I'm in quite a matter-of-fact mood today; for once, I'm not jabbering about high ideals. And what's more, Hitler has even been so kind as to announce to his faithful, devoted people that from now on everyone in the armed forces must obey the Gestapo, and that any soldier who knows that one of his superiors was involved in this low, cowardly attempt upon his life may shoot the same on the spot, without court-martial.

What a perfect shambles it's going to be. Little Johnnie's

feet begin hurting him during a long march, he's snapped at by his boss, the officer, Johnnie grabs his rifle and cries out: "You wanted to murder the Führer, so there's your reward." One bang and the proud chief who dared to tick off little Johnnie has passed into eternal life (or is it eternal death?). In the end, whenever an officer finds himself up against a soldier, or having to take the lead, he'll be wetting his pants from anxiety, because the soldiers will dare to say more than they do. Do you gather a bit what I mean, or have I been skipping too much from one subject to another? I can't help it; the prospect that I may be sitting on school benches next October makes me feel far too cheerful to be logical! Oh, dearie me, hadn't I just told you that I didn't want to be too hopeful? Forgive me, they haven't given me the name "little bundle of contradictions" all for nothing!

Yours, Anne

Tuesday, 1 August, 1944

Dear Kitty,

"Little bundle of contradictions." That's how I ended my last letter and that's how I'm going to begin this one. "A little bundle of contradictions," can you tell me exactly what it is? What does contradiction mean? Like so many words, it can mean two things, contradiction from without and contradiction from within.

The first is the ordinary "not giving in easily, always knowing best, getting in the last word," *enfin*, all the unpleasant qualities for which I'm renowned. The second nobody knows about, that's my own secret.

I've already told you before that I have, as it were, a dual personality. One half embodies my exuberant cheerfulness, making fun of everything, my high-spiritedness, and above all, the way I take everything lightly. This includes not taking offense at a flirtation, a kiss, an embrace, a dirty joke. This side is usually lying in wait and pushes away the other which is much better, deeper and purer.

You must realize that no one knows Anne's better side and that's why most people find me so insufferable.

Certainly I'm a giddy clown for one afternoon, but then everyone's had enough of me for another month. Really, it's just the same as a love film is for deep-thinking people, simply a diversion, amusing just for once, something which is soon forgotten, not bad, but certainly not good. I loathe having to tell you this, but why shouldn't I, if I know it's true anyway? My lighter superficial side will always be too quick for the deeper side of me and that's why it will always win. You can't imagine how often I've already tried to push this Anne away, to cripple her, to hide her, because after all, she's only half of what's called Anne: but it doesn't work and I know, too, why it doesn't work.

I'm awfully scared that everyone who knows me as I always am will discover that I have another side, a finer and better side. I'm afraid they'll laugh at me, think I'm ridiculous and sentimental, not take me seriously. I'm used to not being taken seriously but it's only the "light-hearted" Anne that's used to it and can bear it; the "deeper" Anne is too frail for it. Sometimes, if I really compel the good Anne to take the stage for a quarter of an hour, she simply shrivels up as soon as she has to speak, and lets Anne number one take over, and before I realize it, she has disappeared.

Therefore, the nice Anne is never present in company, has not appeared one single time so far, but almost always predominates when we're alone. I know exactly how I'd like to be, how I am too . . . inside. But, alas, I'm only like that for myself. And perhaps that's why, no, I'm sure it's the reason why I say I've got a happy nature within and why other people think I've got a happy nature without. I am guided by the pure Anne within, but outside I'm nothing but a frolicsome little goat who's broken loose.

As I've already said, I never utter my real feelings about anything and that's how I've acquired the name of chaser-after-boys, flirt, know-all, reader of love stories. The cheerful Anne laughs about it, gives cheeky answers, shrugs her shoulders indifferently, behaves as if she doesn't care,

240

but, oh dearie me, the quiet Anne's reactions are just the opposite. If I'm to be quite honest, then I must admit that it does hurt me, that I try terribly hard to change myself, but that I'm always fighting against a more powerful enemy.

A voice sobs within me: "There you are, that's what's become of you: you're uncharitable, you look supercilious and peevish, people dislike you and all because you won't listen to the advice given you by your own better half." Oh, I would like to listen, but it doesn't work; if I'm quiet and serious, everyone thinks it's a new comedy and then I have to get out of it by turning it into a joke, not to mention my own family, who are sure to think I'm ill, make me swallow pills for headaches and nerves, feel my neck and my head to see whether I'm running a temperature, ask if I'm constipated and criticize me for being in a bad mood. I can't keep that up: if I'm watched to that extent, I start by getting snappy, then unhappy, and finally I twist my heart round again, so that the bad is on the outside and the good is on the inside and keep on trying to find a way of becoming what I would so like to be, and what I could be, if . . . there weren't any other people living in the world.

Yours, Anne

EPILOGUE

Anne's diary ends here. On August 4, 1944, the Grüne Polizei made a raid on the "Secret Annexe." All the occupants, together with Kraler and Koophuis, were arrested and sent to German and Dutch concentration camps.

The "Secret Annexe" was plundered by the Gestapo. Among a pile of old books, magazines, and newspapers which were left lying on the floor, Miep and Elli found Anne's diary. Apart from a very few passages, which are of little interest to the reader, the original text has been printed.

Of all the occupants of the "Secret Annexe," Anne's father alone returned. Kraler and Koophuis, who withstood the hardships of the Dutch camp, were able to go home to their families.

In March 1945, two months before the liberation of Holland, Anne died in the concentration camp at Bergen-Belsen.